"If you are looking for a 'quick fix' recipe approach to motivating your 'boys,' look elsewhere. This book concerns itself with the basic building blocks to character, integrity, and yes, better performance. *Really Winning* is full of common sense and is a terrific resource for the coach who is serious about creating a fun, safe environment for boys to develop in. It is a book for coaches who truly care about boys under their care."

> —Peter Jensen, Ph.D., Olympic performance coach and author of *The Inside Edge*

"Jim reveals the pitfalls to which many coaches and parents are vulnerable. In *Really Winning*, he presents effective solutions by exploring the psychology of coaching and parenting boys. *Really Winning* is a practical handbook that is a must-read for coaches and parents."

> —Tom Lopes, veteran referee of fourteen consecutive NCAA basketball tournaments and Final Four official in 1995

"In *Really Winning*, Dr. Mastrich points to an area in need of much attention—the need for society to place greater emphasis on developing good character in boys—and he shows the way that sports can be used to get the job done. I urge parents and coaches to take heed of the message in this timely book."

> —Leonard Coleman, former president of the National League of Major League Baseball

"In an era where debate rages on what is appropriate behavior at all levels of sports competition, Dr. James Mastrich has come forth with a new book that offers insights and real solutions to parents, coaches, athletes, and even fans. *Really Winning: Using Sports to Develop Character and Integrity in Our Boys* is almost a self-help book for those involved in sports of all age groups. It takes readers on a journey to discovering, then dealing with issues that have been simmering for years. The book's goal, as the author writes, is to take on the problem of 'organized sports all too often producing young men who are characters, instead of young men with character.' From the T-ball coach starting out to the high school coach looking to inspire his players, *Really Winning* can be a valuable tool in teaching young boys and men how to benefit from sports competition."

> —Eric Sondheimer, sports columnist, *Los Angeles Times*

"Dr. James Mastrich is an experienced clinician and author who has integrated aspects of developmental and sport-performance psychology in his book *Really Winning*. His philosophy for developing integrity in boys is empowering yet practical. Dr. Mastrich offers useful and concise strategies for helping parents and coaches to mentor our boys, while also helping them to reach their fullest potentials as young men. The adage that 'sports build character' has been in decline in recent decades. However, Dr. Mastrich shows us that supervised sport participation can still build character in boys and that athletes can be role models again. This book is a must-read for coaches, teachers, or parents who want to play a more active role in the moral development of their boys."

> —Mickey C. Melendez, Ph.D., sports psychology consultant and assistant professor of Counseling Psychology at Rutgers University

"*Really Winning* offers an insightful look into the psychology of boys and provides powerful advice on how to use sports to empower and enrich the lives of these young men."

> —Caroline Silby, Ph.D., sports psychologist, author of *Games Girls Play*, and former member of the United States Figure Skating Team

"With the precision of a scientist, the insights of a coach, and the passion of a parent, Dr. Mastrich gives the reader an extremely informative and useful guide on how youth sports can be conducted in a way that helps boys become mature men of character. *Really Winning* teaches us important facts about the physiology and psychology of boys and suggests practical strategies for using sports to build better communities and better people. This is a valuable book well worth reading."

—Michael Josephson, founder of the CHARACTER COUNTS! Coalition and the Pursuing Victory with Honor sports initiative

"When I think back on my days as a coach, the hits, errors, a great relay, missed chances to score a goal—these all pretty much fade for me. What I remember most is the opportunity I had to help shape the lives of some extraordinary young people, that is, all of the kids on all of my teams. If you've been a really great coach of young boys, you'll begin to know when they start to hit their twenties. *Really Winning* can help you be a great coach by helping you understand the boys you are working with and what really winning really means. Jim Mastrich's accomplishment with this work is laudable."

—Jeffrey Smith, Ph.D., professor of Educational Psychology at Rutgers University

"Integrity is the ultimate winner in Jim Mastrich's *Really Winning*. Mastrich's personal anecdotes, important understanding of boy's psychology, a correct boy-centered philosophical approach, and a critique of the current sports mentality make this a must-read compendium for school and youth-group officials, athletic directors, parents, and coaches of boys. *Really Winning* is a call to action for putting into play sage advise and for implementing a sports code of conduct based on common sense and common decency. Valuing boys' character development over winning at all cost will lead to true winners."

—Carlton H. Tucker, head of upper school of Princeton Day School

"It's truly difficult to overstate the need and importance of a book like *Really Winning*. Yes, it's a book about youth sports, and it's a book about winning. But Jim's down-to-earth message is serious—and oh so seriously needed—and applies far beyond our children's games and fields of play. With its practical wisdom and advice for helping us transform our impressionable boys into *really* good, responsible men, this book should be on anyone's shortlist of timely and essential character-building resources. Do yourselves and your sons a life-enriching service—read this book."

—Russell Gough, Ph.D., professor of Ethics at Pepperdine University and author of *Character Is Everything: Promoting Ethical Excellence in Sports* and *Character Is Destiny: The Value of Personal Ethics in Everyday Life*

"*Really Winning* should be required reading for all coaches in youth organizations and for all active parents. The title truly does reflect the perspective of the book, and the focus is on what youth sports were originally designed to accomplish."

—Don Harnum, men's basketball coach at Rider University

"Dr. Mastrich explains in easy-to-understand language how parents and coaches can help children get the most benefit from the sports experience. Helping them become better all-around people who feel good about themselves is an achievable goal thanks to the practical help in *Really Winning*."

—Mike Schapiro, cofounder of the SAGE (Set a Good Example) Sportsmanship Program

REALLY WINNING

Using Sports to Develop Character
and Integrity in Our Boys

DR. JIM MASTRICH

ST. MARTIN'S PRESS ≈ NEW YORK

www.stmartins.com

Library of Congress Cataloging-in-Publication Data

Mastrich, Jim.
    Really winning : using sports to develop character and integrity in our boys / Jim
Mastrich.—1st ed.
        p.   cm.
    Includes bibliographical references (p. 213) and index.
    ISBN 0-312-28289-3
    1. Sports for children—Moral and ethical aspects.   2. Sports for children—
Psychological aspects.   3. Sports for children—Coaching.   4. Boys—Conduct of
life.   5. Sportsmanship.   I. Title.

GV709.2 .M34   2002
796'.083'41—dc21   2002068361

First Edition: September 2002

10   9   8   7   6   5   4   3   2   1

This book is dedicated

to Zachary and Devin and

all of our boys.

Young people need models, not critics.

—John Wooden

Contents

1

An Opportunity
Squandered

RECORDS HAVE been falling. Times have been slashed. Previously unheard of feats accomplished. Indeed, over the past
twenty years athletes have succeeded in optimizing their performance through physical and mental training. Unfortunately it seems this
success in elevating physical standards has been accompanied by an
overall decline in the character of a great many individual athletes. This
decline in responsibility, honor, and integrity is in no way exclusive to
the domain of sports, but athletics does provide a unique window into a
greater societal problem and some would say societal deterioration. The
good news is that athletics is also a unique arena in which to counter this
trend.

This chapter explores the state of males in our culture and in sports.
This understanding will serve as a baseline from which we can then
formulate interventions for our own sons and for boys in general. For
that matter, boys in general are our sons; for if we do not come together
as a community to provide the guidance they need, we will all lose. *Really*

Winning is about taking concrete steps to make a difference for all of our boys. Let us first take stock of the problem. This will serve as a useful starting point.

✦ Maleness at the Threshold ✦ of the Millennium

Two huge revolutions have impacted on boys and men over the past century. The first has to do with the meaning we get from our work and the second is the dawning of the Age of Aquarius. In the act of doing we derive a sense of satisfaction, mastery, and worth. When the industrial revolution pulled men off the farms and into the factories, it began a radical shift in the ways men would eventually see themselves. There was a transition from a direct and immediate encounter with work and the satisfaction of a job well done, to an increasing sense of alienation from one's work and frequently an almost total disconnection from the end product. Life on the farm may have been difficult, but it provided the opportunity for satisfaction. For instance, in order to grow a peach, a man had to wait many years from the time of the first planting. Over this time, conditions had to be monitored to make sure it was not too dry or too wet or that the impact of insects or animals was minimized. In the end however, there was the peach, moist and sweet and eaten there, right in the field. Furthermore, all the members of the family knew the indispensable worth of the man of the family.

The tremendous technological changes brought about over the past several decades have further impacted on our culture's perception of maleness. On the one hand, while technology has "freed us" it has also widened the gap between people and the fruits of their labor. Furthermore, we could easily ask the question, with the technological revolution yielding so many benefits, How is it that so many more families must now have two working parents in order to pay the bills? In no way am I suggesting that women in the workforce is a bad thing, for we all have the right to pursue satisfaction and meaning in our lives. The necessity of them to do so for the basic survival of the family is a further indication of the dilution of the value of the male. The main point that applies equally to males and females in the workforce is that workers have become increasingly distanced from the finished product. Furthermore, by merely being a cog in the wheel, while meaningful to the extent that he provides for his family, a man forgoes satisfaction and self-esteem and replaces them with alienation and a sense of desperation.

The Struggle Over Maleness

Throughout most of the past decade there has been a battle raging over what it really means to be masculine and how to best go about getting boys to either become it, or according to some, to overcome it. This debate has produced results similar to what happens when cold fronts and hot fronts collide: a lot of noise and sparks flying. The weapons in this battle have been books from the popular culture and the battlefields have been television programs such as *Oprah Winfrey*.

Some have taken the position that traditional conceptions of masculinity are problematic in that they too greatly constrain boys into pre-ordained and rigid social roles. For instance, sensitivity and vulnerability are not considered experiences that a "real" man has, and thus are eventually hardened out of boys. These older versions of masculinity, along with athleticism and aggression, are seen as outdated and have little relevance in today's world. Boys are considered to be placed by society in a gender straitjacket and are automatically limited as to the range of emotions they can be aware of, much less express. Furthermore, the argument goes, boys are also restricted in their ability to think and behave as freely and openly as they optimally could otherwise.

The other camp of authors has been proclaiming that feminists, male and female alike, have ruined boyhood by creating a hostile climate against boys just by virtue of their gender. This line of thought argues that boys' conceptions of themselves have been harmed by a generation of feminist attacks against maleness and that traditional notions of masculinity are sound but need only to be reaffirmed and shored up. In answer to the notion that girls have been shortchanged by society, it is pointed out that girls generally get better grades than boys, are less likely to commit suicide, and are less likely to be victims of violence, or to be perpetrators of violence. It is thought that boys must be armed so that their self-esteem and self-respect as males can withstand the disparaging and demeaning arrows of feminism.

Over the course of this dialogue some "learned" individuals have made grand pronouncements about the differences between boys and girls that seem so extreme in their ideological positions as to make the reasonable person question their credibility; after all, the truth does frequently reside in the middle of such arguments. In point of fact, both sides do seem to make some reasonable points. There *has* been a popular demeaning of what is male and it is logical therefore that this would impact negatively on boys. Some well-meaning people, many who consider themselves feminists, believe that much of what is wrong in the world is a result of a patriarchal culture that kept women down through misogynistic practices and that a reversal is in order. While human history abounds with misguided actions and beliefs, it fails to adequately account for such folly by attributing the full responsibility for this to one gender over the other. Although such a simplistic explanation may be tempting, it fails to be really helpful for either gender. Indeed, this kind of thinking finds it hard to respect the divergent strengths and attributes of each gender, and tends to conclude instead that basically all that is male is bad, while female is good. For instance, competition is bad, co-operation good; problem solving bad, relationship building good . . . on and on along the extremes of the male/female divide. On the other hand, most people know of men who as boys were treated severely and unempathically simply because they were boys. Many of these individuals as adults and fathers are now limited in their range of compassion and affect with their own children.

Regardless of which end of the debate a person favors, both positions share a common concern for boys, that they are lost, and that something needs to be done about it. No matter what it is that must be done, it seems reasonable that fostering a respect for the differences in the genders must be a necessary part. However, in order to begin to chart a course of action we must understand how we got here in the first place. It is my position that neither gender has a lock on perfection. Both are worthy of respect for what they have in common and in how they differ. While men and women have different biologies, brain structure, attitudes, and behavior, they do, in fact, share a common humanity and need to be honored by the other. Being equal does not mean having to be the same.

A Brief Historical Context

Some who are either old enough or who have an interest in ancient history will remember the radical Broadway musical *Hair*. This 1960s classic heralded the dawning of a time of change and hope. Perhaps this wasn't so much a second revolution, but an inevitable outcome of the first. With people being freed up to some extent from the social order that so rigidly bound our culture, men and women naturally began to question the assumptions of roles and duties that had for generations dictated who men and woman were, what duties they performed, and the values possessed by each gender.

Women and girls needed to be empowered to be their own persons and to be encouraged, along with men and boys, to value and respect the feminine. The passing of Title IX by the United States Congress in 1972 had a significant and positive impact on athletics in higher education. Mandating gender equity in the disbursement of funds for men and women's sports not only made a real statement about equal respect and value for each gender, but also was long overdue.

As any history buff or parent of an adolescent knows, when there is a revolution a lot of good gets tossed out of the palace when it is first occupied. It is only later, after the battle for change, that we realize what we may have lost. I believe this was the case as our culture began to shift toward a new appreciation and respect for what is female. In order for women to achieve status as equals to males, many barriers had to be breached. Unfortunately, in the process maleness began to be disparaged. Being strong, having power, being rational, being protective, even the way males communicate, came to be seen as of lesser status to the female. Some women and even some men came to refer to maleness as "testosterone poisoning." This really tells the story. We went from a culture that judged the feminine as weak and inferior to a culture that conveyed a sense of shame and derision in being male, acting male, and communicating like a male.

Fortunately, our culture now seems ready to embrace and respect that which is feminine *and* masculine and to understand and value their differences. *Really Winning* is part of the effort to move this kind of thinking along. One of the central positions in fostering this new paradigm is no longer settling for the rationale that "boys will be boys" as a justification for not helping our boys aspire to develop solid character and integrity. There will be much more on that throughout the book; however, we first need to take stock of the situation in which we and our boys find ourselves. What follows are some snapshots.

✦ Boys in General ✦

✦ "I grew up way too fast today. I want to be a kid again." Those were the words of Tabitha Vess, a Santana High School senior who happened to arrive late for school on the morning of March 5, 2000. She found that during her absence two fellow students were killed and thirteen others people were wounded by a fellow classmate. This attack, which took place in California, was the nation's deadliest school shooting since the infamous Columbine High School shootings almost two years earlier. In that bloodbath two teenagers killed twelve fellow students and a teacher before committing suicide.

In both cases the assailants were teenage boys. To some degree they were considered outcasts and nerds. They were apparently not valued by the majority of their classmates; they knew it and were angry about it. In both cases the boys telegraphed their actions. In stark contrast to adult murderers who are very secretive about their intentions, it is common among young men who commit such crimes to talk about it before they do it. They feel dismissed by the world, and they feel powerless to do anything about it. They talk about wanting to get a gun. The crime eventually comes to fruition when those who are privy to these verbal fantasies dismiss them because they regard the source as equally insignificant. Girls don't commit these crimes. Boys do.

✦ Apparently in an effort to exploit the most base and primitive impulses that lie just below the surface of our boys, NBC-TV teamed up with the World Wrestling Federation to bring the football league XFL to life. In one of the more transparent attempts at marketing, everything about the XFL was pitched as being extreme, pressing the limits of decency, and creating an atmosphere excited by the connection of violence and sexuality. For instance, the normal National Football League rules to protect the quarterback were suspended and some of the "cheerleaders" were provocatively dressed, complete with garterbelts. Teams with names such as the New Jersey Hitmen, the Orlando Rage, and the Chicago Enforcers suggest an attempt to extol an association with the coolness of gangster-type violence. Fortunately for the forces of virtue, the television ratings consistently dropped from its initial big splash. However, the aim of the NBC/WWF alliance was quite clear: exploitation. Just as our culture cannot afford the degenerative influence of the likes of the XFL, the NBC/WWF team eventually concluded that it quite literally could no longer do so as well. By May of 2000 a decision was made to terminate the XFL. This decision was not made as a result of an epiphany of moral insight and virtue, but rather as a function of a diminishing bottom line.

And speaking of the WWF, who attends the "matches," who watches the pay-per-view? Any media marketing person can tell you. The answer is prepubescent and adolescent males, and lots of them. Does this have any negative impact on these viewers? The March 2001 conviction of a fourteen-year-old boy for murdering a six-year-old girl two years earlier is a clear indication that it does. A jury convicted the boy of first-degree murder for battering the girl to death with what he said was an imitation of World Wrestling Federation moves. During the trial, the boy testified that he was emulating the wrestlers he regarded as heroes when he kicked and body-slammed the young girl. Among her injuries were a fractured skull, lacerated liver, fractured rib, and a swollen brain. It was a horrible tragedy for both children.

Daniel Weinberger of the National Institutes of Health aptly pointed out that acts of violence such as the above incident and the rash of school shootings are the result of actions being taken by children who in fact *are children*. Because they are young, these boys naturally have an immature brain. The part of the human brain that enables us to exercise good judgement and control impulses, the prefrontal cortex, is not physically mature at the age of fifteen, which was the age of the boy in the Santana High School shootings. In fact it takes at least two decades to form a fully functional prefrontal cortex. It is Dr. Weinberger's opinion that because the adolescent brain does not have the biological machinery necessary to inhibit impulses in the service of long-range planning, it is important for adults to help children make plans and set rules, and for institutions to impose limits on behavior that children are incapable of regulating. Of course this makes sense, but because teenage boys who may be hurt and angry live in a culture that romanticizes gunplay, and makes weapons all too available, we are hard-pressed to protect our boys and their fellow classmates. In the case of the WWF imitator, it was likely to have been not a question of hurt or anger, but rather of physiological immaturity.

Not having a fully developed prefrontal cortex does not in any way excuse a teenager for his actions. Indeed our boys are responsible for their behavior. We would, however, be taking a rather narrow perspective if we merely let our thinking end there. If we did, the next logical step might be to lower the age of the death penalty and legislate mandatory lengthy sentences for violent youth offenders. "Lock'em all up, boys!" This kind of cowboy thinking is like closing the barn door *after* the horses are already out. It does not address the root problem.

While boys are responsible for their actions, we are responsible for the climate in which they live. They are our flock and we are their shepherds. As parents, teachers, ministers, coaches, school board members, et cetera, we can work together to minimize the chances that our boys might act out impulsively with such serious consequences. We need, for instance, to ensure that our boys don't have access to the weapons that make such moments irreversible. As coaches and parents we need to intervene when we observe aggressive *Lord of the Flies* mentality and behavior on the part of our charges. Every day in high school cafeterias across America the meek are exploited and humiliated by the bigger, stronger, and cooler. Often many of these aggressors are athletes, although hardly the noble warriors they could be. When coaches and teachers turn a blind eye to such behavior, we lose an opportunity to help our boys be the best people they can be. We lose a teachable moment for character development. *Really Winning* is one tool to assist you to do so.

✦ It was a beautiful warm afternoon in New York's Central Park in June 2000. The bands and other participants in a parade had just finished their day's work. Out of nowhere a group of young men sexually assaulted twenty-two women who had been enjoying the festivities. A pair of newlyweds from overseas was also attacked with the groom physically restrained while the bride was disrobed, held down, and groped. This was no organized, premeditated action; in fact, most of the young men did not even know each other. In the newspaper accounts that followed it was revealed that for most of the young men involved these were truly aberrant acts. They weren't normally like that. Yet they spontaneously came together in what amounted to an attack on humanity, of which they are a part.

✦ This event is of a more personal nature. I live in a lovely little town along the Delaware River. It is safe and has a strong sense of community. One Sunday about a year ago I was taking a walk along the canal with my wife and two young sons and passed three boys who were about thirteen or fourteen years old. As young bucks they were playfully butting heads among each other, so to speak; they were busting on each other. Just as we were passing, the one who appeared to be the alpha male of the group called another "bitch." I called out "Hey!" to remind them that a family was nearby and the leader responded with "Fuck you!" Although my blood began to boil in that moment, I moved toward the boy and said to him, "Son, please watch your language around my family." To this he replied, "Fuck you, you're not my father!" seemingly daring me to up the ante. I did, by running to the nearby police station to get some institutional support.

No, he was not my son, but in essence as a member of the community he was. Here was a boy adrift, pushing the limits, bringing a feeling of threat to the place where I am raising my own sons. He had no way of utilizing my status as an older male. Had he, he would have merely said "sorry" and in doing so we would have acknowledged each other with a sense of mutual respect.

✦ Boys in Sports ✦

✦ By the time you read this Dajaun Wagner will be playing basketball for the University of Memphis as a freshman. He deserves a national forum for his talent and natural abilities, and no doubt he put in considerable time honing his craft. In early January 2001, in one momentous game during his senior year of high school, he racked up 90 points while there were still nine minutes remaining in the game. He asked, and his coach granted him permission to continue the assault against the opponent. Wagner went on to score 100 points in the game. By the end of the contest Wagner had taken an amazing 60 shorts in a 157 to 67 blowout.

Make no mistake about it, in terms of athletic prowess Wagner's performance was quite an accomplishment. We do, however, have to ask why any coach would have allowed a player to even be in the position Wagner was in early in the fourth quarter. We also have to shake our heads at how, despite all his years in athletics, the coach hadn't learned when enough was enough or to take pity on a fallen opponent. It is the responsibility of coaches to foster sportsmanship and personal ethics in their young charges. One of the things young men must learn is the responsibility that comes with power (and talent). I am writing about Wagner only because of the manner in which his talent was exploited and raised national attention. Beyond his exceptional skills, he and his coach are examples of what is so common in youth sports.

✦ Last July, during a game against the New York Mets, Boston Red Sox star center fielder Carl Everett was shown by the home plate umpire, Ronald Kulpa, how close he was permitted to stand near home plate. The umpire drew a line with his foot marking the inner edge of the batter's box. Everett became incensed and shouted loudly at Kulpa, who then ejected Everett from the game. A five-minute tirade by Everett followed. He bumped the umpire with his chest, slammed his helmet to the ground, then he head-butted Kulpa as he screamed in the umpire's face. Everett then shoved aside the first base coach who along with the team manager had been trying to restrain him. When he finally returned to the dugout he continued to shout at some teammates and tossed a water cooler. By coincidence, Bobby Cox, the manager of the Atlanta Braves, had just begun serving a suspension for bumping an umpire in an earlier incident.

✦ Former Boston Red Sox great Roger Clemens, now a hired hand with the New York Yankees, made newspaper headlines for his actions in game two of the 2000 World Series. It was the first meeting between Clemens and New York Met star catcher Mike Piazza since he had escaped severe injury or death when a Clemens fast ball hit him in the head earlier in the season. It has long been known in baseball that pitchers have the right to the inside portion of the plate and that batters who crowd it risk being hit. Many batters challenge pitchers' territorial authority and many get hit. While this is generally accepted as a baseball code of ethic, along with it is an implicit agreement that pitchers will not go headhunting; rather, they will aim at the shoulders and below. An exception to this practice occurred in 1920 when Carl Mays beaned Ray Chapman who died as a result of the head trauma.

It was not an incident of throwing a baseball that once again brought notoriety to the Yankees' talented pitcher, it was throwing a bat. The windup . . . the pitch . . . Piazza swings at a blazing Clemens fastball . . . the bat splinters with its head bouncing toward the pitcher's mound . . . Clemens fields it and hurls it across the first base foul line directly in the path of Piazza, who was running to first base. As the bat head shot in front of the runner he appeared shocked, as was most of the crowd and television audience, which seemed hard-pressed to comprehend how Clemens could once again risk injury to another player, much less the same one he had earlier beaned. Afterward Clemens claimed he was just pumped up and that he had no intention of hitting Piazza. However, because of this action and his reputation, one can't know for sure.

As is so often the case with boys and men who "go wrong," they are not necessarily "bad" people or "rotten to the core." More often than not they simply go out of bounds or otherwise push the limits of good sportsmanship. This underscores the need for coaches and mentors to set appropriate boundaries and, by doing so, reining in this excess energy and channeling it for the benefit of all.

Roger Clemens is a case in point. In spite of all of his faults, he has a work ethic and a training regimen that is beyond reproach. He trains year-round and during spring training he regularly arrives at the Yankees' complex before most other players and puts himself through more than an hour of cardiovascular and strength training, including between 400 and 800 sit-ups per day. Only after that does he participate with his teammates in the regular two-and-a-half-hour workout comprised of exercises and running and throwing. In this regard he could be an admirable role model.

✦ The Council of Elders ✦ in Need of Counseling

✦ In Edmonton, Alberta, just two weeks after the Central Park "wilding" incident as it has been called, a hockey father who was also his son's team manager stormed onto the ice and attacked a thirteen-year-old player, grabbing the boy, pushing him and throwing a punch that missed. In a suburb of Boston, soon after the incident in Edmonton, a father who was also his son's hockey coach was beaten into a brain-dead condition by a father of one of his other players after a dispute about how the coach handled some rough play during the team practice session. The father was convicted of involuntary manslaughter. We can only begin to fathom the impact on the sons. . . .

✦ Renowned Indiana University basketball coach Bobby Knight was finally fired after yet another inappropriate action on his part. This time he was guilty of angrily grabbing a student. Tales of Knight's bullying actions are practically legendary. Despite many incidences over the years, ranging from throwing a chair across the basketball court during a game to berating officials, Knight's actions seemed to be subject to executive privilege. He had been treated as if he were untouchable.

In 2000, even after a university inquiry officially determined that he attacked and choked one of his players and physically intimidated and swore at a sixty-four-year-old secretary, he was permitted one additional chance by the university president. Not long after this ruling by the president, which ironically he referred to as a zero-tolerance policy, the choking incident occurred. Bobby Knight has won 763 games as a college coach and his University of Indiana basketball team won three national championships. In terms of sheer numbers, Knight is one of the best in NCAA basketball history.

✦ The mere utterance of the name William Jefferson Clinton is likely to evoke either strong emotional responses—pro and con—or a shake of the head as if to say, "Isn't it a shame." Regardless of one's politics, President Clinton's legacy of a period of economic growth that was unprecedented in the history of the United States will be forever tainted by scandal. Not only did he demonstrate poor judgment and lack of personal ethics in the Lewinsky affair, but also, by putting himself in that position, he weakened his effectiveness in pursuing his legislative agenda. Furthermore, his status as moral pariah forced the Gore campaign staff to decide to marginalize him in the vice president's failed election effort.

We need not rush to judge this man who grew up as the son of an alcoholic father. His mother as a single parent raised him. No doubt she did her best. And no doubt Clinton did the best he thought he could.

Blessed with a brilliant intellect, he used it to compensate for his dysfunctional roots and spurred himself on to considerable academic success. For that he could well serve as a model for many boys raised in adverse circumstances.

So far we have provided incidences in which overindulged athletes act out in ways better suited to a two-year-old. We have cited several incidents in which boys in general do considerable damage to themselves and others as they career through the world, and lastly we have taken a glimpse at the actions of some grown men that are shameful, harmful, or simply embarrassing. There is no simple explanation for why so much of this is happening, but clearly our boys are lost . . . and many of those who would be their guides are themselves lost. Many boys of all ages carry deep emotional wounds. These wounds naturally affect each boy's sense of identity and their actions. Our boys need to know what it is to be male and they need to find a solid footing of maleness within themselves. *Really Winning* can be a useful resource to help us create the conditions for the sound development of character in boys who are truly comfortable in the special qualities of their maleness. It is essential, therefore, that the elders of the tribe—the leaders, coaches, and parents—are out in front as quality role models.

✦ The Sins of the Father Are ✦ Bestowed Upon the Son

The famous quote that serves as the heading for this section has long been attributed to Sigmund Freud, although its original source is the Bible, Exodus 20 and 34, verses 5 and 7 respectively. Whether they know it or not, when a person decides to be a parent, they automatically take on the burden of being the best person they can be. Because children learn primarily through observation, how a parent carries him- or herself has a direct impact on the values and character traits developed in the child. Similarly, it is a fact that fathers, coaches, and mentors have a tremendous responsibility when a boy is entrusted to their care. By virtue of who they are, how they behave, what they value, they teach maleness to these young squires.

What impact does President Clinton's unethical or immoral behavior have on boys of today? How has Bobby Knight's fiery temper and win-at-all-costs attitude influenced the young men he coached or the legion of fans that followed his career with great interest? There is no way to determine with any certainty, but we do have reason for concern. One person was the leader of the free world for eight years and the other an esteemed coach for many more. These questions are analogous to the long-debated issue of whether television violence inadvertently produces aggressive behavior in children and young men. While Hollywood has perennially cried foul at this suggestion, child-development and behavioral psychologists have long known otherwise. The fact is there is a direct correlation between what children observe and how they behave. Furthermore, the more they look up to the person they are observing, the greater the influence that "teacher" has on the "student's" behavior.

Both big boys and little boys generally hold presidents, famous coaches, and athletes in high regard. It is because of this connection that we do our best to ensure that the fathers atone for their sins. First impressions are frequently lasting impressions. No coach, mentor, or father need be perfect, but because of the weight of their influence, just for being who they are, we need to be assured that they have as a primary goal the development of sound character and integrity in our boys. In chapters 7 and 8 we will explore some of the ways that communities have already initiated efforts to clean up youth sports.

As we review the snapshots provided in the preceding sections we are forced to ask the question, What is happening to our boys? It is a sad state of affairs that almost on a daily basis, magazines and newspapers recount tales of violence and aggression perpetrated by boys and young men. The ones listed above are only a small sample of the many that occurred over a very short span of time.

Stories of star high school athletes accused of assaulting young women or of Super Bowl heroes becoming murder suspects, for instance, give new meaning to the famous line of the 1919 Chicago Black Sox gambling scandal, "Say it ain't so, Joe." This doesn't mean that everything about boys these days is all bad news. However, many boys do appear to have lost their way in the world and the evidence of this is almost everywhere. If boys are squires, then the knight who is their master needs to teach them. In our effort to provide an honest appraisal of the "state of the male" it must be realized that a considerable number of star athletes looked up to by boys are, but for their biological age, themselves boys. The same caution holds for the leadership of sports programs as well. The fact is that some of the men coaching our sons can also be considered to be boys housed in the powerful bodies of men. This rampant immaturity has a profoundly negative impact on our boys. We will explore this further in the next chapter as we talk about the psychology of boys.

✦ Where Have You Gone, ✦ Joe DiMaggio?

In early 2001 James Shulman and William Bowen wrote what is considered by many to be one of the most important books on higher education to be published in the past two decades, *The Game of Life*. Bowen is a former president of Princeton University and is currently the president of the Andrew W. Mellon Foundation, where Shulman serves as the financial and administrative officer. In short, these are smart, accomplished fellows who crunched a lot of numbers about athletes at thirty-two elite colleges and universities, and here is some of what they found.

Since the 1950s there has been a general and consistent decline in the SAT scores of athletes admitted to college and in their academic performance as college students. Whereas student-athletes were originally all-around achievers and measured academically as fairly equal to their nonathletic colleagues, they have now become a breed unique to themselves. By 1989, for instance, male athletes' SAT scores averaged 118 points lower than those of other students.

The authors point out that there are almost no varsity sports walk-ons. Over the years athletes have been specializing in particular sports at earlier and earlier ages, leading to an emphasis on their particular athletic talent. The result is a significant change in the relationship between athletes and the rest of their classmates: from being indistinguishable from their nonathletic peers to *very* different not only in terms of academic aptitude and achievement, but more important, in their values and interests.

The authors tell us that athletic virtues no longer automatically translate into positive social virtues. They report instead that the main thing athletes carry off the field and into life is the belief that competition is good. While there certainly can be considerable benefit to this notion when applied judiciously, it contrasts starkly with the original goals of a liberal arts education, which was to make people more imaginative, open-minded, and humane.

The romantic notion of the scholar-athlete is placed in considerable doubt by the information provided in *The Game of Life*. Indeed, when one takes a serious look at how male sports has evolved in the United States, the kind of role model that Paul Robeson stood for has been eroded by the very system of college athletics. Robeson was a brilliant scholar, a courageous athlete, a dynamic singer, and like Muhammad Ali, and Lance Armstrong decades later, he was a man who made his personal beliefs a priority in the face of great obstacles and challenges.

A friend of mine told me that his nine-year-old son, Jared, asked, "Hey, Dad, when's Darryl getting out of rehab?" It was particularly troubling that he did so with the same naïve excitement that someone a generation earlier might have asked about Mickey Mantle. During that more innocent time, the general public, and certainly America's youth, knew nothing of Mantle's battle with alcoholism. They were concerned solely with his recovery from ankle and knee injuries so that he might be able to continue his assault on Babe Ruth's home-run record. When Jared inquired about his hero Darryl Strawberry, he was concerned about a very different kind of recovery. To this nine-year-old, alcohol and drug abuse had become commonplace enough for him to be rather matter-of-fact about it. The good news is that people, in particular, athletes with substance-abuse problems, can finally come out of the closet and get the help they need. The bad news is that so many of them hold positions of high status during their active addiction and are looked up to by boys and young men. During this phase of their abuse of alcohol and other drugs, many of these individuals wreak havoc on their health and well-being, on their personal and professional lives, and by being role models, on the psyches of boys who look up to them. I use Darryl Strawberry only as an example. It must be noted, however, that many professional athletes and other prominent figures manage to become poor role models entirely without the use of alcohol or other substances.

The frequency and severity of these incidences have become such a part of our popular culture that we have to face the reality that there has been a severe erosion of the athlete as role model. This is not to say that they are not role models. The fact is they still are, but only a few represent ideals for boys to strive to emulate. Despite Charles Barkley protesting, "I am not a role model," he still is one. Fortunately there are still athletes and men who are available to show the way for boys and young men. And we must not forget them, or else our exploration of this issue would turn into an exercise in frustration and despair.

✦ Real Heroes ✦

As a player Joe DiMaggio was sleek, strong, and graceful. He carried this sense of dignity throughout his retirement. Contemporary writings have revealed some of his darker side; a side that all people have. He was said to be moody and reclusive, but no one has ever questioned his integrity. During his playing years as a spokesperson for a then fashionable cigarette company, or as a promoter for a financial institution, or as Mr. Coffee, as many young people came to know him in his retirement, the Joe DiMaggio endorsement was a coveted prize for many an advertiser. The reason for this was simply because he was the real deal and everybody knew it. DiMaggio sold because of the strength of his character. He was like George Washington, who as a boy is alleged to have declared, "I cannot tell a lie. I chopped down the cherry tree."

Another role model from a different generation who shares much of the integrity of DiMaggio is Muhammad Ali. This boxing legend is everything a boy might aspire to be. As he used to say as he mugged for the cameras, "I'm so pretty." He was a beautiful specimen of maleness. He was handsome and strong. In the boxing ring he would, as he said, "float like a butterfly and sting like a bee." Ali was smart. During the early part of his boxing career he was a relentless warrior; agile, quick, and powerful. In the latter days, as his athletic gifts began to wane, he shifted strategies and employed a willful determination while lying in wait and playing what he called "rope-a-dope."

Ali also proved himself to be a man of conviction outside the ring. In the 1960s, before the all-volunteer military, he refused to be drafted into the United States Army. Many at the time thought this was a cowardly act and Ali received a great deal of criticism. Over the years, he has since won over the majority of the public for having spoken up early about what most now consider an unjust and unnecessary war. "Keep asking me no matter how long. On the war in Viet Nam I sing this song:

I ain't got no quarrel against the Viet Cong," Ali proclaimed at the time. As a consequence of being a man who was true to his convictions, Muhammad Ali was suspended from professional boxing for over four years and was stripped of his world heavyweight crown. Through all these trials and tribulations he remained steadfast in doing what he believed to be the right thing.

Heroes are not people who seek recognition. They do what they do because something inside of them directs them. We can call this inner voice character. DiMaggio and Ali clearly had it. Strength of character is manifested in countless forms every day and usually without much fanfare. Former National Hockey League star Pat LaFontaine is but one example.

It is not what LaFontaine did on the ice that I am talking about. If we were to examine his stellar career we would talk about his courage and leadership on the ice and his considerable talents as a goal scorer and a skater who demonstrated a great deal of finesse. In 1996 as captain of the Buffalo Sabres, LaFontaine suffered his sixth concussion. In the months that followed, he was no longer able to sustain his high level of play. In fact LaFontaine lost the clarity of thought and purpose that had been so much a part of his approach to the game. "It felt like someone had reached in and pulled all the spark, all the enthusiasm right out of me," LaFontaine reflected, speaking of his troubled time. He eventually recovered and went on to continue his high standard of performance.

In 1998, after yet another head injury LaFontaine retired from the National Hockey League. Instead of mourning over having his career cut short and withdrawing from life, he did just the opposite: he chose to give back. He increased his ongoing activities on behalf of children's hospitals, redoubled his fund-raising efforts, and enthusiastically recruited other NHL players to visit infirm children. "We don't know when adversity will strike us, our only choice is how we will respond," said LaFontaine, who has since written a book about athletes who have faced severe challenges. *Companions in Courage* tells about those who have had to deal with and overcome obstacles ranging from cancer to deafness. LaFontaine considers the common denominator among these courageous athletes to be their inability to hear the word "can't."

No discussion of heroes would be complete without talking about three-time Tour de France champion Lance Armstrong. Like LaFontaine, Armstrong refused to hear the word "can't." In 1996 he was diagnosed with testicular cancer that had also spread to his lungs and brain. He was given a fifty percent chance of survival. He underwent brain surgery, which was followed by chemotherapy. He lost his hair, his strength, along with twenty pounds, yet he refused to lose hope. When he encountered medical professionals who did not have the belief and confidence that he would survive, he fired them and found positive-thinking doctors. "I just wasn't going to be around people who thought I was going to die," he said. He recovered from the cancer, resumed his training, and won the grueling three-week, 2,774-mile bicycle race through the mountains of France. And then he did it again and again!

Like LaFontaine and former major league baseball star Dave Winfield, Armstrong sees the meaning of his life as going beyond his sport. He created the Lance Armstrong Foundation as a vehicle for cancer research and is very invested in seeing it grow and produce results for the benefit of others. Heroes see beyond themselves and look to give back to others. This is a function of the normal process of mature, healthy adult psychological development. When this happens naturally, an individual does not experience any suffering from the sacrifice of time, energy, and money. Rather, he does it quite willingly. As Armstrong said, "It's important for me to know that something like the Lance Armstrong Foundation will be here in 20 years, whereas the Tour de France will not be here in 20 years . . . at least it won't for Lance Armstrong." Indeed, all glory is fleeting, but men with integrity and character don't seek to hold on to it. They move on to the next phase of life, frequently deriving meaning from contributing to make things a little better for everyone.

Sportswriter and National Public Radio commentator John Feinstein recently wrote a book about some other heroes. In *The Last Amateurs,* Feinstein tells the story of the college basketball players of the Patriot League. This is one of the NCAA's smallest Division I conferences and is comprised of colleges such as Colgate, Holy Cross, Lehigh, West Point, and Annapolis. Few of these players have athletic scholarships, they all carry full loads of academically challenging courses and virtually none of them ever leaves college early to join the National Basketball Association.

The players of the Patriot League play for the love of the game, the satisfaction of being the best they can be, and for the yearly League Champion, the challenge of facing the much more powerful and privileged teams in the "March Madness" NCAA Tournament. In the Patriot League, Feinstein describes his having found college basketball played with the passion and integrity that it once inspired. The story of these Davids playing for honor and glory and eventually facing the Goliath in the form of North Carolina, Duke, or Indiana in the NCAA Tournament stands as a beacon of hope. It contrasts greatly with what much of college sports has become as reported in *The Game of Life,* which we discussed earlier. There *is* still hope for our boys.

The remainder of this book *is* about hope. It is about what we can do about these challenges that face our boys and that face those who care about them. It is about who boys are and how we can help them. It is about the efforts that have already begun to formulate the answers to the myriad of questions regarding boys and about the positive impact parents and coaches can increasingly have.

Earlier in this chapter, I told of the confrontation with the boys by the canal. Ironically, it was at just about the same spot about six months before that another very different incident took place. It was a warm Sunday last fall and we were returning from a family stroll. Although it was a beautiful day, the wind was given to occasional strong gusts. About fifty yards ahead a friend was walking her three-year-old daughter while at the same time pushing her baby in a carriage. In as brief a span of time in which the first incident took place, Lauren bent down to tie her daughter's shoes and in that instant a gust of wind literally scooped up the carriage, baby and all, and deposited it upside down into the water of the canal. As strong and protective mothers are always apt to do when faced with threats to their children, Lauren reacted immediately and was in the water in an instant attempting to pull the baby out. In the next moment three boys who were about eleven or twelve years old were also in the canal. They stabilized the carriage that was now heavy with water, righted it, and rescued the infant. These heroes happened to be fishing downstream and sprinted to Lauren's aid. Miraculously, the baby was not harmed, but it took several days for her mother to stop shaking. Several other passersby helped out, offering assurance, a nearby place to wash up, phone calls to a doctor, and a ride home. We all felt good about joining together and helping out and these young boys were the central players. When their work was done they disappeared as suddenly as they had come. It turned out that they lost several pieces of fishing equipment in the water in their hurry to assist Lauren and her girls. In doing so they knowingly sacrificed some things of high material value to them for the welfare of another human being.

Like the hero in the old television show *The Lone Ranger,* they quickly disappeared. They picked up what remained of their fishing poles and tackle and moved on. "Who was that masked man?" was the statement repeated in the television show. No one even knew their names, but they were genuine heroes. And like most heroes they acted because it was the right thing to do, not out of an interest in notoriety or to be praised. Afterward, like most heroes, they no doubt felt genuine contentment at having given for the greater good. Sports is such a fertile ground for developing character and integrity in our boys, because it provides numerous opportunities for them to work hard for a meaningful cause. Furthermore, when our boys come under the influence of mature and honorable coaches, they frequently develop into heroic and honorable warriors.

As Michael Gurian in his insightful book *The Wonder of Boys* points out, boys are naturally drawn to find out what their roles are in the world, what their purpose is, and what constitutes their birthright. As inherently tribal beings, boys seek guidance, recognition, and acceptance from the elder males of the tribe. Unless a boy is received into the male kinship system he will be inclined to seek to prove himself worthy elsewhere, perhaps in another tribe. This has particular implications for violent gangs such as the Crips. As Gurian says, "Boys who do not learn what their birthright and role is from their tribe will often create a gang in which to manufacture them. The boy will defend that new birthright, however misguided, with his life."

If the tribe a boy chooses is not grounded in the mature values of the adult male world, he might mistake dangerous acts of aggression and antisocial behavior as the path to proving self-worth and becoming a man, while forgoing honor, respect, and responsibility. In short, boys need a gang, and if we do not provide one for them, they will create one of their own . . . and that may not be such a good idea. Well-structured sports programs, run by coaches and administrators with an eye toward character development, can be the gang they choose.

I'd like to share a personal observation on the natural inclination of boys to move toward tribal affiliation. This occurred when I served as a coach on my six-year-old son's T-ball team. At the first practice the kids were given some instruction in the art of throwing and catching, and they all practiced together for about an hour or so. Just before the end of the session the league administrator divided the kids into two teams, the Reds and the Blue Jays. The head coaches for each team (the tribal elders) then slipped brand-new Blue Jay and Reds jerseys over each child's head. When this was done they placed individually fitted baseball caps onto each of their players. As this ritual was going on, I observed the kids just soaking it all in. It concluded after about ten minutes, and at that point each team spontaneously began to cheer its own name: "Blue Jays, Blue Jays, Blue Jays" and "Reds, Reds, Reds."

Although they all joined the league because they wanted to play T-ball, they instantly saw themselves as members of one tribe opposing the other, merely by virtue of a random assignment that had occurred only a moment before. I was of course delighted by the kids' glee, but equally impressed by how easily the gang and group mentality can form. The latter made me more mindful of how important it is to have the kind of leadership that can temper such enthusiasm into good sportsmanship and respect for each other . . . and how if this leadership is present, sports can really serve as a medium for character development.

Sports is a play, a drama, and literally a game in which we put ourselves all out for the cause. It is a game through which we offer boys the opportunity to practice at being noble, while they are busy having fun. It is also a medium to develop a sense of mastery in the world. Our boys are the equivalent of young squires honing their craft as baseball, basketball, and football players, and during that process they are available for us to teach them the art of chivalry. As we, who are their guides, learn to consciously focus our thinking on these goals as we organize and coach youth, secondary school, and college sports, we will create a culture that increasingly fosters development of the honorable warrior. In so doing, we will also create an environment for the emergence of the future Joe DiMaggios, Paul Robesons, and Muhammad Alis along with their more contemporary manifestations such as Tiger Woods, Michael Jordan, Lance Armstrong, and Don Mattingly. But mostly we will be helping to build what will eventually become good men.

Obviously not all boys can run, ride, jump, hit, and throw at the level of these gifted individuals. They don't have to. Vince Lombardi once said, "Winning isn't everything, but striving to win is." It is not surprising, given how distracted sports has become from its mission of centering on honor and sportsmanship, that Lombardi has been frequently misquoted throughout the years as saying, "Winning isn't everything, it's the only thing." The original quote really hit the mark. It *is* through striving that we become better at the skill we are exercising. With the correct coaching and mentoring, striving and working hard in sports can also help our boys to develop as whole persons.

Thomas Jefferson said, "I'm a great believer in luck, and I find the harder I work, the more I have of it." In spite of his failings, which were largely due to the times in which he lived, Jefferson was a genius whose hard work bore the fruits of countless inventions and acts of statesmanship. I have enormous respect for the value of hard work and for those who perform it at any place along the continuum of work activities, from physical to mental. I owe it to my sons to help them learn the value of persistence, dedication, honesty, and hard work. We all owe it to our boys.

As we stand at the beginning of the new millennium, we find, if we dare to look, that a great many of our boys are adrift in a sea of opportunity. Because they are so rudderless they are unable to take advantage of the resources that abound all around them. Through no fault of their own they are lost. They are certainly responsible for any foolish or reckless actions they may commit, but we all share the responsibility to give them direction. Once they have a mission, our boys will soar, as they are born to do. In order to prepare them for their flight, we first need to understand about their internal workings, how they differ from girls, and how they differ from grown-ups. We also need to develop empathy for what it is like to live in their world and what it looks like through their eyes. The rest of this book is about understanding who boys are and how to foster sound development of their character.

2

The Psychology
of Boys

BOYS WILL BE BOYS because they are boys, and when they stretch themselves toward their potential for goodness and greatness, they are indeed wondrous beings to behold. Boys may lack the maturity and insight of men, but they possess a capacity for psychological health and well-being, and constructive creativity, that can be seen throughout each stage of their lives. If adult caregivers provide a suitable environment, the seeds of their massive potential will blossom and thus set the stage for their evolution into active, curious, and industrious boys and dignified young men. This chapter explores the spirited nature of boys. It examines their potential for productivity and psychological health as well as their capacity for self-defeating and antisocial attitudes. The reader will come to understand who boys are, what boy psychology is, how they think, and what they need from parents and coaches. We begin by getting to know some boys.

✦ As a sixteen-year-old John presented himself as somewhat shy but likable. He was always eager to please, as puppies are inclined to be;

always waiting attentively, right by his master's side, eager to be loved. His mother brought him for counseling primarily because of his long history of getting poor grades and because she believed he had low self-esteem.

Like his brother before him, John was a wrestler, but he never seemed to live up to his abilities, nor to his own expectations that he achieve athletic success equal to his older brother's. In point of fact, John never really believed he could wrestle as well as his brother. Deep down he knew it was only a pipe dream. Soon after I met John, I had a conversation with his coach. I learned that John really had the skills, technique, and work ethic necessary for success as a wrestler. In middle school he had done well, but for some reason, since he entered high school his performance had been mediocre. "I don't understand it," the coach mused. "He works hard and does everything right in practice, but at some point in the match, it all goes to hell." A conversation with his guidance counselor confirmed the same phenomenon. He began each academic quarter with eager attentiveness, only to fade over the term. John would loose focus in class and daydream, forget to hand in assignments, and, not surprisingly, have dismal test results. Periodically John's frustration with his lot in life would manifest itself in the form of loud arguments with his girlfriend in the hallways at school or in getting into fistfights with other boys who he felt had slighted him in some way.

✦ Josh presented himself very differently from John. This college senior carried himself with an arrogant swagger that conveyed the message, I don't care what you think of me: I'm just fine. As an athlete, Josh was gifted with a natural talent that many of his football teammates might covet. He was strong, had explosive speed, great leaping ability, and soft hands; all the equipment necessary for being a lethal wide receiver. Yet as much as his teammates appreciated how his abilities helped to position the team to win, most of them despised him.

Josh would frequently arrive late to practice and he would only occasionally press himself to really work hard. The same was true in game situations. If he knew the pass wasn't going to him, or if the play was to be run on the opposite side of the field he tended to make only a gesture toward running out his pattern. His teammates saw this and hated it and resented him. So did his coaches. They all reacted to the attitude he carried which basically said, "If it's not about or for me, I'm not interested." Josh's self-centered arrogance had even gotten him into scuffles with teammates on the sidelines during game situations. When asked why he didn't work harder in practice he laughed, shrugged his shoulders, and said, "Why should I have to, it's what I do in the game that counts." It was true that when the plays were going to him, he performed very well. When his coach suggested that he could be that much better if his approach to practice was more diligent, he said, "What for? I'm fine." Josh simply did not know how to let himself be coachable.

✦ Patrick was almost six years old when he joined his first T-ball league. In comparison to the other boys and girls on the team, he seemed like a young six. He was shy in dealing with the other kids and apprehensive as he approached the ball and the bat. Like many kids his age he did not seem to know quite what to do with the instructions the coaches gave him. But he seemed more uptight than most of the others and carried his body rather stiffly. As a coach, I was drawn to look out for him in order to help make this a positive experience for him.

It wasn't until I was fitting him with his batting helmet in the on-deck circle that I noticed his parents talking *at* him. The on-deck circle is next to the fence that separates the stands from the field, and it was there his parents sat. Patrick was the only child who brought his own helmet, bat, and batting gloves to the game and no doubt his parents were quite generous in purchasing these tools of the trade for him. However, they were rather meager in their emotional support for him. As he struggled to put on his batting gloves they yelled, "Hurry up, Patrick, hurry," and then they seemed to laugh at his folly with the people sitting with them. A similar exchange took place prior to his other time at bat. At that point I whispered to him, "Don't hurry, Patrick, you've got all the time you need." His parents loved him enough to buy his equipment; they did not seem to see the shy person he was. What was worse was laughing at his expense in a manner that suggested, What am I going to do, my kid is such an idiot! It's not my fault.

Ironically I saw him in the grocery store later that same day and he waved to me from his shopping cart. As I checked out I saw him again. He and his mother were in line at another cash register. She was in the process of scolding him in front of everyone and he was in tears. His eyes were lowered. He seemed utterly humiliated.

✦ Andy was the kind of young man a person would want their son to grow up to be and their daughter to marry. He was hardworking and clean-cut and had a sense of dignity that was evident in his dealings with his girlfriend, how he approached his college course work, and the diligence he brought to his work as a member of the lacrosse team.

With so much being said about what is wrong with boys, he stands as an example of a decent young fellow. When he and his teammates agreed not to drink beer in the days before the lacrosse matches, he followed through. When others settled for a C average just so they could cruise through and still be eligible for athletics he regularly made the dean's list. When he found out that his girlfriend had taken up with another guy, he asked her about it in an honorable manner, dared to feel his hurt and tell her about it, and moved on. It wasn't that this twenty-three-year-old was a straitlaced goody-goody; he wasn't. Rather, Andy just seemed inherently balanced and grounded.

✦ It is easy to presume things about people based on their status in the community and the way they present themselves. This was the case with Vince. At fifty-five he was the successful owner of a long-established family business. Vince was quite affable and to all who thought they knew him he was the life of the party and a regular good guy.

He was in fact a good guy, but he was tortured by having to be the well-respected man, as the old Kinks song goes. What people did not know was that he was secretly resentful and mistrustful of others. Furthermore, although he had long been married to a lovely woman who was attractive, intelligent, and her own person, he felt trapped in the marriage. For a long time he had secretly lusted after other women at the office and at cocktail parties, and for the past four years he had been having a clandestine relationship with the wife of a neighbor.

An individual has the right to get out of a marriage if that is the course one prefers to take. But Vince didn't take that option, as many don't, and one day his wife found him out. He had no interest in hurting her and vowed to repent, but he could not keep himself away from the other woman. As a man who wanted his cake and to eat it too, Vince regularly vowed repentance, but continued to hurt his wife. He wanted them both, but he was not prepared to be a full and honest partner with his wife. She repeatedly caught him in his lies and when this happened she felt terribly betrayed and he was sickened with feelings of shame and despair. Yet he persisted.

✦ As an eight-year-old Alex seemed to be the epitome of a fine young boy. His sparkly eyes darted out beneath his buzz-cut blond hair as he enthusiastically talked about his adventures in youth wrestling and pee-wee football. As he spoke, he wiggled around on the couch and fidgeted with his water cup or the leaves of the plant that sat on the end table. He told of the challenges he faced in his upcoming wrestling matches. He wanted very much to advance in the district tournament to a higher level than he had the previous year. He also wanted to make a good showing against a very talented boy with whom Alex had had difficulty during the regular season. Although his overall record had improved from last year and he had a good winning percentage, he was totally dominated in the two matches against his nemesis. It was clear to me that he wanted to prove himself to be a worthy opponent by making the match competitive this time. He was very concerned about this.

What also worried Alex was the reaction of his father, who had wrestled as a boy and until recently was an assistant coach on his team. That Alex's father loved him was not in question, but he sometimes seemed to blur the lines around the purpose of Alex's involvement in sports and his purpose as a coach. Unfortunately on several occasions his dad lost it on him over his sports. Once during the previous season when Alex had trouble handling an opponent in the districts, he stormed out of the gym after Alex came off the mat, saying, "I don't know why I even bother coming out here!" Alex then collapsed in tears. A similar incident occurred when his father was guiding him through a training session in their basement. Alex had a match the next day and in order to make weight he had to drop four pounds. It did not matter to him which weight class he was in, but the coaches, including his father, preferred the lower one. Alex was hungry and wanted to eat, but his father ordered him to only drink a protein shake. During the session that followed, Alex, dressed in his sweats, was made to continuously jump rope to the sound of blaring rock music while his father sat, kinglike, in a cushioned chair opposite him barking admonishing commands with the intent of motivating Alex. Alex wept throughout the session. Fortunately his mother came home and interceded.

We were all first introduced to the "lost boys" in James Matthew Barrie's famous children's classic *Peter Pan*. These boys ranged in age from middle childhood through adolescence and shared one common condition that was their bond; they either did not have parents or did not have parents who were prepared to welcome them, love them, and guide them. As different as they may be, Josh and John are lost boys and as such they are in part cut off from themselves and their natural potential for greatness. Their success is an expression of an imbalance, for their strength in one area is negated by gigantic vulnerabilities in others. They could be much more than they are, but because they are lost, they don't know how.

✦ Boy Psychology ✦

There definitely has been a lot of hullabaloo around the issues of who boys are and what they really should be. Questions as to whether they should be more feminine or more masculine; whether they are fine just the way they are; and what it really does mean to be a man are among the issues at the center of the commotion. This controversy has frequently been punctuated by some of the "experts" on the topic presenting themselves as convinced that their position has an exclusive lock on the truth. I know enough not to claim to know it all when it comes to the psychology of boys. I do, however, believe our boys can all be better served by taking a more down-to-earth, common-sense approach. Fortunately, well-grounded information is already available to assist us in our efforts. And as the years go by, we will likely gather additional data that can help to fill in the blanks.

In order to understand what really comprises the psychology of boys, I will present several different ways to understand them. Each is in essence a theory that will help us to form a composite picture of boys. Just as contrasting colors and shades help to enrich the detail of a photograph or painting, I believe that the way in which we approach our boys can be enriched by an appreciation of all that a reasonable person can know about them. Although we may find ourselves drawn to a particular point of view, each color, so to speak, offers something that can help us understand the boys we are parenting, mentoring, or coaching.

It is my hope that the reader will consider these theories as different pairs of glasses. Through a particular pair we can understand and see something that is not seen quite the same way through the other pairs. In fact, no specific pair of glasses can claim to have a more accurate perspective than the others. Rather, they each offer something important to consider as we attempt to understand who boys are. It naturally follows that when we undertake this kind of pragmatic approach to understanding who boys are, we are likely to develop a greater breadth of knowledge about them. As a direct result of this increased empathy we will be able to be more flexible and grounded in our day-to-day dealings with our boys. Simply put, if we are more informed, our actions and communications with them will reflect this understanding. Fortunately, because no two boys are exactly the same, we might find one set of glasses to be more effective in helping us understand one of our boys at a particular age or stage of development, and another set more helpful at a different point in time.

What follows is an examination of the psychology of boys that is presented in three tiers, the first two in this chapter and the third following in the next chapter. In the first tier we will briefly touch upon the characteristics of males that are clearly brain-driven and hardwired into their psyche through brain structure and brain chemistry that is gender specific. In the second tier we will explore the psychological and social developmental processes that occur in boys and girls with a particular emphasis on boys. This will be done by considering the specific issues that are especially salient during particular stages of the child's life. Chapter 3 begins with the third tier, in which we contrast the psychology of boys to the psychology of men while emphasizing both the healthy as well as the dysfunctional qualities of each. With all that under our belt we will be in a good position to get on with the rest of *Really Winning* and discover ways to help our boys become good men.

Boys Will Be Boys: The Physiological Facts of Life

The heading of this section is not meant in the way it is most often applied. For at least the past few generations the phrase "boys will be boys" has been used to excuse the irresponsible behavior of boys. Some boys who break things, steal things, fight with each other, along with some boys who hurt girls either as young playmates or by sexually exploiting them in adolescence and later, are given permission to continue these kinds of asocial behaviors when parents and other caregivers think this way. When boys are not reprimanded they become less than they can be and the integrity that they are capable of developing becomes hollow. Another thing that accompanies attachment to the "boys will be boys" belief is that caregivers absolve themselves of their own responsibility to hold themselves and their boys to a standard of behavior that fosters the development of sound character. This is a principal tenet of *Really Winning*.

My saying "boys will be boys" is not intended as an excuse, but as a statement of fact. Because of their physiology boys *can only be boys*. Nothing need be done about that except to create the conditions that will enable them to grow to be the best men possible.

What, then, is the physiology that makes boys unique to themselves? Let us first state the obvious. Young men differ from young women in that they have a penis. In fact, their entire genitalia are external. They are physically bigger and have more muscle mass, and their voices are significantly deeper. They really look different. But how did this happen?

The principal factor in this difference is the large amount of testosterone in boys and men. Simply put, this hormone regulates the development of everything that makes a boy a boy. Its presence first makes its influence felt in the womb and by adulthood a man might have up to twenty times more testosterone than a woman. The level of testosterone available to the fetus determines whether it will become either a boy or a girl.

From a man's deep voice and his penis to his desire for adventure and aggression, maleness is driven by testosterone. This hormone is the fuel that creates the biological imperative of young men to seek young females with whom to mate. The gleam in a mother's or father's eye that appears when the word "girlfriend" is mentioned reveals our pleasure as parents that our boy is fulfilling his role as a healthy young man. We may very well not want him to have sex with numerous young women and we certainly wouldn't want him to engage in sexual behavior at too early an age; nevertheless, his biology pulls him to do so. Part of our job is to compassionately guide him through these dangerous waters. Like Ulysses and his men struggling to resist the call of the sirens, in their adolescence our boys will experience a mighty sexual pull that is bio-chemically driven.

Boys may well be boys, but not all boys carry the same level of testosterone. While it is certainly true that boys carry higher levels of it than girls, there can be considerable variability within each gender as to the level of testosterone possessed by a particular boy or girl. As a result some boys with lower than average levels may appear physically softer and may in fact be more sensitive and empathic to others, characteristics typically attributed to females. All the same he is a "real" boy. He, like all other boys, will begin to generate an average of six daily testosterone surges beginning in late childhood. While they have traditionally been thought of as stereotypically negative female phenomena, behavioral and mood swings also occur in males and are directly influenced by their own hormonal surges. A boy's outgoing and engaging behavior, aggressive behavior, or sullen and withdrawn mood can all frequently be attributed to a rush of testosterone.

Boys are different from girls in so many ways and the differences, which begin *in utero,* are evident throughout their infancy. The more aware we become about the influence of testosterone on aggression, sep-aration, and tension-release behavior, the more capable we can become in effectively responding to a boy displaying such behavior. Infant boys engage more physically with their environment. This could take the form of exploratory behavior and hitting other children. Even in the most nonviolent-conscientious-objector-type households little boys will turn objects into guns and swords and engage in mythical battles against the forces of evil. Teenage boys will tend to engage in mock fights with their friends (frequently in the presence of females of the same age). In ob-serving this from afar, one becomes aware of the parallels between human courtship and the behaviors displayed by big horn sheep and elk during rutting season, as shown on television shows such as *Wild Kingdom.*

Boys need to separate from parents earlier than do girls. This hormonally driven behavior does not mean that they do not need or want their parents' or coach's approval or affection; rather, they are driven to become independent. Boys frequently need more physical space and they need to be the ones to regulate contact with parents. A six-year-old leaning on a parent's leg while watching a movie is every bit as meaningful an encounter as a hug. If the hug were forced on him, the boy would most often flee. Only by successfully completing the biochemically driven psychosocial activity of separation can a teenager ready himself for engagement in the adult world, including having successful and mature relationships with young women.

My boyhood memory of listening to the New York Knickerbockers broadcast on the radio by Marv Albert is centered on his use of one word: "Yes!" In a crucial moment in the game, at a time that called for courage, determination, and perseverance, when Bradley, Frazier, Reed, or DeBusschere would sink a basket, Albert would respond with a resounding "Yes!" I loved the sound of him saying it and still do. The sense of urgency, the buildup, the excitement, and the release that follows are a function of the interwoven relationship between testosterone and tension. It not only manifests in battle situations as in sports, but also in the male sex drive. The primitive nature and function of tension and release is easily seen in battling to protect the tribe or in spreading one's genetic seed by mating with females. Of course, just because boys and men may be driven in part by primitive biochemically instinctual behavior doesn't mean they have to act it out in socially inappropriate ways. However, knowing that this behavior is hardwired into boys can assist us in helping them learn to enjoy the benefits of it as well as to manage it.

A boy's brain is the martini shaker where the hormonal cocktail of testosterone and other ingredients comes together. The physiological structure of boys' brains along with the particular levels of chemicals at hand are part of the standard operating equipment unique to boys. It's kind of like formulating a cocktail. If you add more of one ingredient, less of another, or leave out one altogether, you will end up with a different beverage. Let's take a brief look at some of the highlights.

On the one hand boys' brains are at least ten percent bigger than girls' brains. On the other hand, boys' brains develop at a slower rate than do girls' brains. Does this mean that one is better or smarter than the other? No, this simply means that boys and girls, men and women, are different; so let's come to know, respect, and celebrate the difference. The following are just some of the ways in which these differences are manifested. Male brains grow in a more one-dimensional pattern than do female brains. That is, male brains are more oriented toward right-brain activities, which include spatial relationships and abstract problem solving, while female brains develop with a less skewed and more balanced processing. Although the left brain, which is responsible for more rational activities that we generally associate with thinking, develops at a slower rate than the right brain in both genders, female brains have a more equal balance between the right and left brain hemispheres. This results in little boys generally being much more active in manipulating objects, such as blocks or LEGOs, and much more active in exploring their environment, than are little girls. Not better, not less than, but different.

Another brain structure difference resulting from the different pattern of growth is that of the corpus callosum, which in essence is the bridge linking all communication between the left and the right hemispheres of the brain. Because of a combination of more rapid and more balanced hemispherical growth in female brains, their corpus collosum is able to process a greater coordination of activities between the two sides of the brain. This is not unlike the way a computer hooked up to the Internet through a DSL cable line can access and process information much more rapidly than through a traditional telephone line. The numerous gender differences that accompany this high-speed access, so to speak, range from males lagging behind females in their readiness and ability to read, to males feeling and actually being less accurate in their ability to process interactions with others, especially if emotionally laden. The latter fact has a direct impact on the emotional fragility of boys that so frequently goes unnoticed. Just because girls are more likely to express upset outwardly through tears and verbal expression, this in no way makes boys tougher, more resilient, or insensitive just because they are inclined not to express themselves this way. Good for girls that they are hardwired to get emotions out so easily. Boys, however, are frequently burdened by social stigma that they should not emote in ways that show their pain or upset. Moreover, they are more fundamentally burdened by not being able to so readily process emotionally laden material. Rather than being supermen with bullets bouncing off their chests, because of their brain physiology, they possess fewer conduits to process emotional information. Boys are at risk of becoming particularly fragile because of how their brain handles and processes such material. The stuff that bothers them can get stuck inside! It is all too easy to mistake stoicism for insensitivity or the swings between withdrawal and anger as not caring. A parent, teacher, or coach mindful of boys' brain physiology can become much more effective in their interactions with them. They might then find a patience, understanding, and compassion that they might not otherwise have felt toward our boys.

An additional functional difference is males' tendency to focus in on one task. In doing so they may get truly upset when their concentration is interrupted. This can apply equally whether it is a seven-year-old playing with LEGOs or a seventeen-year-old working on a report for school, or more likely, watching *The X-Files* on television. There is another frequent occurrence resulting from this uniquely male way of processing. Parents, teachers, and coaches tend to feel disrespected when a boy they are talking to acts as if he is ignoring their words. It is understandable that they would feel troubled if one of their charges were in fact ignoring them; however, sometimes what seems to be true, in fact may not be. While it may be true that the boy is not listening, this sort of selective listening frequently happens without his conscious intent. And that makes a very big difference in terms of what adult response is called for. For instance, in a particular circumstance a boy may be trying to blow off the direction or instructions that the adult is attempting to provide. When this is the case, the adult needs to respond accordingly. This would, however, entail neither crushing the ego of the offender nor allowing the manipulation to succeed in making the adult's request that he, for example, clean up his room be successfully ignored. Both of these extreme responses would negatively impact on the boy's sense of self. In the first case the self would be devalued, while in the latter case the self would be overly indulged. On the contrary, an adult response, informed by an awareness of the uniqueness of boys, would calmly but firmly get the boy's attention so that he might do what must be done.

The long and the short of it is that boys, and all people for that matter, navigate through their lives as they are directed to do so by their brains. Their brains serve as their computer. It is abundantly clear that the operating system in boys' computers is fundamentally different from the operating system in girls' computers. The actual brain structures and the levels of various chemicals and hormones differ according to gender.

This results in the behavioral, attitudinal, and cognitive differences we have already discussed. There are other differences, of course, but an exploration of them would go beyond the scope of *Really Winning*. However, we must remember that each gender is issued these systems as its own standard equipment. There are no other options from which to choose. When it comes to boys we need to be informed by this biochemical difference and adjust our dealings with them accordingly, just as we need to adjust when dealing with girls.

The genders *are* different and we need to teach, coach, and parent accordingly. Boys are more messy, antsy, and need a lot of territory to exercise themselves mentally and physically. That boys naturally tend in this direction needs to be respected and we need to accommodate our homes, classrooms, approach to teaching, structure of youth sports to reflect these differences so that we can reach boys as they are instead of demanding that they become something that they are not. We will explore how to accommodate the needs of boys in sports settings in the next few chapters.

Anyone who has spent time with boys of almost any age will notice the attraction that objects such as balls have for them. They are fascinated by such objects and tend to lock onto them and track their movement. Like hunter animals such as felines, little boys and big boys can become singularly focused on these objects moving through space. It is reasonable to consider this brain-driven interest and behavior as a vestige of the ancient archetypal directive to develop their skills as warriors so as to protect the tribe. It is only natural that organized activities such as sports would appeal to this basic instinct. Sports contain so many of the basic elements rooted in human history that pull at maleness. Among these is a tribal coming together (the home team) to meet a common threat (the visitors) by using one's body to manipulate objects through space (balls). Because our boys are naturally drawn to playing such games, a significant opportunity presents itself for us to use their interest to not only develop their physical skills and confidence, but also their character. These are opportunities we had best not squander. After all, boys will be boys.

Psychosocial Development

Despite the main differences I have noted, boys have far more in common with girls than they might appear to have at first glance. This is only logical given that they share a common humanity. Although there are developmental, psychological, and physical differences, it is wise to begin with an examination of what they share.

An excellent way to understand the developmental processes through which all young people pass is the psychological and social developmental theory of Erik Erikson. In a nutshell, Erikson believed that beginning in infancy, people go through a series of stages of development during their life. Depending on the age of an individual, they are "in," so to speak, a particular stage. Accompanying each stage is a critical period in which a particular aspect of their psychological and social development is ready to be addressed. This is not the only time in a person's life in which the particular issue can be dealt with, but it is a period in their growth that provides a unique opportunity to do so. For instance, between the ages of six and twelve, boys and girls are particularly geared toward addressing the issue of whether they will develop a sense of themselves as competent and capable or inferior and inadequate. Because of this, it is crucial that parents, coaches, and organizers of youth sports shape their interactions with kids accordingly. A coaching style that is loud and demanding and an atmosphere that is excessively competitive will not only turn off a lot of kids in this middle-childhood/preadolescent period from sports, but will wound their sense of self as well.

Each stage provides a window of opportunity to help shape the kind of person the child is capable of being. This "readiness" to go to work to resolve a particular aspect of their personality and self-concept is a solid point of commonality between girls and boys. The same issues present themselves to both males and females throughout their lifetime. Depending on one's gender, the manifestations of these windows of opportunity may differ, as may the venues in which they take place, but this progression of development which contributes to the formation of the self is part of our shared humanity. Therefore it is crucial for those who work with young people to have their approach to them informed by the knowledge of what psychological and social issues are ready to be shaped. We want to take advantage of these opportunities to develop a positive sense of self and a solid character. What follows is a general overview of each stage of development.

Trust

The first psychosocial stage of development occurs during the first year of life. In addition to growing like crazy, all babies are given an opportunity to begin to address the issue of whether they will grow to eventually sense the world as a place that is safe and reliable or whether they will perceive it as inconsistent and dangerous. This is what is known as the trust crisis. As all crises are not necessarily bad but may well serve as opportunities to make a change and a difference, the trust crisis lays a foundation upon which the child's sense of self will be built. This period in the child's life also creates the opening scenes of a play in which he will form a sense of the other and begin to act in ways that confirm his expectations of what is to come in encounters with others. In short, the paradigm for trusting and relying on others, or not, begins to be set in motion with the law of self-fulfilling prophecy leading the way. Those of us who have coached in the early years of organized youth sports, with four- and five-year-olds, know all too well how guarded, tentative, and uncertain these children can be regardless of the warmth, understanding, and support of the coach. Some of these children are particularly at risk for making a quick exit from sports. This is most unfortunate, for in doing so they will forgo an opportunity to use sports as a medium to form a positive relationship with their own body, develop a sense of mastery in being-in-the-world, acquire social skills and a sense of belonging necessary in all aspects of their life, and last but not least, develop character and integrity.

Autonomy

The second psychosocial stage occurs between the ages of approximately eighteen months to three years. The vital issue at this stage of life is how the child resolves the question of whether he comes to see himself as an autonomous being or one entangled with feelings of shame and self-doubt. Like the trust crisis this crisis is an important milepost on the way to the development of a healthy personality.

This is a period of life in which the toddler's muscular system allows for independent walking and a greater control over the use of fingers and thumbs. The child can navigate through the world with greater independence as well as hold and manipulate objects with a greater degree of dexterity. Simultaneously, the child is gaining mastery over language and is challenged to use complex phases to accurately convey his needs and wants. He may also begin to feel anxiety over toilet training. This might manifest itself in the ambivalence of being drawn toward being a "big" boy and the lure of delaying this increase in social status by lengthening his time as the pampered baby whom most families tend to center around. The bottom line is that these young children have to deal with numerous tensions and stresses without having yet developed the necessary coping mechanisms.

The job of children at this time of life is to learn to regulate their own behavior so that they fit in socially with other people. During this learning process children will demonstrate the tendency to demand to be in charge. The job of parents is to blend permission for the decisions two-year-olds can handle with prohibitions against actions they cannot adequately manage. For example, a great deal of tact is not required for a parent to permit a child to choose between having yogurt or peanut butter and jelly for lunch. It will, however, require a great deal of loving patience as the same parent refuses to let the toddler throw the puppy down the stairs to see whether it can fly.

Among the challenges for a parent of a toddler is to set limits that are neither too confining nor boundless. The goal is to shepherd the child away from dangerous activities without crushing the self that is emerging. Setting a good example by enforcing the boundaries with a positive intervention is ideal. Saying something like, "You're being silly, puppies can't fly; why don't you roll the ball to Spot," directs the child to an appropriate activity while allowing the child's sense of autonomy to continue to blossom.

Independence Day

After the child has resolved the crisis between autonomy and shame, by about age three he will begin to confront a new crisis centered on the resolution of having initiative versus timidity and guilt. This period will last into the sixth year and basically boils down to two clear consequences. A child who is rewarded for showing initiative and risk taking will develop a sense of purpose and direction. On the other hand, a child who is taught through his experiences that trying new things and showing initiative frequently result in failure and criticism will develop a sense of inhibition and guilt. How this psychosocial developmental stage is resolved can have life-altering consequences. For instance, it is most often the case that the children who were rewarded for displaying initiative and taking risks in their preschool years are the very children who tend to be successful academically and exude a sense of self-confidence. It is as if they have a distinct advantage as they begin their foray into the world outside their family.

In a fashion similar to that in the previous stage wherein the issue of autonomy was at hand, there is a need at this time to balance the guidance and restrictions placed upon the child with trust and respect for the child's personal autonomy. This has particular relevance for the use of sports as an important activity. By now most boys and girls who are likely to be involved with organized sports in elementary and middle school and beyond have joined a local soccer or T-ball league. Regardless of whether they watch or coach, the approach that coaches and parents take with their charges goes quite a way toward determining whether these children will continue in sports, and, more important, how they will come to see themselves in positive or negative terms.

Children whose attempts at taking initiative are thwarted by anxious, hovering parents are as much at risk for experiencing feelings of guilt and inhibition as those children who are given so much space to operate that they repeatedly suffer from failure and frustration because they have exceeded their capacities. The fact is that all children need coaching. This is true regardless of whether they are playing sports or not. They need coaches that are very much involved, but not overly so. Catching the grounder and trying hard to catch the grounder should at this stage be considered of equal value to the parent/coach. All movements on the child's part and any efforts he or she makes should be greeted with a hearty and sincere "Way to go!" Not only is this approach sensible, but the research in optimal performance sports psychology shows that this kind of support for young athletes is *the* way to pave the way for excellence in performance and self-esteem later on.

Patrick's story from the beginning of the chapter is a good example of what not to do. Of course it is both wonderful and silly to find it necessary to have batting gloves in T-ball, but that's part of the fun of allowing a child to experience being a "big guy." His parents missed this point by hassling him to "hurry up" and put his batting gloves on. In doing so they only increased his anxiety and consequently slowed the whole process up. The shaming that continued in the grocery store provided further evidence that this boy will likely resolve this period's crisis with a strong sense of timidity and guilt imbedded into his concept of himself. This is not to say that he will not be able to develop a sense of purpose and direction, rather it will be harder for him to do so because the conditions are not conducive for this to occur.

To Be or Not to Be

Between the ages of six and twelve children go through the crisis of industry versus inferiority. This is an especially unique time of life. At the start of this period the child goes through the rite of passage of beginning first grade and really entering life outside the immediate world of the family. By the end, at about age twelve, the child marks the passage from childhood into early adolescence.

Because this is a time when children are very eager and ready to learn how to do things, sports can be a constructive medium for developing a sense of industry. In virtually every culture this readiness is accompanied by the beginning of some form of systematic instruction. Children look to parents, teachers, older siblings, and coaches to teach them how to perform various tasks. As children pass through this stage they not only want to do things, but they want to do things well. The potential to develop a sense of mastery is the central theme of this stage and thus it is incumbent upon the adults who have access to children in this stage to orchestrate such a positive outcome. At this time role models begin to play a major part in the child's imagination. Parents, coaches, and sports superstars are all looked to in order to find their way.

In order for our boys to develop a sense of competence, they need to feel that their efforts at being productive achieve positive results. It is important for them to know that they planned something out (e.g., learned how to catch a ground ball), followed through (put in the time outside the game situation to practice it), and performed well in the actual game. If a child does not have enough of these positive experiences, he will develop a sense of inadequacy and inferiority. When this happens, children sometimes begin to withdraw from activities and involvement with peers who are perceived to be more competent. The fine line that parents and coaches must walk in this stage is to show the child the way with support and encouragement, without fostering dependency. Children need to have their efforts recognized, their successes praised, and their mistakes used as opportunities for new learning, not as evidence of failure.

Because of Patrick's age, he borders two crises: the attainment of a sense of initiative and a sense of competence. His situation is also a good illustration as to how a negative resolution of a crisis from a previous stage can undermine a successful resolution in the current stage. In Patrick's case, he already carries a sense of shame and self-doubt, which makes it much more likely for him to develop a sense of inferiority. The reason is logical and simple. Because he is highly anxious and doubts himself it will be difficult for him to learn new things and perform them well. Anyone who has ever attempted to field a ground ball when feeling uptight knows how this decreases the chances of fielding it cleanly. This is a snowball effect that can move in both directions. If we field it cleanly, the next one will be more easily handled. If we muff the first one, the next one will be even more difficult. In Patrick's case, it will be really hard for him to do well when he feels that his self-worth is at stake every time the ball comes to him. This is all the more reason to encourage kids to just have fun.

If the conditions change for Patrick, that is, if he is blessed with good coaches and teachers, if other, more sensitive and insightful members of his extended family get involved, or best of all, if his parents attend parenting classes or family therapy and see him as a young person needing their patience and support, then he might relax enough to become comfortable with himself. As he feels more at ease he will be able to allow himself to do well at T-ball or other tasks. When this is the case he would be able to use his success in T-ball as a medium to compensate for his prior negative feelings about himself.

Obviously sports is only one medium to utilize in the development of a sense of industry and mastery, but it is a good one. It can be lots of fun, and unless either a harmful coach or an overly anxious parent has previously contaminated the experience of sports activities, kids will continue to be drawn to such popular games as soccer, football, softball, and Little League. Overinvolved parents and overinvested coaches can really kill off the fun that is inherent in sports activities. Parents need to work hard to see their middle-childhood to preadolescent child as a person separate from themselves. Parents need to be mindful as to whom they are rooting for: for their child, or for themselves through their child.

Although Alex is two years older, and much more successful as an athlete, he like Patrick is wrestling with developing a sense of himself as a productive and competent boy. What is interfering with the successful resolution of this crisis is his father's overidentification with him. It is fine that Bob has been willing to invest his time and energy in coaching his son, but clearly some of this effort has been more for himself than for his son. On many occasions Alex has felt that he has let his father down, even though he has consistently worked hard and never given up.

To Bob's credit, he was courageous enough to come for counseling with Alex and has really made efforts to be the father he wants to be for his son. Through his efforts in some individual sessions, Bob has even developed some insights as to how he had been vicariously living through Alex's success as an attempt to quash his own self-doubts and shame. He realized that he had acquired these feelings about himself as a result of his mother's harsh parenting. Alex's dad is a strong, handsome, and physically fit man who from outward appearances would not in any way project self-doubt, but like all of us he is only human.

Coaches and parents like Bob need to ask themselves for whom they wish to achieve a victory. If it is for the children then, for instance, all will be given a chance to participate in the game and the score will never be run up on an opponent. We who work with children as parents and coaches need to stand guard to make sure we don't inadvertently use our boys to compensate for our own prior failures or otherwise vicariously live through them. Unless we rein in these impulses, our boys may very well develop a sense of inferiority and inadequacy. In subsequent chapters, I will explain and give more examples of how this can happen even with young athletes who are highly successful.

Independence Day II: Who Am I?

This question pretty much sums up what the struggle of adolescence is all about. From about the ages of twelve through nineteen and beyond, teenagers are wrestling with the crisis of developing a sense of identity verses role confusion. This stage varies widely as to when it begins and when it ends. Some young people may begin to enter it as early as age ten, while others are not quite done in their middle twenties. Besides Who am I? such questions as Where is my place in the world? and How can I get them to like me? accompany feelings of insecurity, confusion, as well as excitement.

This stage begins with the adolescent's attempts to integrate childhood experiences into a new understanding of himself. This is no small task. When we consider the dramatic emotional, cognitive, social, and physical changes that are taking place at this time, it is little wonder how difficult it is for such a man/boy to find a role for himself. The boy is turning into a man, but is not yet one. His body is changing, hormones are flowing, and desires are springing to life that never before existed and simultaneously produce feelings of anxiety as well as the promise of great pleasure and of grand things in store.

In an effort to resolve their psychological crisis, teenagers must ultimately distinguish their own sense of themselves from other people. But along the way they will experience the disturbance of role confusion. This can manifest in the form of self-doubts regarding their intelligence, competence, physical attractiveness, and even their sexual identity. This is a disturbing process for the child and his parent, but it is natural. When a child is allowed to progress through this stage, this crisis is not unlike a summer storm: we see it coming; we are fully entrenched in it, obliterating our sense of perspective; then it begins to move on. Parents sometimes encourage a premature resolution to the crisis by pushing their child into a career choice, e.g., to be a doctor or a ball player, or by demanding that their child be compliant, highly achieving, or a "good" boy. When this is the case, the results invariably backfire. There usually is a crisis of confidence. Rebellion occurs either during adolescence or it simmers for many years only to erupt in one's mid-thirties. When this upset occurs in the teenage years it frequently takes the form of poor academic performance, quitting the sport he had always loved, sexual acting out, alcohol or other drug use, and/or involvement with the legal system. It is just as tragic when the upset occurs later in adulthood. Marriages are disrupted. Romantic entanglements outside the marriage develop and the normal routine and stability of the lives of the now grown-up boy's children are negatively impacted. In order to avoid such dreadful consequences parents and coaches need to handle these confused, hormonally charged young men with a sense of respect and understanding.

At the end of this stage, the adolescent who has successfully resolved this crisis has come to know who he is. He has a sense of his strengths and can now better tolerate the knowledge of his limitations. He no longer tends to see himself in dichotomous ways: good/bad; attractive/ unattractive; smart/stupid, et cetera. By understanding the adolescent process parents and coaches can minimize their impulse to overreact and instead guide boys through the turbulent storms they face.

Josh and John are two young men who could really benefit from having a safe harbor and a beacon to guide them through their storms. They differ greatly in age and this is characterized by marked differences in their size, beard, voice, and experience with women. One appears to be a man while the other seems like a boy. In reality, however, they both are young men at different phases of the same life stage. They are both in search of themselves.

John's uncertainty as to who he is and his desire to please make for a very transparent understanding that this is a young man who is searching, but who is not yet at home with himself. On the other hand we mustn't be deceived by Josh's arrogance and swagger, for he and John are but flip sides of the same coin. They are both young men not fully grounded in their identity. The challenge is to confront them with this knowledge and to assist them toward the successful resolution of this crisis.

When we encounter young men who present themselves like John, we can easily fall into perceiving their accomplishments as gifts they present to us, as the mice left at the front door by a cat for his master. We must be vigilant not to inadvertently reinforce a boy's sense that he needs to perform and please us in order to be accepted and affirmed. We must walk a fine line between thanking them for what they've brought us, and at the same time letting them know that we value them whether they bring us something or not, whether they *hit* that bases clearing double or score the winning goal. In the case of John, we need to encourage him to achieve excellence in academics and athletics *for himself*. We need to let him know that we are proud of the effort he has put in and that we are especially pleased that he is more in charge of his life and is doing the things that he believes are worthwhile.

On the other side of the coin is Josh. As many of his teammates and the coaches he has had over the years have came to know, he is a guy who is easy to dislike. If we are his coach, he is almost baiting us to do so. And if we get hooked we will join the ranks of those who despise him, but, more important, of those who don't really know him. Despite his arrogance, Josh is a sensitive guy who has used his athletic prowess and conceitedness to keep others at bay. And he has been very effective at doing so. Few people know of his troubled family life and the uncertainty that dwells inside him. The challenge for a coach is to demand integrity in Josh's behavior in a manner that does not trigger his oppositional behavior. Josh needs a coach, a father, and a mentor who would not be put off by his attitude. This man/boy needs a father who would be neither intimidated by him nor disgusted with him. He needs a wise and patient man who would respect the person inside and in doing so create the conditions for him to emerge. As the real Josh comes to the surface, he would move toward self-acceptance and the successful resolution of this crisis of identity. This is not an easy job, but it can be done. Helping young men like Josh is why fathering, in all its forms, is such a worthwhile activity. And sports is a very convenient medium for these efforts.

Developing the Capacity for Intimacy

The next stage occurs as our boy has truly become a young adult, from about age nineteen through age twenty-eight or so. It is during this time that the crisis of intimacy versus isolation emerges. What this means is that the boy will either learn to form close relationships, including friendships and especially love relationships, or will come to feel alienated from others and alone. Although there are more stages in the psychological and social development of men, for the purposes of understanding the psychology of our boys, we will conclude our examination with this stage in which he seeks to develop the capacity for intimacy.

During this period of time young men are very much on the move. Typically they are in college or engaged in some other activities related to their development of a career. They might be involved in a trade, college, or graduate school, participating in various social or political activities, entering the military, working, and/or becoming involved with a special girlfriend. When they are at home, they are there in name only. Always out. Always busy. This occurs much to the chagrin of younger siblings, who miss the presence and attention of their older brother.

Regardless of the particular focus of activity, there are two general factors at play. The first is that the young man is out of the house and into the world. The second is that whether or not he is involved with someone, there is a strong pull toward a relationship. Clearly the activity of greatest emotional significance at this stage is commitment to a partner. The success at each stage is in part a function of how well he has resolved the crises of the preceding stages. This is especially true now that he is entering adulthood and seeks to make meaningful connections with others and perhaps commit to a lifelong mate. In order to make such a commitment he must have a reasonably solid sense of who he is. With such a positive sense of self he might then become ready to love and care for others.

The negative consequences are quite clear as well. If the young man does not know who he is, he is likely to develop unhealthy and potentially destructive relationships. As a young man who straddled two stages of development, Josh was at risk in the arena of relationships. Because he had not adequately come to know and accept himself, Josh fell prey to always needing to have a pretty woman on his arm in an attempt to shore up his self-esteem. As a handsome young man, he had no trouble finding lovely candidates. This of course never really works and in his case it occasionally triggered off insecurity and jealousy that on one occasion led to assault charges pressed by one of his girlfriends. Men who hit women are not yet men, they are boys in men's bodies. They act "strong," but feel weak. Josh's eventual success in developing a capacity for intimacy depends on having a clearer sense of himself as an adequate person and in building his capacity to know and tolerate his limitations. Our job is to help create the conditions necessary for Josh to obtain a sense of strength by becoming more accepting of who he is.

People tend to seek out others at their own levels. Consequently if a man feels wounded, inadequate, unworthy, he will likely find a partner (if he finds one at all) who will reinforce his perception of himself. A young man who lacks a clear sense of identity may isolate himself. But if he does venture out to form a relationship with a young woman he will tend to find one who will most likely fit one of three extremes: one who is as sad and feels as inadequate as he, thus sharing and reinforcing a common negative experience of the world; one who will be emotionally abusive and critical of him, thus reinforcing his low self-esteem; or one who because of her own wounds would be drawn to mother him, thus reinforcing his sense of inadequacy and dependency.

Responding According to Stage

At each stage of our boy's psychological and social development the stakes are enormously high. This is evident as we observe him entering the stages of the teenage and young adult years. By this time we have a sense of the boy's enduring personality traits as well as his social skills. But make no mistake, what we see in these later stages is clearly a function of what has come before. What we do with our boys at each stage makes a difference. Sitting side by side with a three-year-old and putting a puzzle together, teaching a five-year-old how to swing a bat, rough-housing with an eight-year-old, sharing a quiet moment on a fishing trip with a twelve-year-old are among the meaningful opportunities to connect with a boy. All our actions do count.

An otherwise well-meaning client once shared with me his interest in being involved with his children and grandchildren only "after they were housebroken." In saying this he revealed to me how he had missed the point of giving to these children in the ways in which they needed him to, as well as when it was needed. Furthermore, in failing to do so, he was forgoing the opportunity to experience and share in the wondrous early experiences of little boys. A normal instinct built in to older males is to feel drawn to give guidance and to mentor the young ones. Because Bob was not guided in his boyhood and into his young adulthood by his own father, he was not provided with the kind of role model that would instill a similar behavior toward his own son and grandsons. This is an unfortunate situation for all concerned.

The strength and depth of character that will eventually develop in our boys, as young men, depends very much upon our respectful involvement with them *at their level* and *at each stage* of their development. It is the *quality* of the interaction that makes these exchanges meaningful ones. What must come first is the willingness of the adult to genuinely lend himself to the boy. For instance, this may translate into engaging with young boys by getting on the floor and looking at the world from the perspective of their eye level. Whatever the age, whatever the medium, be it a board game, a sport, or a book, adults who are willing to lend themselves are able to see, feel, and experience the world as if through the eyes of the child. Children always know when this kind of relating happens, and it not only fosters a bond between them and the adults, but the child also feels affirmed in the process. When the child feels this kind of positive affirmation, the natural childhood egocentrism built into the boy will attribute it to qualities that reside within him. As this happens he develops a sense of himself as valuable. As you can see, developing a positive self-concept is a simple process, but not an easy one.

Knowing what stage of development a boy is passing through can be very helpful to a coach or parent in appreciating what is the most current theme that they can positively influence through their interactions with the child. It is also true that the developmental issue at hand is an avenue *into* the child. By following the child's lead, so to speak, through our knowledge of his boy psychology, in essence we are shown the way to engage with him. If we interact in a child-centered manner with a four-year-old knowing his need for taking initiative or with a fourteen year-old knowing his need to have a clear and positive identity then we put each in a better position to receive what we have to offer. When we do this as a parent or coach, we will be more effective in teaching a particular skill *and* simultaneously conveying a respect for the self that resides in that child. If we also impart sound values through our own words and actions, then we also foster the development of character and integrity in the boy.

In this chapter we have explored a process of psychological and social development that is shared equally by boys and girls. Although the manifestations of the behavior underlying a given developmental issue may differ by gender, the psychological and social issues at stake are exactly the same. For instance, a nine-year-old boy's fascination with a major league first baseman from his favorite team and the daily efforts he exerts to emulate him as he plays baseball is parallel to the efforts of a like-aged girl in refining her skills with watercolors in an art program. Both children are addressing the developmental task of coming to feel like competent individuals. They both do this by learning skills that lead to the accomplishment of real tasks that they find interesting and meaningful. I want to emphasis that it is not my intention, by this example, to gender-stereotype. Just as a normal middle-childhood-aged girl may be interested in mastering the art of soccer goal tending, a normal middle-childhood-aged boy may similarly be interested in perfecting his skill as an artist. My point is that boys and girls, while sharing a similar process of psychological and social development, are nonetheless different. This is something to which people who have raised, taught, or coached boys and girls can all attest. It is also a fact that idealists and ideologues who are convinced that the genders are the same and that any differences are due to societal influences, a history of patriarchal domination, and so on, find abhorrent. Real involvement with boys and girls can serve to inform an individual who previously was guided by a preferred notion or a particular theory. In the next chapter we focus on those aspects of psychological processes that are particularly unique to boys.

I want to encourage you to learn more about what comprises the psychology of boys by looking through the list of books and other resources provided in the Appendix 1. By expanding your knowledge of gender differences in psychology and physiology you will learn more about yourself and that can only help you as you encounter the boys in your life. It is also self-evident that being able to "read" where the particular boys you are raising and coaching are coming from will equip you to more effectively respond to them and guide them in their journey toward manhood. We will talk more about this in the next chapter.

3

In Order to
Coach Boys We Must First
Understand Them

I N THE PREVIOUS CHAPTER we laid the foundation of our understanding of our boys by examining some of the psychological and behavioral characteristics of boys that are rooted in their brain structure and brain chemistry. We also explored the psychological and social development of boys as they progress through a biologically preprogrammed series of stages. Imagine each of these bodies of knowledge as transparencies. Each explains some particular qualities about our boys, but when laid on top of each other they provide an even richer understanding.

This chapter begins with the addition of one more important body of knowledge about our boys. Continuing with the analogy, this particular transparency focuses exclusively on four specific dimensions within the psychology of boys *and* how they evolve into the psychology of men. When the healthiest dimensions of boy psychology are fostered, our boys develop into men with a healthy adult male psychology. However, when the conditions are set for the less functional qualities to develop, our boys grow into emotionally immature men. When this third transparency is placed upon the first two we will be equipped with enough information to have a pragmatic and workable understanding of the psychological makeup of boys and of the men they can become. This knowledge can help us to be mindful of creating the conditions necessary to foster high esteem, sound character, and integrity in our boys.

✦ Archetypal Psychology ✦

The writings of the psychoanalyst Carl Jung have long been regarded as having rich psychological meaning. In particular, his work has facilitated the understanding of some of the dynamics of the masculine and feminine human qualities that reside in all people. More recently, writers such as Marion Woodman, Robert Bly, Ann Yeoman, Robert Moore, and Douglas Gillette have continued to elucidate the yang and yin of the psychology underlying the genders. What follows is a rudimentary explanation of Jungian psychological principles that can assist us in better conceptualizing boy psychology. Please understand, Jung wrote volumes, as have those carrying on his legacy through the C. G. Jung Institute in Zurich, Switzerland, and other institutes. Therefore I dare not suggest that his entire work can be summarized in the following paragraphs. I merely wish to present enough of it to whet the reader's appetite and to provide a clearer sense of the person residing inside that boy who is being coached or otherwise parented.

Part of the brilliance of Jung was in his understanding that human beings for the most part cannot be characterized as all one thing or the other, rather their personalities tend to possess degrees of many different elements or characteristics. For instance, we might not accurately know who a boy is if we see him in the extremes of being either independent or dependent. Rather he might best be served if we were to know him as a boy who is independent or dependent to a certain degree. He might be even better served if his coach understood him as a boy who in particular circumstances, and under certain conditions, could function with greater independence. A coach who is equipped with understanding might know that this particular boy needs a pat on the back as opposed to a kick in the pants. The coach might even know when the metaphorical kick in the pants would be helpful.

Another example is in seeing a boy as neither exclusively introverted nor extroverted but rather as one who has certain qualities of each that may be increased or decreased depending on social conditions in his milieu and in how his coach approaches him. Similarly a young man might have characteristics that could be considered either more stereotypically feminine or masculine within his personality. A boy in the former case may be more sensitive and empathic toward others and may shy away from aggressive action. This does not make him any less male, but rather helps us to understand that this particular male has a personality that is not characterized by exclusively "male" qualities. Indeed, just as the level of testosterone does in fact vary from person to person in both genders, boys and girls *will* have characteristics that are stereotypically male *and* those that are stereotypically female.

Because boys' personality characteristics operate much more on a continuum between two extremes, rather than being locked in at one of the extremes, a one-size-fits-all approach to teaching, parenting, or coaching our boys would miss the mark. If it works well for one group of boys, it tends to make the others feel as if they do not fit in. In order to reach all our boys, a boy-centered approach is required. We will talk more about that in chapter 6.

Who Knows What Evil Lurks in the Hearts of Men?

The answer to that question from the classic story is that "only the Shadow knows." Whether Jung could have fathomed that one of the central tenets of his notion of the unconscious human mind would become a central character of a comic book, television program, and movie is purely a matter of ironic speculation. Although it is comprised of an interweaving of several complex elements, the shadow represents the dark side of human nature. What feeds the shadow? According to Jung we each have both a cultural history and a personal history. Within each person there are irrational and primitive impulses and beliefs that may be thought of as residing just on the edge of our conscious awareness. Greed, fear, lust, envy, hatred, sadism, and a passionate displacement of all that is evil and ugly in oneself upon others (thus justifying any and all acts of aggression upon them) are manifestations of the shadow. It can be a disturbing experience when this dark knowledge rises to the surface in dreams or conscious thoughts or feelings. In some individuals and groups of individuals the floodgates of this underworld open and they act out with horrific results. Nazi Germany's Holocaust, the more recent ethnic cleansing in the Balkans, parents attacking each other and referees in youth sports, and the sexual assault by the young men in New York's Central Park cited in the first chapter are but the tip of the iceberg.

While a courageous individual can learn from these shadow impulses, it is also natural for people to deny or repress them. According to Jung, when they are repressed or otherwise neglected their psychic energy disappears into the unconscious mind only to be manifested in disguised forms later. An otherwise decent person may sometimes spill over, so to speak, and say or do something regrettable. As Vince Lombardi said, "Fatigue makes cowards of us all." We are especially susceptible to being less than the best we can be when we are depleted physically, emotionally, nutritionally, or spiritually. We *and* our boys are all capable of having our actions directed by our shadow. Our only hope is that we are strong enough and grounded enough to dare to know our whole self. The humility we gain as we struggle for self-knowledge will help us considerably as we guide, counsel, and coach our boys who are in so many ways susceptible and governed by their own fears.

The Elements Within the Psychology of Boys

Jungian personality theory is useful for understanding who boys are and for giving parents and coaches a handle on helping them to emerge in adulthood as whole men with sound character and integrity. There are four components, which Jung would call archetypes, in the psychology of boys. In its most healthy form each component is balanced and reflects the ideal qualities we look for in our boys. Within each of the four components are two extreme shadow forms that hold the potential for pathology and dysfunction. Robert Moore and Douglas Gillette in their book *King, Warrior, Magician, Lover* do an excellent job of exploring these concepts in boys and men. Their title helps identify the four components that comprise the psychology of mature men. If we do a good job in helping our boys become whole, then they will grow to acquire the most mature and healthy forms of the psychology of men. However, if we don't create the conditions that would foster this growth, then our boys are at great risk of evolving into men who are guided by the unhealthy, shadow forms of their king, warrior, magician, and lover components. The precursors to the development of the healthier adult male forms are boy psychology archetypes specifically applicable to athletics and sports: the leader, the hero, the strategist, and the loyal teammate. We will now discuss each.

The Leader
The leader represents the part of the self that fosters a love for life and for developing a capacity to find contentment. In the adult mature form, as king, it is manifested as the wise ruler who knows his power, understands his responsibility for it, and does not exploit it. The two extreme shadow forms of the leader are the exploiter who is basically a demanding narcissist, and the perpetual infant. Both shadow forms are the result of overindulgence.

Two of the young men from the beginning of chapter 2 demonstrate elements of each. As a sensitive child who was wounded by a father who in effect had abandoned him, John was to some extent overindulged by his mother, who sought to make it up to him as best she could. In doing so, however, she reinforced some of his self-doubts and insecurities. These were manifested in his being overconcerned with pleasing his mother and coach and underperforming while under pressure. A boy who feels abandoned by his father irrationally attributes his father's actions to his own inadequacy and in not being lovable. He then simultaneously feels rageful and weak. John is no weakling, but a piece of the perpetual infant shadow was inadvertently reinforced by overindulgence.

On the opposite extreme of the shadow we find Josh. As a gifted athlete, he is a classic example of one of the major things that can go wrong in male sports. At each higher level of competition, as the athlete's degree of skill increases, he is held to *decreasing* levels of accountability for personal actions. As the big man on campus he is indulged by parents and coaches, sought after by young women, given passing grades by teachers, and given special dispensation were he ever to get into trouble. In response to his considerable athletic success, Josh was overindulged, but in his case it was manifested in the shadow form of the self-centered exploiter. He used women, thought only of himself, and was convinced that the teammates and coaches who were upset with him really had a problem that had nothing to do with him.

The leader has a significant influence upon the other three archetypal components of boy psychology. If the boy manifests this balanced sense of self, then balanced and healthy forms of the others will naturally follow. This also holds true for the adult male psychology. As this boy emerges into adulthood he will likely be directed through the world by the king. When this is the case, the healthiest dimensions of the warrior, magician, and lover will be manifested as well. The king knows himself, including his weaknesses and insecurities, yet does not run from them. He is strong enough to know everything about himself. He is capable of tolerating awareness of his shadow and consequently he is less likely to be ruled by it. Because of this he is capable of being compassionate and reasonable in his dealings with others. Our boys who grow to be men guided by the king are strong, grounded individuals who have an enormous sense of fairness. They become the men we want to run our companies and to marry our daughters.

We need to remember that part of growing up is struggling to learn about oneself. As we discussed in the previous chapter, the processes of individuating and separating are central to that adolescent experience. Given that the resolution to these crises may not come until our boy is into his twenties, even a boy guided by his leader is likely to pass through dark forests and rough seas before his king self begins to take hold. Struggle is part of the emergence of the self even in the most well-adjusted young man, so we need to be prepared to be patient and ready to lend a hand along the way. As coaches and parents we need to keep our faith in our boys who have come through in the past and have faith even in the ones who have yet to do so. This can be considerably frustrating at times, but it comes with the territory.

Carl Jung's writings have explored in depth how it is naturally built into human beings to (consciously and unconsciously) look to the promise of the leader child. Joseph Campbell's exploration of mythology, folklore, literature, and religion chronicled the theme of the leader, referred to as the divine child, as a central component of the human psyche. His work has demonstrated how this theme has been on the minds of all people across cultures and throughout the length of human existence. I have personally experienced this with the birth of each of my sons. Many new parents are similarly deeply touched not only by the miracle of birth, but by the profound sense of hope and of the divine. Some even experience a feeling of redemption, as if there is now a chance that what is wrong and evil in the world may be put right. There is such promise with new life.

We must carefully nurture the leader component in our boys. As we parent and coach we must be mindful of fostering its ideal form while guarding against reinforcing the elements of the shadow. As we are doing this we will be directing them toward letting the king in them emerge as they mature.

While it is only natural for children to be egocentric, the leader consistently considers the overall needs of the team. An example from baseball is when a player "gives himself up" by hitting to the right side of the infield in order to advance a runner who is on second base. The leader as batter would be out at first base, have no statistical credit either in the form of an improved batting average or an RBI, but would get the job done for the sake of the team. Another example is when the leader gives emotional support to teammates. A pat on the rear end or a tap of baseball gloves accompanied by a "don't worry about it, you'll get him next time" when a teammate makes an error is yet another. Or when the leader makes an out he might encourage a teammate to manifest his own greatness by the simple statement "pick me up."

When a child manifests this leader behavior it is imperative that the coach recognize him for it. This can and should be done publicly and privately by the coach. The coach in either setting can acknowledge and support the actions of the leader in such a manner that sends a clear message that *this* is the sort of behavior and attitude that is worth aspiring toward. The coach has several options. He may make affirming statements directly to the leader, making sure they are overhead by his teammates. "That's the way we play on this team!" or "Way to give your self up, way to go!" The coach may also use the actions of the leader as an instructional tool. "Did you see the way John gave himself up and moved the runner over? That's the right attitude. You need to ask yourself what is best for the team." Last, but certainly not least, when a coach models the attitudes and behavior of the king, our boys will see a good model. When this happens they will increasingly move toward the leader in their own boy psychology. However, please remember that all boys, like all men, have shadows. It is our job to help keep them in balance and to be guided by their own ideal form.

The Hero

This is a balanced boy who is not pulled off center by his impulses. He has a mission and he moves toward it. He has a strong sense of right and wrong, and is guided by his principles. When the hero is manifested in our boys they are frequently very courageous in how they rise to meet a difficult challenge and they convey a sense of responsibility for their actions. Sports is a particularly useful forum for the emergence of the hero when boys test their emotional and physical limitations. In the mature male it takes the form of the warrior who, having the full resources of the adult male, can be a powerful force for virtue and the betterment of the community. He is a man who really comes through for us.

The two shadow forms for the hero are the hot dog and the quitter. In the former we see a boy who seeks to impress others. Because he truly does not believe in himself, he is threatened by others who doubt him and may act out aggressively toward them. This is a manifestation of the primitive instinct to kill off a threat. On the baseball field, we might find his actions saying, "Look at me, look at me," as his ball sails over the outfield wall for a home run. The hot dog, motivated by his sense of inadequacy, is very much a *me* player not a *team* player. In the latter we see just the opposite. The quitter is also resentful and angry, but hides it. He is also very apprehensive about declaring his position whether physically or intellectually. In baseball, he is the boy who won't go after a ball, but rather lets the ball play him.

Vince, from the last chapter, is a good example of a man who in many respects is a man only in years. By his refusal to leave either his wife or his lover and his continuing to hurt both himself and his wife, he vacillates between the two poles of the shadow. He is both a hot dog and a quitter. His actions toward his wife have a sadistic element. It is as if he is saying, "I refuse to incur the guilt for making the choice to leave you, therefore I shall put you in a position through my repeated betrayal in which you will be so hurt, you will have to be the one to call it quits. When this happens, I will feel hurt, I will feel that I deserved it, I will feel guilty for hurting you, and I will feel relieved." This position is an expression of both passive aggression and cowardice.

In stark contrast to Vince are the boys from chapter 1 who rescued the baby who had fallen into the canal. In the true sense they were heroes. They acted purposefully and without hesitation did what had to be done. As we raise and coach our boys well we will help them move toward the warrior they are capable of becoming as men. The word "warrior" can be disturbing to those who do not understand the nobility and sense of duty that it carries. Its shadow forms are frequently mistaken for the real thing. A man who has a developed warrior self carries a sense of mindful purposefulness. He has a sense of perspective and fully engages with life. The hero and the warrior are fellows we want on our team, whether it is the volunteer fire department, school board, or sport team.

In *The Hero with a Thousand Faces,* Joseph Campbell explores the central theme of the hero in the human psyche as demonstrated through mythology. Invariably the hero comes from common human origins, but is uniquely gifted. He encounters a struggle, rises to meet the challenge, and contributes to the betterment of mankind as a result. Prometheus, the Buddha, Lance Armstrong, and Michael Jordan are heroes, and through their struggle and victory we all benefit. Organized sports have the potential to be a wonderful medium to help the hero emerge in every boy. By engaging in a dedicated struggle the boy becomes more confident and comes to believe in himself.

A good example of hero behavior is when a boy manifests a never-give-up attitude. When Joe Montana had the football you always felt that anything was possible. When Jerry Rice was running a deep fly pattern you were always sure that he not only could catch a difficult pass, but was a credible threat to deek the defense and score a touchdown. When one of our boys in Pop Warner football comes to be known as a "go to guy," he has most likely demonstrated the consistent just-give-me-the-ball attitude of the hero. Michael Jordan's failure to make his high school basketball team initially brought him to tears. However, his mother's wise counsel that he must use the energy from his upset productively was a strategic intervention. She simply told him to use the energy to make the team and to show his coach and teammates that the wrong decision had been made. Jordan himself gives credit to the ceaseless effort he exerted in ultimately making the team for being a major building block in his character development. Years later, after losing an important game six to a young and strong Utah Jazz team and facing a difficult game seven, Jordan said with a sense of assurance, "We may have weak legs, but we have strong hearts."

As coaches we need to reinforce this never-give-up attitude and behavior in our boys. Believing in the hero in each child, not just in the star players, and conveying this belief is imperative. Given that sports is only a game, it is particularly important that the coach recognize and encourage the hero/warrior in all his boys, for this is something that can clearly be taken off the field or court and brought into all aspects of their life. As with the leader, both public and private acknowledgment of hero actions and attitudes is very powerful. The boys will naturally feed off this. Their ears will perk up when a coach tells stories of Michael Jordan or Lance Armstrong and the never-say-die attitude that leads to success. They will also be interested to hear about the coach's own struggles as a younger ball player. Similarly a teenager or young man with "women problems" would also be positively impacted by a caring coach telling of how as a young man it affected him when a girlfriend broke up with him and how he dealt with it. Courage, of course, is something needed throughout a boy's life. Most important, when a coach demonstrates his belief in his boys as individuals and as a team it encourages his boys to believe in themselves. When this happens we all really win!

Heroes are sometimes the result of the right person happening to be in the right place at the right time. The Bucky Dent home run in the famous 1978 playoff game between the Boston Red Sox and the New York Yankees will be forever remembered by Sox fans. He was an unlikely hero, a hitter who did not usually hit home runs, coming through in the clutch. Coaches at the college level and below are encouraged to find and create situations that might provide an opportunity for an average player to manifest his hero form. An example in early youth sports is when the coach runs over to high-five the not-so-athletic boy as he runs hard all the way to first base and beats the throw. A coach of a high school baseball team might choose to let a player hit for himself in a crucial situation to convey his belief in him. When a coach is not just interested in winning, but in building character along the way, he constantly scans to find these moments for greatness.

When we coach with an eye toward developing the hero in boys, we must go beyond encouraging the never-give-up attitude. The noble hero merely begins there. We want to coach to encourage effort *and* good sportsmanship. We need to reinforce the efforts, not the outcome of their efforts. Of course we celebrate successes, but we want to put the emphasis upon the hard work that leads to success. We also want to teach that success achieved in any way dishonorably is tainted and not to be savored. Winning at all costs is not really winning. Winning achieved through injuring another player or cheating is winning in name only. We want our boys to grow up to be honorable warriors. When we coach a boy to be an honorable sportsman, he becomes a more complete person. As we as fan, parent, or coach observe this hero, we feel that all is right with the world.

The Strategist

One of the most wondrous qualities of boys is manifested when we see an industrious and intellectually curious child working on a project in which he is completely immersed. The activity itself is unimportant, it is the act of being so thoroughly engaged that activates his desire to learn and develop a sense of mastery that makes this boy a strategist. In early childhood it shows, for instance, in a boy's fascination with a prism placed in his hand or by the continual stream of "why" questions. "Why is it raining? Where does the water go when it goes down the drain? Why is there a rainbow? By middle childhood the boy's expertise in baseball statistics, building rockets, or computer games is enough to astound the imagination. I have taken personal advantage of this on several occasions at Yankee Stadium when I was curious about what a batter did the last time up or whether he still leads his team in home runs. I turned to the nearest eight-year-old for the information he was more than willing to dispense.

The two extreme shadow forms of the strategist are particularly relevant for youth sports coaches. On the one hand is the wanna-be. This is a boy who has some skills or knowledge, but mistakes what he has for all that there is to know. The wanna-be who uses the pretext of being a master of a particular body of knowledge is really being a master faker. This is a boy who is covering up his own self-doubts and insecurities with an "I'm the one who knows, you're so stupid" attitude. Our football friend Josh frequently sent these messages to his teammates and coaches. In so doing he created divisiveness among his peers, he instilled self-doubts in younger ones, and he presented a façade of knowing it all so that coaches found him unreceptive to their counsel.

One of the challenges in coaching is working to help our boys become coachable. By this I mean creating the conditions that make a boy open to feedback and guidance from his coach. The wanna-be can deceive himself into thinking that any further input from the coach is superfluous and unnecessary. As coach we have to walk a fine line, relaying to the boy that it is okay to not know everything and that therefore he might benefit from a few moments of a coach's counsel. While doing so it is imperative to convey a sense of respect for the boy's psychological territory. The wanna-be can be easily threatened by a confrontation, but it is worth the risk in order to reach him. While it is only natural to want to avoid an unreceptive child, as coach or parent we nevertheless must take on this difficult task. We owe it to him not to walk away and leave him to his own devices. It may feel uncomfortable for both parties, but a caring and constructive confrontation need not be offensive. It can be a very positive and potentially transforming encounter.

The benchwarmer represents the opposite shadow form. Boys with this shadow activated present themselves as unresponsive and incapable. Their seemingly dull and distractible intellect frequently gives rise to frustration in coaches. In athletics, the benchwarmer can seem very much out of his element and disconnected from his own body. In T-ball he can't seem to let himself grip a bat with the strength he possesses. In soccer he watches the others as if he has no right or capacity to kick the ball. It's as if this boy was not in full command of himself . . . and he is not. These are the very boys who really need the involvement of men and other boys with skills, but who so frequently are ignored at best or ridiculed and abused at worst. The benchwarmer also presents himself as uncoachable. Like the wanna-be, he requires great persistence and genuine interest from his coaches. In the face of the frustration that coaches invariably experience when encountering either of these shadow forms, we must be guided by our goal of reaching the boy. We must recognize that his attempts to put us off are attempts to maintain a fragile sense of mastery. Coaches need to know this and must not take offense from such players.

What we are referring to as the strategist in boy psychology is manifested in the mature adult as the magician. This man is a person who has the capacity to see beyond himself and in so doing has an observing ego. Consequently he possesses knowledge about his inner experience of himself and also knowledge of the outer world. He knows interesting things and he is willing to pass it on. As Moore and Gillette observe, it is magician energy that drives our modern civilization. The investigative and creative forces behind the technology that is such a central part of our world are manifestations of the magician. However, as many of us are all too aware, we have the capacity through its shadow form of producing questionable science at best and incredible destruction at the worst. Genetic engineering, scientific fraud, space-based weaponry, and seemingly endless quantities of nuclear waste are but some examples.

However, the issue at hand is reinforcing the most balanced form of the strategist in our boys. As coaches we want to emphasis brains not just brawn. I have already told my own sons a story my father told me about how, in essence, his strategist was activated in him as a boy. My father told me of watching a big parade in the town where he grew up. There were marching bands, dignitaries, and representatives of the military. It had rained heavily the night before, as was evidenced by the large puddles that gathered on the street. He told of how impressed he was as the army marched in formation down the street and through the puddles as if they were not there. He told of how the marines unflinchingly did the same thing. But he was most impressed by the navy. They kept in unison, as did the others. But just before the puddle, they split formation and marched around it, never missing a step. On the other side of the puddle they re-formed their ranks and continued as before. The inventive and creative solution to the problem of the puddle cast a lasting impression on my father's young mind. Years later he chose to enlist in the navy to fight in World War II.

Another example of the strategist/magician is Michael Jordan's strategy in dealing with Karl Malone in the NBA championship game in 1998. Jordan had noticed Malone not protecting the ball from behind when he made defensive rebounds. He decided to retain that knowledge for later use when the game was on the line. In the final minutes when the circumstance presented itself Jordan made his move and stole the ball and in doing so helped move the Bulls toward another championship.

We want to encourage boys and reinforce them when they come up with strategies to outwit an opponent. A coach who will ask boys why they think he decided to call a certain play are fostering this sort of inventive thinking. Similarly a coach who is open to suggestions and input from the kids on his team is respecting the strategist in his boys. If encouraged, boys will begin to understand that creative and strategic thinking is a skill their coach expects them to develop.

The Loyal Teammate

The first relationships that boys develop are with their parents. In particular, the most primary and vital one in infancy and early childhood is with their mother. By definition one of the central components of the psychology of boys is the central involvement of their mother in their lives. They, quite literally, owe their lives to these women. Make no mistake, it is a goddesslike act to give birth to new life. How the mother and son manage this rich and important relationship has a great deal to do with how effective the boy will eventually be in forming healthy and mutually respectful adult relationships with women. The relationship a boy has with both parents also sets the stage for how effective he is in relationships with his peers and how he deals with the authority figures he will encounter throughout his life. The loyal teammate archetype represents this connectedness to others as well as the dynamic of how connected he is with the world around him. The balanced loyal teammate feels his life fully, has a strong appreciation for his internal experience, and is intrigued by the world around him. It is from this archetype that a boy develops a sense of spirituality. He is introspective and has a capacity for having an empathic understanding of others.

The two shadow extremes of the loyal teammate are the pleaser and the dreamer. In the case of the pleaser we have a child who is overly involved with his mother. He frequently is too dependent upon her and very sensitive to how she feels about him, but also may feel an inappropriate responsibility for her feelings. This excessive neediness and boy-caretaking-of-mother dichotomy frequently leads to a boy feeling trapped. As a young man he frequently is trapped by being drawn to women as if they were essential for his psychological well-being, thus feeling dependent upon them. The other half of the equation is that he also feels the need to push women away so as not to suffocate. *The Casanova Complex*, by Peter Trachtenberg, did a good job of describing young men who were caught in this pattern in which women are objectified. Josh's use of women as "hood ornaments" is indicative of the exploitative tendency of the pleaser. The loyal teammate manifested in the pleaser focuses on constantly pursuing beautiful women, but does not know how to have a relationship of substance and true intimacy with them. The pleaser uses his charisma and athletic achievements to seduce women. Consequently, women drawn to him for his many charms are frequently hurt and disappointed.

This young man not only treats women as objects, but also, in doing so, he objectifies himself as well. He acts as if he is an "it" who needs those "its" in order to feel whole. Despite his outward confidence and beauty, the pleaser is haunted by feelings of inadequacy. Despite his seduction and plunder of the opposite sex, he does not really feel enough like a man. Ironically, it isn't that he merely uses women—he is dependent upon using them in a misguided attempt to shore himself up. Once he woos and conquers a woman, gets her to fall in love with him and open herself up to him, he does not know what to do with her. Then he runs.

At the other shadow extreme is the dreamer. Whereas the healthy loyal teammate feels a connection with his inner world and the world around him, the dreamer is markedly disconnected. Whereas the pleaser is actively, although counterproductively, maneuvering in the world, the dreamer is more rigid and passive. He dreams dreams that he has no chance of ever implementing. Whereas a healthy boy's dreams are an exercise in imagination, a creative expression, and fuel for future actions, the dreamer's are locked into an exclusive exercise of fantasy. He is frequently depressed and isolates himself from others. In an organized sports setting his behavior will provoke his teammates and peers to reinforce the isolation. Reaching this lost boy is a real challenge to a coach.

Like the benchwarmer, the dreamer takes a passive stance in the world. He may want to catch the bus, so to speak, but he does not get himself to the bus stop on time. Consequently the bus and life pass him by. The dreamer is not inclined to last long in organized sports and is likely to be there only because his parents made him join. It is therefore imperative that coaches in early youth sports make a conscious effort to bring him into the game, into the team, and thus into the social world. It can be very tempting to high-five and stroke those boys who are naturally gifted as athletes, but the benchwarmer and dreamer need this kind of affirmation and inclusion *at least* as much.

As with the other positive components of boy psychology, coaches need to consciously reinforce the attitudes and behavior that denote the loyal teammate. An example is when a child senses another player feeling down on himself for having made an error or dropped a pass and then uses that understanding to be encouraging by either words or gestures. A coach observing this can let the loyal teammate know he appreciates what he is doing.

Another mark of the loyal teammate is when a player has the capacity to put the game and the meaning of the game into perspective. For instance, after the loss of a game, a comment such as "We'll get 'em next time" reinforces the notion that all is not lost and to focus on preparing for the next contest. More important, the child who manifests the loyal teammate archetype realizes that there are more important things in life than a game for the sake of a game. This isn't to suggest he doesn't care; on the contrary, if his leader, hero, and strategist are activated he is a hardworking, dedicated player. The boy with a strong and balanced loyal teammate within is both there for his teammates and has a child's version of a philosophical perspective on the game as being a training ground for things yet to come. In that sense he knows that it's only a game. Sometimes this is manifested by being a balancing presence in the locker room or on the bench. He knows when it is the time to joke, and with whom, and when quiet conversation is in order. Even if they are injured, loyal teammates can be effective just by being there. They sense what is going on with individuals and teammates and intuitively know how to respond appropriately. To some extent this cannot be taught, it has to develop in a boy. But it certainly could be reinforced, and it definitely can be modeled!

It is well documented that modeling is one of the most powerful and effective forms of teaching. A coach can model and reinforce loyal teammate behavior by sensing what his players are feeling individually and as a team and responding in ways that work best for each player. Joe Torre of the New York Yankees is an extremely effective manager because of his ability to "read" and understand the psychology of each of his players. As a result he has been able to adjust his interventions according to the personalities of each of his players. When a coach does this he is not only modeling the capacity to understand and to have an empathic understanding of another, but also, because he is not force-fitting his players into one mold, he is able to get the best out of each one.

If all goes well, our boys will emerge into adulthood with a grounded and positive sense of self. In these young men the more balanced and healthy form of the adult male will be activated. I don't mean to suggest that our boys would not have any shadow forms, they will. We all do. Rather, because as men their king will govern them, they will be better equipped to manage them.

Having a sense of the four manifestations of boy psychology and the corresponding psychology in men is indispensable in order to understand where we are with our boys and where we hope to go with them. Furthermore, I believe that being able to identify when the shadow forms emerge is important in order to be good shepherds. I especially encourage you to read *King, Warrior, Magician, Lover* by Moore and Gillette, who did a fine job detailing the theoretical transition from boy psychology to man psychology. Furthermore, it is vital for us as men who are parents and coaches to understand the components and manifestations of our own shadows so that we can make a conscious choice to be the best man we can.

✦ The Shadow Method of Coaching ✦

There is no official "shadow method" of coaching, but because it is so common it is worth commenting on. It is imperative that coaches, fathers, and mentors be mindful of their shadows. As long as they have a reasonable degree of awareness, these men will be able to focus on the important things our boys need. Unfortunately most everyone can recall experiences with gym teachers and coaches that serve to reinforce the stereotype of the "dumb aggressive jock." An episode from the popular *Seinfeld* television show epitomized this by flashing back to George Costanza's high school days when his gym teacher nicknamed him "can't-stands-ya" and encouraged George's jock-type classmates to harass him.

There is no end to the variety of manifestations of a coach's and father's potential shadows in sports, but we will briefly discuss two. One particular form of this darkness is what we can safely call abusive coaching. The two primary ways that coaches become abusive is in the end-justifies-the-means way of thinking and acting, and in assaults on the self-concept of a player.

The End Justifies the Means

When a coach is guided by the notion that the end justifies the means, anything goes as long as he is able to bring his team to victory. No doubt if this were a real war situation such a position could certainly be justified. Sports, however, is only a "play war" situation. It is only a game. The survival of life as we know it is not really on the line. But the long shadow of an unenlightened coach could certainly get him to act as if it really were a war to the death. In 1974, Martin Ralbovsky first exposed this darker side of coaching in his book *Lords of the Locker Room: The American Way of Coaching and Its Effect on Youth*.

Giving credit where credit is due, I must acknowledge that such shadow methods are able to engender a strong work ethic in their players. In fact, many such coaches are able to build sports programs with fine winning percentages. But successful programs do not in any way have to come at the expense of developing the components that comprise integrity in our boys. In fact, the value of hard work could be so much more meaningful if learned in the context of being an honorable warrior. Nevertheless, these coaches take their players under their wing and with "proper" training, they turn out fighting machines. It is unfortunate for all of us that the whole person is frequently sacrificed for the development of a shadow warrior; a man-boy who is trained to manifest his aggression on command like an attack dog. I once counseled Barry, a young police officer who told me with delight a story of an army boot camp experience. They were playing war games and as a result of being captured he was brought before the commandant. Upon presenting his prisoner to his commanding officer, the "guard," thinking the game was over, lowered his weapon. At that moment my client, his prisoner and his fellow recruit, grabbed the gun and smashed the butt of it into his jaw and took his captor prisoner. Although the "guard's" jaw was broken, the commandant was mighty impressed with my client and his aggressive ingenuity. If this had been a real enemy his actions would have been impressive. Unfortunately both Barry and his commanding officer were unable to see the folly in perpetrating such harm upon one of their own.

Those who have relationships with such a shadow warrior and care about him will suffer and he will also suffer. He may not notice it on the day of the big game, but because he has been trained to be one-dimensional, life will be harder for him. He will not know how to decode his inner voice and he will not know how to best communicate to those who love him. He may not know how to best take care of himself and he probably will not know how to mentor, coach, or parent. It is not terribly surprising that Barry came to me at the urging of his wife, saying that she found it impossible to communicate with him. Because all glory is fleeting, a shadow warrior, like Barry, may very well carry an emptiness inside that he might eventually bestow upon his own son or upon players he might coach. As we said earlier in the book, the sins of the father are bestowed upon the son . . . unless he musters the courage to face his shadow.

Injury to the Self

The shadow of abusive coaching can also cast its pall over the developing self-concept of the players who are subject to it. Some players may respond with higher levels of performance to the use of meanness, insults, and derogatory comments as the primary means of motivation. However, a sense of negativity is injected into the coach-player relationship through these hostile acts. Even players who do try harder or perform better subsequent to a dose of abuse absorb this negativity and conditional regard from their coach directly into their self-concept.

Derogatory comments regarding one's talent, attitude, physical appearance, ethnicity, race, or religion can be very wounding to a boy or young man, yet many who employ the shadow method of coaching continue to abuse their boys under the guise of "making them tough" or "treating them like boys."

I recently contacted a high school soccer coach in his mid-twenties named Bill. He had a client of mine on his team. Derek was bright and hardworking on the field and in the classroom, but due to a combination of immaturity and having a problematic learning style he began to run into conflicts with some coaches and teachers. Although he did not let it be known to others, he felt terribly ashamed when he was not able to perform to the high standards imposed upon him by his parents. The fact that he had a learning disability made it particularly difficult for him to tolerate the frustration of not "measuring up," as he would say. As an attempt to cover up his embarrassment, Derek would sometimes become quiet and act as if he did not care. To the world of coaches and teachers this seemed like copping an attitude. Bill, his soccer coach, responded to this by getting in Derek's face and taking an aggressively firm stance with him. Bill did this out of a sincere attempt to get Derek to "not give up on himself" and to try harder. Although getting in a player's face can certainly have its place in coaching, Bill's one-size-fits-all method of motivation got Derek to work harder only half the time. It turned out that the energy Derek did put into digging out the ball and putting his foot into it was rooted in his hatred for Bill for treating him poorly. The rest of the time it served to demotivate Derek. He thought that his coach did not believe in him and he became convinced that Bill did not like him. The point is that although Bill was not a malevolent guy, his shadow was slipping out and in doing so was inadvertently contributing to Derek's wounded sense of himself. Being a young man himself, Bill lacked the wisdom that years can sometimes provide. However, regardless of our age, we need to be mindful of how our approach to our boys may affect them. By not seeing boys as individuals and assuming that they are all able to respond to the same aggressive (in this case) coaching method, Bill was less effective in developing Derek's skills as a player and esteem as a young man. Our shadows leak out when we take similar coach-centered versus boy-centered approaches.

In terms of injuries to the self, what is even more pervasive is the tolerance on the part of coaches for players picking on and making fun of their own teammates. When this happens with a boy who has a fragile or somewhat negative sense of self, he can't help but feel that he is less worthy than the others. Furthermore, when a coach tolerates this sort of behavior and attitude toward players on another team the character of our boys is further diluted by the addition of poor sportsmanship.

Winning Is Everything

Another manifestation of the shadow method of coaching is the "winning is everything" mentality. There is nothing inherently wrong with either winning or with competition. I personally love to win. When and if there are problems with competition it is because of what coaches sometimes do in the name of competition and because of their overemphasis on winning. I do not offer this as an excuse, but some coaches' distorted notion of winning and competition reflects a point of view shared by many people and frequently portrayed in the media as "normal" thinking. It may be normal for some, but it is not healthy and does not in any way reflect the mature form of masculinity.

When a coach overemphasizes winning, he injects his own shadow into the young men and boys entrusted to him. This sort of coach sacrifices working toward the development of character and integrity for the sake of winning. When a coach's priorities are skewed in this way it does not necessarily mean his team will win more or that his players perform better. However, it does reinforce the body of research that asserts that as boys advance, especially in aggressive sports such as football and basketball, they are held to *decreasing* levels of personal responsibility for their actions. Not only does it hold that the more talented and successful a young man is, the more he will be treated by his peers, parents, coaches, and community as if he is privileged, but such boys come to develop a perverse sense of entitlement. Of course it is not particularly surprising that their worldview is egocentric. If the only problem were a boy developing poor social skills, it would be bad enough. However, all too frequently the perception that the world, and frequently women, are subject to their whim creates serious problems for all concerned. Do not make the mistake and think that this is a case of pampering that got out of hand. There is nothing beneficial here for our boys. On the contrary, the "benefit" is only for those doing the pampering: the coaches who wish only to win or who can't be bothered confronting a player's attitudes and behavior off the field; the parents who feed vicariously off their son's athletic prowess or who could never consider that a son of theirs might be wrong; or the alumni community who cares only for the numbers in the win column. In point of fact, these "pampered" boys are really exploited objects.

What does it look like when our boys are pampered and privileged? When the normal standards of conduct and integrity are not applied to them, by virtue of their status as an athlete, then the disservice of privilege is committed. Among the acts of indulgence is a lack of accountability for cheating on the field or in the classroom; for bullying and other acts of aggression toward peers, especially those of lesser social status; for noncompliance with academic standards; for noncompliance with alcohol and substance abuse rules; and for exploitation of females. Research has shown that this privileged treatment begins in the youth sports programs of eight-year-olds and continues throughout the college years and beyond. One of the central reasons *Really Winning* was written was to address the problem of organized sports all too often producing young men who are characters, instead of young men *with* character. Fortunately, we can do something about this.

✦ You and Your Shadow ✦

As with all the archetypal elements in the mature male psyche, great caution must be taken to ensure that the healthy, balanced, and beneficial qualities of the magician are activated. Regardless of whether you are a father or a coach, your willingness to look at and know your own shadows is essential for mentoring the next generation. One of the central problems with youth sports is that for so long, in many schools and programs, men who are not conscious of their own shadows have held leadership positions as coaches and athletic administrators. In order to really win with our boys, conditions have to change so that there is no longer room for these dangerous individuals. The impact of their destructive qualities is just too great. A man who is a good coach or teacher always has elements of the magician activated. He need not be a perfect man, but he must be a conscious and caring one.

Our boys are strong and resilient but they also have fragile self-concepts and are enormously malleable. The latter makes them especially susceptible to their environment. Depending on who their team leaders or coaches are, they will have either the functional or shadow components of their personality reinforced. We must do our best to ensure that the adult males they are exposed to model the mature forms of adult male psychology. It is all too easy to come under the spell of bullies and otherwise inadequate men who get their kicks out of turning boys into fighting machines instead of noble warriors. Since these men are uncomfortable with their own introspection, they would naturally feel threatened by a sensitive boy on their team. Such a coach would likely not recognize that he felt threatened but rather judge the boy as being too soft or a bit of a wimp. His interventions with our boys would result in their being less than fully integrated as whole people. Instead, their own shadows would be fostered, in particular the exploiter, hot dog, quitter, and wanna-be. Fred Engh in his book *Why Johnny Hates Sports* speaks to this as a problem that is rampant in organized youth sports. The system has been failing our kids and the simple fact that many are not having fun is proof enough.

I remember being told by a vice president of human resources of a major corporation for which I consulted that he made a decision to get rid of an employee because "We don't like wimps around here." It is notable that the employee happened to be quite competent at his job. It is also notable that the man doing the firing was a man who did not seem to know how to have a mutually respectful relationship with his own wife. He tended to buy her showy things, but could not muster the courage to have a genuinely intimate relationship. Eventually when he told her of his decision to seek a divorce she said, "I guess he fired me too."

Coaches and leaders who are directed by their shadows live vicariously through the victories of their charges. Because they are themselves not whole they will focus on one-dimensional coaching. The it's-all-about-winning attitude is among the cluster of little-boys-in-men's-bodies beliefs that has cast such a negative pall on things masculine. Many people, men and women included, had come to mistake such a pathetic example of male mentality and behavior for the real thing. It is not the real thing; it is only a shadow of the real thing.

As I have said, in order to be an effective parent, mentor, or coach it is vital to know your own shadow and vulnerabilities. Unless we know our shadows we are likely to employ shadow coaching to some degree in our dealings with boys. Ironically, one of the best mediums for accessing this knowledge is the very boys you coach. Try this exercise for identifying your shadow issues. Identify the two or three players whom you like best among the boys you coach or have coached. Now identify the two or three players to whom you have the strongest negative reaction. Note the qualities and personality traits of the "positive" players and do the same for the "negative" players. It is the latter players who, through your strong reaction to them, will show you your shadow.

You have disliked these players. You have benched them or have otherwise limited their playing time. You have found them either frustrating or irritating. These are the ones that bug you and because of that you can use them to guide you to your shadows. Although you feel what you feel toward them, *it is not they who make you feel this way*. Rather it is *you creating your own feelings in reaction to them*. Because of this you are in a position to learn about your own shadows. This sort of introspective learning is not for the faint-hearted; it does take a great deal of courage. Our shadow exists whether we face it or not. The way I see it, it's best to know what is there, because it's there anyway.

Make a list of all the negative feelings and attitudes you have toward these players. It might look something like this:

I don't like his whining . . . he expects me to take care of him
He's afraid to work hard . . . and he gives nothing in return
He doesn't know how to follow through . . . he disgusts me

He's weak and afraid . . . I don't like my own sense of cowardice,
so I don't like it in others

I hate this kid . . . I don't have any use for him

He's a bad apple and I want to get rid of him . . . he makes me
feel like a bad coach

Now that you have identified your negative shadow reactions, the way
to understand and be productively guided by your own shadow is to take
a counterintuitive approach. For example, if you do not like his whining
or cowardice then turn your gaze back at yourself and understand that
you also don't like your own ability to whine (even if you do not actually
manifest that behavior) and your own cowardly feelings. After all, the
more grounded and solid we are, the less reactive we will be to the in-
adequacies of the boys we coach. It is only natural that we are not going
to like a boy's cowardice, but the more grounded we are, the less we will
use it to kick up our own personal "stuff." The less stuff that is kicked
up, the more capable we will be of responding in ways that help the boy
move beyond being a coward.

Jerry Lynch and Al Huang in their book *Working Out, Working
Within* provide a very helpful exploration of the experience of fear. They
talk about using fear as a teacher that can help us become better and
stronger. Instead of running from fear, they encourage the counterintuitive action of turning to face it. This is what must be done with all
manifestations of shadows in order to learn from them. Michael Jordan
did a similar thing in consciously choosing to find out what his weaknesses as a basketball player were and making a commitment to himself
to make them his strengths. When we do not face our shadows, sooner
or later they will manifest themselves. Sports history buffs know all too
well the story of legendary Ohio State football coach Woody Hayes.
While he was with Ohio State, Hayes's Buckeyes won three national
titles, four Rose Bowl victories, and thirteen Big East titles. On two occasions he was honored as Coach of the Year. Despite all he had accomplished, his shadow leaked out while he was coaching Ohio State in the
1978 Gator Bowl. When a Clemson player made an interception and in
so doing thwarted an Ohio State scoring drive, Hayes reached out as the
player made his way up the sidelines and "clotheslined" the kid onto the
turf. Because he was not sufficiently aware of and in control of his
shadow impulses, Woody Hayes's career ended abruptly that day.

The point is this: we all have shadows. The shadows show up in the form of negative emotional reactions. I am referring to this as our "stuff." The more we are aware of our own shadows, the less we will be blind-sided by our reactions. When we learn from our impulses we know more about ourselves and are in a better position to help our boys. Taking the counterintuitive approach can not only teach us about own shadows, but can also guide us to know how to respond to the bad apple, the coward, the frightened or antagonistic boy. For instance if we feel disgust we can reposition ourselves to provide compassion or if we feel anger we must come to feel acceptance toward those who evoke such feelings. I encourage you to be mindful of the importance of keeping **SCORE**.

Stop and observe your internal reaction to the boy
Control your impulse to act
Orient yourself by owning your experience as self-generated
Respond in a boy-centered manner
Evaluate whether your intervention moved the boy forward

Sometimes the few seconds that remembering to keep **SCORE** takes will be all you need to gather yourself to be the best coach you can be. Kids and young men don't usually plan their shadowlike actions and consequently you are likely to be hit out of the blue by them. Having a simple tool like keeping **SCORE** at your disposal will help you to let your own balanced, kinglike self emerge.

✦ Modeling and Mentoring ✦

When mature and psychologically balanced men are involved with mentoring boys and young men only good things can happen. Many of the unsung heroes that we encounter in our daily lives attest to this fact. In contrast to the ancient stereotype, when our boys are fortunate enough to have a gym teacher who is grounded, skilled as an athlete, and fun, they learn so much more than they even are aware of. Mr. Boone is the gym teacher in my local elementary school. He is young. He is handsome. He is athletic. He is fun and the kids love him. All the kids, boys and girls, future athletes and future nerds, experience the sense of inclusiveness he creates. He helps the children to acquire athletic skills, but it is readily apparent that he is guided by the intent to foster self-esteem, self-acceptance, and feeling comfortable with oneself. Literally all the children adore him and think he is the coolest guy around. He is modeling how a balanced man behaves.

My friend Ed Adams is a psychologist who has a small gallery in my town where he displays and sells watercolor and acrylic paintings he has created. He has also become accomplished as a sculptor. In fact Ed has become so successful at his art that he has dramatically reduced his private practice, except for one small but significant piece of it. Years ago he began a group for men called Men Mentoring Men. It has continued for almost twenty years and has been both a therapy group and a support group. Some of the original members still belong. On occasion I have bumped into Ed and some his guys at a local coffee and bagel shop and whenever I do I am struck by a profound sense of being in the presence of a positive force. I do not mean to come off as New Age, but these guys have worked together in fostering the emergence of their king archetype and it is evident. It is even evident in how they treat my young sons. When they have been with me, my sons were given a sense of recognition and acknowledgment for the boys they are and the men they will become. This does not come with fanfare or psychobabble, rather a respectful acceptance of them is conveyed. It has been very pleasant to experience. These are good guys. These guys are the kings.

As psychologist Erik Erickson has written it is a natural and healthy expression of psychological and social development for an experienced man of years to want to give back to the next generation. This does not come with an ego investment in having a protégé. It simply feels like the right thing to do, not out of a sense of morality or a should; it comes out of the center of their being. Good coaches are drawn by this instinct to give back and when the conditions are right the players are ready to receive.

A good example of old warriors giving back is what happens with the New York Yankees during spring training. There is a tradition for the great Yankee players of the past to pass on their knowledge. The current crop of players knows that the former stars are a fount of knowledge, and are eager to receive. Everywhere one looks in spring training the likes of Reggie Jackson, Don Mattingly, Yogi Berra, Ron Guidry, Goose Gossage, and others are present to offer their thoughts and input to the players currently playing their former positions. First base prospect Nick

Johnson said it best in reference to working on learning how to play that position with Don Mattingly. "You just have to listen. To have guys like him around, and not to take advantage of it, that would just be wrong." Among the Yankee traditions passed down is the creation of the conditions that make young players like Johnson coachable. Manager Joe Torre commented, "It's amazing, what they do here with all these guys hanging around every spring. It really gives you an appreciation for what's gone before you, and it's great to see that our guys appreciate it."

No amount of mentoring or modeling would be sufficient if the mentors did not have an appreciation for the psychological state of the newcomer. The Yankee heroes who return every spring seem to have a respect for the younger players' position. This sort of player-centered orientation not only helps create the conditions that make the players receptive to input, but furthermore, it is the only way the mentors can effectively know what is needed. Regardless of their age, our boys need us to be centered upon them. I do not meant that they should be focused on in a way that would reinforce egocentrism or narcissism, rather as a means of understanding and respecting the experience of the boy whether he is two, ten, fifteen, or twenty-two.

Carl Jung sees our young heroes as having three stages of development. Carefree play is the hallmark of the first stage. A pillow fight and a squirt-gun fight are good examples. The reckless thrill-seeking of adolescence occurs in the second stage. Driving fast or performing other dangerous, silly stunts are examples. As the boy develops into a young man the last stage occurs. At this point he is prone to take up idealistic causes. Self-sacrifice frequently accompanies these missions, whether it is a stint in the Peace Corps or joining a protest about global warming. Boys will be boys and therefore when they behave according to the stage of psychological and social development they are in, their coach, father, and mentor need to honor them.

✦ Heroes ✦

When Lance Armstrong won the bronze medal at the 2000 Olympics there was a good deal of consternation among some in the media as to his "failure" to win the gold medal. All this clamoring over the loss of the gold medal revealed some of the shadow qualities of our broader culture. We have become so obsessed with winning that even placing third among a large field of the best athletes in the world was seen as not coming through. I'm a psychologist and I can assure you, that is insane. In a similar fashion, paying a sinful amount of money to a guy who throws a little white ball real fast, while elementary school teachers scrape by, is also insane. It reveals how out of balance our culture has become. It also reveals what kind of work we have to do with our boys.

However, it is encouraging to know how Armstrong handled the press. When he was asked to "explain" his bronze medal he stated simply that he rode as fast as he could; that he received the bronze medal for his efforts; he acknowledged that the other racers were faster; but that he did his best and was pleased with his medal. To know the Lance Armstrong story is to know the story of a true hero. His struggles, his near death, his sportsmanship, and his dedication to his sport as an honorable warrior reveal him to be one of the thousand faces of the hero. Joseph Campbell pointed out how difficult it is to walk the hero life in these modern times. Campbell said:

> It is not society that is to guide and save the creative hero, but precisely the reverse. And so every one of us shares the supreme ordeal—carries the cross of the redeemer—not in the bright moments of his tribe's great victories, but in the silences of his personal despair.

I suspect that Lance Armstrong would scoff at the notion of being a hero. This fits rather precisely, for a man who is directed by his king archetype is not one to feed off his ego. He simply does not find it gratifying to focus on the self. He does what he does because it is the right thing to do. This is not unlike the boys who saved the baby from the canal in the first chapter; they did what they had to do and then they went home. Creating the conditions that foster these kinds of selfless acts is our target.

Remembering Vince Lombardi's statement that "striving to win" is everything can really put the usefulness of sports into perspective. Our boys are not playing for our benefit or for our glory. Through our help they are engaging in becoming honorable warriors. Boys and young men who are encouraged to work hard and follow through in their respective sport are developing a solid character. When we coach them to do the

right thing, play fair, and honor their opponent, we cultivate sound values and personal integrity in the next generation. Our boys become real
heroes when we create the conditions for their physical, emotional, and
spiritual development. Our attitudes toward them, and their successes as
well as their miscues, will send very clear messages as to whether we
believe that winning is everything, or that striving to win is everything.
We will carry this theme into the next two chapters as we talk about
building integrity training into our coaching.

4

A Guide to
Sports Psychology for
Parents and Coaches

O VER THE COURSE of the millennia many coaches and athletes have angled to obtain a competitive advantage over an opponent. Some have sought to do so by various acts of chicanery and poor sportsmanship. Ben Johnson's doping in order to increase his efficiency as a sprinter; Johnny Mackenzie, the Boston Bruin infamous for biting opponents during the occasional NHL scrum that so taints the sport; Mike Tyson doing the same to Evander Hollyfield's ear in a boxing match; and the major league baseball pitchers who have been guilty of "doctoring" the ball are but a few examples of athletes seeking to elevate their own performance through dishonorable means. Fortunately, throughout the history of sports many have sought an advantage, not by denigrating their sport or opponent, but by simply trying to bring out their own personal best.

If we were to study athletes at the elite level of many sports we would notice that there is a great deal of parity among them. For instance, most competitive sprinters have access to comparable training facilities, nutritional and conditioning trainers, and coaching. Consequently, despite differences in physical endowment that can be attributed to an individual's genetics, there is remarkable similarity in the physical attributes these athletes possess; they can all run very fast. Given this equal playing field, so to speak, how can we account for those who are consistently more successful than the others? When we rule out physical advantage, the difference comes down to what is between athletes' ears. Not their brains, but how they think and how they mentally approach the game. The attitudes, beliefs, and other techniques employed to optimize an athlete's mental preparation for competition are what we call sports psychology.

No one knows for sure when people first began applying psychology to sport, but it is reasonable to speculate that the ancient Greeks must have. Because it is known that their philosophers reflected on the relationship between the body and the mind, it is reasonable to consider that the idea of mental preparation was employed by some who competed in the ancient Olympic games.

Norman Triplett was one of the first to document the influence of an athlete's psychological condition on his physical performance. In the late 1800s he observed cyclists under different race conditions and found that their athletic performance was enhanced by the presence of other competitors. Simply put, he consistently observed an increase in cyclists' speed when they raced against other cyclists as opposed to racing only against the clock. Since all the other conditions were the same, Triplett concluded that the presence of other racers affected the cyclists' psychological state and that therefore one's state of mind can substantially affect one's physical performance. In the 1920s, the father of American sports psychology, Coleman Roberts Griffith, established the first laboratory devoted to the study of the influence of one's mental condition on athletic performance. He went on to serve as a sports psychology consultant to the Chicago White Sox baseball team.

Since these early days the field of sports psychology has gradually expanded until it really flourished in the 1960s. Thanks in part to the political climate of the cold war, the East, notably the countries formerly known as the Soviet Union and East Germany, and the West, in particular the United States, Canada, England, and Australia, invested a great many resources into research on ways to enhance the performance of athletes. The aim was to ultimately reign victorious at the Olympic games and to exploit this achievement as "proof" of the superiority of one's political system. Fortunately we are the beneficiaries of all the time, energy, and money that went into this research that was originally intended for the exclusive use of elite athletes, for it is equally applicable for all ages and at all levels of sports.

✦ The Five Skills of Mental Fitness ✦

There are five mental fitness skills. When we use them to help our boys to maximize their abilities in a sport it is called sports psychology. When we use them to help them do well in other areas of their life it is called optimal performance psychology. The skills are:

1. To develop an active awareness of themselves
2. To hold as a constant a positive mental attitude
3. To effectively manage their energy
4. To employ an effective goal-setting strategy
5. To use imagery to guide them toward these goals

What follows is a description of each mental fitness skill along with some practical suggestions for using and teaching them with the boys you coach or parent.

✦ Active Awareness ✦

In this first skill of mental fitness we teach our boys to have a greater awareness of themselves. Developing such awareness is crucial in making any significant changes in how a boy approaches a sport, or for that matter how he approaches his studies. We know that beliefs, attitudes, and mood can affect performance for better or worse. Unless a boy becomes tuned in to his beliefs and how these influence his thinking and his behavior, his performance may be negatively impacted. In a similar fashion, how he is feeling emotionally and physically may also have a direct influence on how he approaches his sport and his subsequent performance in it.

When we help our boys to develop the skill of active awareness we are training them to be more conscious of themselves, more awake, and more present with themselves. Most people walk through their daily lives with minimal conscious experience of themselves despite the fact that our mind, our feelings, and our body are constantly sending a stream of information to us. This information is, in essence, a feedback loop. It is continually feeding back sensory data and information that we can use to make sound decisions and judgments. This information can be very useful to our boys, who can then make the necessary adjustments in order to excel in their sport. A boy can only take advantage of this information if he develops an active awareness of himself.

Beliefs and feelings such as "it's too hard for me," "others are better than me," or "I can't do it" do not have to play themselves out in a poor performance. Such negative thinking needn't plague an athlete, although he shouldn't try to deny that these thoughts exist. Quite the contrary, the more he is aware of them, the more he will be able to play an active role in adjusting these messages so that they better serve him. For example, if the endless internal tape is playing messages that are negative and disaffirming, our boys can be taught how to transform them into messages that are affirming. "I can't do it" and "I might as well give up" can be transformed into "I can do it," "I can trust myself to follow through," "I can work hard," and "I do not give up." I will specifically explore how to implement strategies to transform such negativity in the next section when we discuss the second skill of mental fitness: developing and maintaining a positive mental attitude. But first let's take a look at the three steps that must be taken in order to master the mental fitness skill of active awareness:

1. Become the observer
2. Become the one who chooses
3. Become the one who takes action

Become the Observer

The first step of active awareness is to tune in to our *thoughts, feelings,* and *bodily sensations.* The way to do this is by simply observing. A walk in the woods becomes a richer experience when we stand silent for a minute and listen to the sounds of the wind passing through the leaves and animals rustling in the underbrush. A mouthful of our favorite food becomes a complex mixture of flavors and textures when we forgo shoveling it down, but instead take a moment more to actually taste it. Similarly, a boy who is tuned in to the subtle messages his internal tape is sending him can find these to be a source of valuable information. Some messages are positive and some are negative. With practice, after they have been gleaned for any meaningful information, the negative ones too can be transformed into positive messages. A boy or young man so positively affirmed will be running on all cylinders. But first we have to do the prep work required in order to accentuate the positive.

Most people find it disturbing to discover an unpleasant thought or feeling, and it is only natural to move to block out these things from our awareness. A blocked-out negative thought or feeling does not go away, but instead merely goes underground where it can continue to exert its destructive influence. It is therefore imperative to circumvent this counterproductive attempt at "self-protection." Boys being boys, they will need us to help them tolerate what may be troubling feelings or beliefs. We need to encourage boys to tune in, but not be lost to the negative feelings or thoughts they may find. Sometimes helping boys imagine they are a movie camera observing themselves can help them obtain the kind of detached perspective that is helpful.

Nevertheless boys, as any of us might, will be inclined to mistake a negative attitude or belief for a truth. For instance, a boy who feels afraid might think that he is really a coward and that he must hide this shameful truth from others. He might also think that due to this "weakness" he might not be able to meet the challenge that awaits him. If his critical notions remain unchecked the probability that his performance will be negatively impacted will increase. A string of negative performances can reinforce his negative beliefs about himself, which can beget more negative performances. Therefore, we need to help our boy learn to tolerate this kind of negativity and identify it as being *merely* a feeling or thought, nothing more. We need to let him know that brave boys and men often have such feelings and do not have to run from them. We also need to let boys know that being a man means facing our fears, it doesn't mean not having them. We also want to help our boys learn that these fears and feelings of negativity can be used as teaching tools and as sources of personal wisdom.

Jerry Lynch and Chungliang Al Huang did a great job of exploring the virtue of athletes facing their fears in their book *Working Out, Work-*

ing Within. As they explain, when we fight or attempt to force away fear, inner turmoil, tension, and anxiety result, which will then interfere with performance of all kinds. We need to encourage our boys to be brave by feeling the fear, but not being lost to it. When a boy is able to maintain the kind of perspective that "being the camera" can provide, then he is better equipped to decipher the message that his fear offers. As Lynch and Huang put it:

> Whether you fear injury, failure, falling, looking bad or not "making it" rather than moving ahead in this frightened state, allow the fear to instruct you as to what needs to be done . . . Think of ways in which you may get better prepared: more practice, better coaching, safer equipment. By responding to fear in this way you create an important shift in consciousness where you begin to feel a kind of spiritual expansiveness, a freedom that enables you to be more integrated with the Tao, the way things are naturally. With this attitudinal change, you cease to regard fear as a limit, and you focus instead on its sacred value as a guru helping you progress forward in a safe fashion.

It is particularly relevant to our work with boys that we teach them to not cut themselves off from their internal experience, in this case of fear. As they increasingly understand that being masculine means respecting and listening to their internal experience, they move a great deal further towards being fully integrated, whole boys and whole men.

Thoughts

There are two dimensions of thought our boys can become aware of: beliefs and conscious thoughts. Beliefs are sets of assumptions we have about ourselves of which we may not necessarily be aware. They may either be rational or irrational. Furthermore, beliefs may not necessarily be accurate. It is particularly troublesome to have negative irrational beliefs in operation because they are frequently unknown to us. Like the puppeteer pulling the strings of the puppet, these forces exert a direct influence on the actions of an unwitting boy. For instance, if a young man has a belief that says, "I will never be able to hit a low curveball, on the outside edge of the plate," then the probability of him mastering that skill will diminish. If he were to eventually master it, such success would come with considerably more struggle than is necessary. By learning to listen to his internal voice he can access very valuable data about himself. I have often suggested that we need to put our ears to the ground, as the Native Americans once did to detect the presence of buffalo or an approaching enemy. We figuratively need to help our boys put their ears to the ground and simply listen.

Conscious thoughts are quite literally the stuff we hear in our internal dialogue. This seemingly endless string of self-talk is something that occurs in everyone. Because we tend to believe what we say about ourself, it is always wise to make sure we are saying the things that help us. One way or another our conscious thoughts eventually become self-fulfilling prophecies, for we tend to act in a manner that is consistent with what is in our thoughts. I once worked with a football player who after dropping a pass would say to himself, "Don't drop the next one! Don't drop the next one!" Although he didn't mean to, he was actually setting himself up to drop the next one. Instead of an affirming thought about accomplishing the task at hand such as, "Bring it to me, I'm catching this one. Stay focused," his self-talk was focused on *not* doing something bad. Until he learned to correct this habit, he tended to string together a series of dropped passes. This was most disheartening for him. But once he become aware of these thoughts and learned to substitute positive ones, he became a more effective and consistent wide receiver. As our boys become practiced at all the skills of mental fitness they will eventually learn to make sure their internal dialogue aims them in the direction that really serves them.

Feelings

When I talk about becoming aware of our feelings I am referring to the various emotional states that move through us. Some feelings are complex while others seem quite simple and clear. Some feelings are subtle and barely detectable, while others sweep through us like the deluge of a summer storm. Regardless of their form, feelings reveal an emotional state that can directly affect how we approach a sport on a given day. And as with thoughts, if we are not aware of our feelings they may make us less effective than we would want to be. As I mentioned earlier, feelings such as fear can be used to our advantage if we do not seek to avoid them. Not only can they be a teaching tool to guide us toward ways to better ourselves, but they can also serve as a source of energy if channeled for constructive purposes.

Our boys are likely to receive messages from their feelings telling whether they are safe or unsafe, connected with their teammates or isolated from them, confident or frightened, relaxed or anxious, and focused or scattered, et cetera. The odds makers in Las Vegas would be sure to know that it is a much better bet to be safe, connected, confident, relaxed, and focused. In order for our boys to foster these positive emotions they must first be open to all of their feelings, including the less positive ones.

Bodily Sensations

Becoming aware of the information our body is sending about itself can also be critical to optimally performing in a sport. Sometimes this information can be taken for granted. Nevertheless, it provides direct feedback about the state of the machine. An athlete attuned to his body who is preparing for a hundred-yard dash would be inclined to detect a subtle tightness in his right quadriceps. As a result of this awareness he might either make an adjustment in how he runs his race or prepare for the race with particular emphasis on stretching and loosening up this muscle group. A young man who was not as aware might run the race as usual only to pull up lame.

When we teach our boys to be more mindful of the state of their bodies, including what they put into them, we are also helping them to have a greater respect for their bodies and a greater degree of responsibility for it. As our boys become more attuned to their bodily sensations they will be more aware of the messages they receive from their bodies as well as the messages they send to them. For example, a boy's body can inform him how strong, rested, or tense he is and he might in turn send a message about what he thinks about his body, whether he likes it, feels comfortable with it, or trusts it. As is the case with increasing awareness of thoughts, feelings, and bodily sensations, being forewarned is forearmed.

A simple, but effective exercise for developing an active awareness is to have boys practice finishing the following sentences. "Now I am aware that I am feeling _____. Now I am aware I am thinking _____. Now I am aware that my body is saying _____." It can be very informative to conduct this exercise in quiet settings as well as in contexts that may give rise to anxiety such as before examinations, before asking girls out on dates, or before athletic events. This is an exercise a boy can complete on his own or with the guidance of a coach. Sometimes the use of a journal in which a boy enters the thoughts and feelings he experiences on a daily basis can also be effective in increasing awareness of himself. The boy may be counseled to use the journal to specifically focus on sports. For example, a boy might be instructed to note his thoughts, feelings, and bodily sensations prior to a game and then repeat the exercise after his performance. This type of journal could then, with the boy's consent, be reviewed by a coach or parent. Because of the personal nature of an adolescent's journal, assurances must be given to respect his privacy. He must also be prepared to be responsible for keeping the journal in a location that is safe and secure. Of course a boy need not engage in either of these exercises. However, we do want to convey to him the importance of paying attention to himself. And if he gets out of his own way, so to speak, all he has to do is look and listen to what is happening inside and to learn to accept that sometimes we all have self-doubts. The first step is to simply observe.

Become the One Who Chooses

The second step in developing an active awareness of self is to make a choice as to how we would like to feel, think, believe, and behave. This goes beyond focusing on what troubles us, and uses that information to establish our right direction. It is about choosing to turn the coin over and following the direction that is provided on the other side. Our wrestler friend John provides a good example. John wanted to please people, especially those who were important to him. This distracted him in matches if he knew his father was in attendance or when he mistakenly thought he owed it to his coach to win with a pin. John frequently underperformed as a result of his heightened anxiety and lack of focus. I worked with him to turn the "external focus" and "pleasing others" coins over. Instead of these distractions, he chose to wrestle for himself as opposed to for others and to focus on being the best wrestler he could be in the moment. He used his negatives to provide a positive direction for himself.

Other examples of being the one who chooses is to want to *feel* strong and relaxed; to want to *think* in a positive and confident manner; and to want to *behave* consistently with our ideal picture of ourself at bat, on the ice, or on the gridiron. We give our boys a gift as we help them learn that they can actually make these choices.

Become the One Who Takes Action

The third step in developing an active awareness is to choose to take a specific course of action. This choice should be directed by what was learned from the first two steps. It will become obvious as we discuss the other skills of mental fitness that there are a number of pragmatic techniques that can be used to implement the choices a boy makes. The point here is that change only occurs if a specific plan is formulated and followed through. In particular, when we discuss the mental fitness skill of goal setting we will learn to provide our boys with a concrete, rational, and winning formula to move toward their desired goals. All they have to do is follow through in a consistent and practiced manner. These choices and actions will serve as a North Star for our boys and will show them the way to their targets. If they ever lose their way, they can always turn to their plan for taking action. As you will see, among the actions our boys can take to support the choices they have made are to learn to breathe differently, talk positively to themselves, create desired images, and move their bodies differently.

Obviously young men and older boys who are more mature and psychologically sophisticated can readily understand the value of tuning in to thoughts, feelings, and bodily sensations and then to make choices as to how to behave differently. Younger boys can also be encouraged to do so, but in a more down-to-earth manner. A coach might say to this group:

> Hey guys, I know some of you might be a little nervous about the big game, but remember, all you have to do is try hard and, most important, have fun.

The hidden message here is:

> I am well aware that most of you have feelings of anxiety and are worried about how you will perform today, and your stomachs might be feeling a little tense. I want to let you know that it is

okay to have these feelings and thoughts. It is quite normal to have them, especially before an important game. However, we can consciously choose to substitute more positive feelings and beliefs, and remembering to have fun is an effective tool for increasing feelings of relaxation.

Saying all this would be boring as all hell for a group of nine-year-olds and would most likely fly right over their heads. Given our understanding of boy psychology, specifically psychological and social development, we can always effectively adjust our message in order to reach the boy where he is. In the next section I will discuss offering our boys several tools for transforming negativity, fears, and doubts into a positive mental attitude.

John

One of the keys to John's eventual success as a wrestler was learning to see things for what they were. While previously he found himself lost in a muddle of feelings, and frequently angry as a result, I helped him develop the skill to be actively aware of his mind, body, and emotions much earlier. In addition to the "Now I am aware of feeling————" exercise, and talking in weekly sessions with me, John made good use of a daily journal of his thoughts and feelings. He gradually became more aware and eventually increased his effectiveness in deciphering what he was really feeling and thinking deep down. With this increased clarity he was prepared to employ other mental fitness skills to help manage his thoughts and feelings *and* to use them as personal assets and sources of important information, and thereby became one who takes action.

✦ Positive Mental Attitude ✦

In this second skill of mental fitness we teach our boys to maintain a positive and optimistic perspective regardless of the circumstances in which they find themselves. Whether it is a critical moment in a big game or other high-pressure situation, an ability to accentuate the positive helps ensure that one's best can be brought out. Sometimes in particularly distressing situations, such as being down by three touchdowns late in the game or having fallen on the first jump of a figure-skating routine, learning to make lemonade out of lemons can help salvage what seems like a disastrous situation. It is sometimes not easy to be optimistic and positive. Severe challenges such as the distressing situations cited above, or negative beliefs that our boys may have been taught at home, or the self-doubts that invariably accompany youth can make it difficult to see the positive. However, if our boys are to succeed in sports and in their lives, choosing to maintain an optimistic can-do-it attitude is the only realistic choice. There are two pragmatic techniques for achieving a positive mental attitude: *reframing* and *self-talk*.

Reframing

When we help our boys to learn to look for opportunities even in the midst of difficult situations we are teaching them to employ the technique of reframing. It is a mental skill that we can use to identify *any* positive possibilities in apparently negative circumstances. In the act of reframing we consciously choose a perceptual framework that emphasizes any aspect of a crisis situation that can provide a fertile ground for growth, learning, getting better at an aspect of our sport, and excelling. It is a method of responding to a problem that sees the challenge the problem provides instead of the immovable obstacle it seems be at first glance. I am told that the Chinese character designating the word "crisis" is the same character used to convey the concept "opportunity." In this spirit, the key to reframing is knowing we have a choice in how we view a given situation *and* actively choosing to see a situation in a way that benefits us. Philosopher-without-letters and former New York Yankee center fielder Mickey Rivers was once quoted as saying:

> There ain't no use worrying about things you don't have control over, because you don't have control over them. And there ain't no use worrying about things you have control over, because you have control over them. Therefore there ain't no use worrying.

Rivers was talking about having an optimistic perspective and using reframing in order to support that perspective. Good coaches, tending to be amateur psychologists, have always been naturally drawn to employ strategies that emphasize the virtues of having a positive mental attitude such as reframing and self-talk. Many of the signs and posters that are the hallmark of team locker rooms convey an optimistic spirit through a never-say-die attitude.

Reframing is important when our boys find themselves in a situation determined solely by the luck of the draw. I recently observed an example of this when I attended a Little League homerun-hitting contest. It was held on the final day of a tournament that took place over three consecutive weekends. All the boys who hit homeruns at any point during the tournament were automatically entered into the contest. The boys advanced through three rounds in which those hitting the most home runs advanced. The contest came down to two twelve-year-olds during the final round and they were each given ten consecutive swings. A coin toss decided who went first. Whether they knew it or not, at that point each boy was charged with having to reframe his position in the order of batting to his best advantage. It would do him no good to focus on the other's position or to envy it; rather, what would serve him best was to see the advantages that *his* own position provided. The first batter could reframe being the first to hit as being able to set a standard that would put pressure on the boy who followed. He could also see the relief in getting to go first. The second batter could conceptualize his as an opportunity to take advantage of seeing how many home runs the first boy hit so that he would clearly know what target he had to shoot for. He could also see that because of his position, he had a greater feeling of control over the outcome of the competition. Similar circumstances exist in Olympic figure-skating competitions when the order of skating is also determined through a random process. Regardless of whether a person finds himself skating first, third, or fifth, reframing can be very helpful in finding the opportunities for excelling.

Reframing can be very helpful at various times in all sports, in particular when an athlete or a team find themselves in an unfortunate position. Regardless of how we got there the fact is that it is third and twenty from our own three-yard line, or we have just double-faulted for the third time and we are down five games to one in the first set, or the umpire has squeezed us on two consecutive pitches and we are facing a batter with a three and 0 count and the bases are loaded. The common denominator in all of these situations is that if we could have written the script in advance, it wouldn't have been crafted this way. Let's take the baseball scenario as an example for reframing. Three and 0: I have the advantage because I know the batter probably has been given the "take" sign. I lay in a solid strike. Three and one: I'm coming back. I know he probably has a hit sign if he really likes the pitch. I'm going to throw a strike, but no way am I giving him a fat one. I paint the outside corner just inside of where the umpire squeezed me. He takes it for a called strike. Three and two: I'm back now and we both know it. The bat hasn't left his shoulders. I'm in control. I bust him inside. If I don't get him the first time, I'll put it there again. If he fouls that off, I'll take him outside.

Regardless of whether the pitcher is ultimately successful in getting this batter out, he is creating a scenario that will maximize the probability of being successful. He is optimistic and he is positive and with each success along the way his confidence builds. Because he has taken the time to practice the physical skill of pitching and the mental fitness skills, his momentum increases as he finds himself increasingly in his zone. Even if he ultimately walks that batter after achieving a full count, he knows he came back from being way down and can use that to inspire himself to continue to "tough it out." When we encourage our boys to utilize reframing, we help them to incorporate the never-say-die attitude that always seeks the opportunities that lie hidden in difficult circumstances.

Self-talk

Self-talk is literally the stuff we hear inside our own head. Don't worry, you are not going crazy, we all have it. If you listen, you will find an internal intrapsychic chatter between yourself and yourself. You are telling yourself things and because you are listening to what is being said your actions are so influenced. The subjects of this dialogue are frequently things of importance to us, i.e., job, wife, finances, fitness, sex. The tone of this dialogue reflects the attitudes, beliefs, and assumptions we make about the world and ourselves. For example, Person A has a belief that he is capable of meeting any challenge that he faces, he is confident, and trusts his capacity to work things out for the best. On the other hand Person B harbors an irrational belief that he is less worthy than others, he doubts himself and consequently worries about his ability to obtain favorable outcomes. Because we really do listen to and are influenced by what is being said in our self-talk, it is extremely important that the *right* things are being said. In terms of our boys, we need to make sure that the self-talk they have is positive, affirming, and moves them forward toward their sports goals, as well as toward being the most decent and honorable men they can be.

Whether they know it or not all of our boys have an internal dialogue. Their self-talk is naturally centered on matters near and dear to them in their lives, such as having fun and doing well in sports, acceptance by peers, doing well in school, maintaining their job, being attractive to girls, managing their place in the family, and pimples. The tone of their self-talk is often fraught with the struggle to simply feel okay. The world looms large and boys frequently perceive that others find their way in it more easily than they do. Attitudes and beliefs that suggest a discomfort at making mistakes for fear of being exposed as inadequate, worries about acceptability, and an underlying sense of self-doubt are the kinds of things said underneath the disguise of "looking good" and being "cool." In short, most of our boys need the reassuring balm that our positive contact with them can provide, especially if we model and directly teach them about reframing and self-talk. Robert Bly remarked once that when a boy and a father spend time together something like a spiritual food passes between them. Our boys are hungry. Fortunately we have much to offer them.

John

John was anxious about an upcoming wrestling match, so I encouraged him to reframe his anxiety by getting himself ready for what was to come. I also helped him compose an affirmative paragraph in his own words that addressed the things that concerned him as a wrestler. We began by identifying his negative beliefs and conscious thoughts. We then turned the coin and arrived at the following statement:

> I can be a good wrestler. I am a good wrestler. I have the skills and talent for success. I can use my skills and talent. I am successful. I am confident. Distractions do not pull me away from my mission. I can be focused. I am a focused and competent wrestler. I am performing only for myself. The only thing that exists is being a wrestler in the present. I love to wrestle. I am a wrestler.

John then began and ended each day by repeating this to himself and eventually memorized it as his own personal affirmation. He began to see that he could *choose* how to look at a situation, and that this choice could have a beneficial effect on his performance.

✦ Energy Regulation ✦

We all need energy in order to do what must be done; however, our effectiveness in performing a task is largely a function of how well we regulate our levels of energy. When we teach our boys the mental fitness skill of energy regulation we give them a valuable tool in making sure they psych themselves up and not out.

Energy regulation builds on the foundation of the skill of active awareness. As with the other mental fitness skills, its effectiveness is hinged on a person being tuned in to himself on the level of cognition, affect, and body. When a boy is informed in this way he is positioned to know when and what he must do to adjust his energy level. For instance, as a function of noticing whether he is up enough for a game or whether he might be a little too "high" because of excitement or worry, he can use some specific and practiced techniques to move himself into his personal zone. When a boy is in his zone he is neither too high nor too low, but rather is energized at the correct level in order for him to perform optimally.

The reason a boy will play better when he is in his zone is twofold. Playing in your zone means having fun. As I've stated before, fun, relaxation, and a positive mood enhance performance. But the improved performance is also about how the human brain processes information. There is an inverse relationship between a person's ability to focus and his level of arousal. What this means is that the more highly energized, aroused, and psyched up a boy becomes, the less he will be able to focus on the performance of a task, particularly if the task in question is complex or requires considerable mental processing. For instance, a young man in the middle of a rugby scrum can simultaneously maintain high levels of arousal and performance as a player. This stands in contrast to a quarterback in football who needs a more moderated level of arousal because he must receive the hike, fade back to pass, "read" his receivers in their patterns as well as "read" the defensive coverage and the pass rush. Because the quarterback performs more complex physical and cognitive tasks, it is imperative that his level of arousal be within reasonable bounds. Serving in tennis, hitting a baseball, shooting a free throw, executing a series of jumps in figure skating, and sinking a fifteen-foot putt are a few of the sports functions that also require a moderate level of energy in order to perform optimally. Some activities in which a player can tolerate and even enhance his performance by maintaining elevated levels of arousal are initiating a pass rush as a defensive lineman, breaking up a double play as a base runner, and diving to block a penalty kick in soccer.

A more complete understanding of this phenomenon can be gained by picturing an inverted U. Performance is enhanced with moderate levels of arousal and is then compromised at higher levels. This of course varies with both people and tasks. Many elite athletes, for instance, can tolerate and take advantage of very high levels of arousal in high pressure situations and even thrive on it. Reggie Jackson was implying this when he referred to himself as "the straw that stirs the drink." However, the inverted U also informs us that energy regulation is not exclusively focused on managing the high end. We must be up enough in order to perform adequately. Consequently regulating energy also involves bringing one's arousal level up so that one is in his zone. Successful athletes tend to have pregame rituals that serve the purpose of raising their energy so that they peak in their zone when the contest begins. Music is frequently employed for this purpose.

Boys being boys, they sometimes tend to move toward the extremes. They might become discouraged in reaction to a lack of success in performing their sport and might let their frustration take the air out of their balloon. In this case we would need to help them raise their level of energy so they get psyched up. On the other hand they sometimes might become so excited, or overconfident, or overwhelmed that they are flooded with too much energy and as a result lose focus. When they become psyched out like this we need to help them refocus, pull themselves in, and bring their level of arousal down and back into their zone. As we guide our boys in these ways we are teaching them to know when such energy regulation is called for and how to do it.

Centering

The primary device used to help regulate energy is to center oneself. In order to maintain perspective, reframe a situation in a positive light, or see the humor in it, a person must be practiced at centering activities. The purpose of using centering activities is to help our boys come to a calm and familiar place inside of them. We want to teach them to find a safe harbor that they can return to again and again, especially during times of high seas and high stress. Among the many resources for further application of these techniques are such useful books as *The Relaxation Response* and *The Centering Book*. Both are listed along with many other resources in appendix 1 in the back of *Really Winning*. As you will see when you look through these and other books, there is nothing complicated, tricky, or difficult about learning how to center and relax oneself. The only thing that is required is a willingness to follow through with practice.

Watching the Breath

The primary means of helping a boy to center himself is to teach him to relax by watching and using his breath. The first thing to do is to ask him to sit quietly and be aware of his breath. Ask him to notice it. Is it shallow and quick (indicative of nervous and unfocused energy) or is it deeper and easy like waves washing upon a shoreline (indicative of calm and more grounded energy)? Have him pick a number on a scale from one (extremely calm) to ten (highly aroused) that would indicate where he is. Regardless, ask him to have his breath carry a message to his body to have it relax. Easy in, easy out. Easy in, easy out. Have him imagine breathing in a calm and relaxed centeredness, and imagine breathing out tension, doubt, and worry. After about five minutes ask him to pick a number that now indicates his new level of arousal. Invariably, if not the first time, with another relaxation session or two, he will experience a sense of being calmer.

This is something that a boy can practice on his own and as he does he will learn that he can begin to regulate his own levels of energy. As he comes to master this skill, he will be able to bring his energy up or down as needed. By becoming proficient in this centering activity he will gradually learn to be more self-directed from the inside, rather than reacting and possibly being thrown off center by external forces. He will be better able to manage his reaction to a hostile crowd, adverse weather conditions, being way behind in the score, or having committed errors of omission or commission.

When a boy learns to listen to his breath, he has instant access to a barometer that indicates his internal state. If it needs adjustment he can make it. If it doesn't, it reinforces that he is in his zone. There is an old saying in the yoga tradition that the mind follows the breath and the body follows the mind. This breath-centered focusing assists his efforts to foster a positive mental attitude and helps to bring the function of his body in line with his personal goals.

Progressive Relaxation

A boy can use his breathing by itself to help to center himself or he can incorporate an additional technique. After using a couple of minutes of rhythmic breathing to center himself, he can then proceed to do what is call a progressive relaxation exercise. In this exercise he brings his awareness to particular parts of his body, breathes in and tenses those particular muscles while holding his breath for a count of ten and then simultaneously breathes out and releases the muscles. He progressively directs his attention to the next muscle group until he has scanned and relaxed his entire body. I think it is helpful to begin with the extremities and move up toward the head. It goes something like this:

Focus your attention on your feet. Notice whether there is any tension. If there is or not, with your next inhalation tense the muscles in your feet. Hold, hold (count of ten), and release. Breathe easily and calmly. Breathe in calm and bring out tension. Now focus on your calf muscles and on your next inhalation tense the muscles in your calves. Hold, hold. And release. Breathe out any tension and breathe in a sense of well-being. Now focus your attention on your thighs. Note whether any tension is there. Now breathe in and tense the muscles in your thighs. Hold it. Hold it and release, breathing in a calm confidence and breathing out any doubts or worries.

Your need not follow this model exactly, for you need to find the words that work best for you and the boy or young man with whom you are working. As the relaxation progresses throughout the body help bring the boy's attention to his buttocks, stomach, chest, hands, forearms, biceps, shoulders, and face. After a few times of a boy being "taken through" a progressive muscle relaxation he will be able to practice it at home on a daily basis by himself. Once our boy has put himself in a calm and centered state he needs to be directed to read or say the affirmation statement that he constructed as he learned the skill of maintaining a positive mental attitude. Regardless of whether he uses the breathing-centering activity by itself or along with progressive muscle relaxation, it is imperative that he repeats his affirmative self-talk during this period of calm.

Our boys should be encouraged to engage in these exercises twice per day, preferably at the beginning and at the end of the day. The need for this regular practice must be emphasized. Once this mental fitness skill is mastered they will be able to call it up whenever it is needed, even on short notice. For instance, if in an instant a batter finds himself flipped over on his back, the result of a high, hard brush back pitch, he can *with one or two breaths* bring himself back to his zone. In order to ground himself in an instant he needs to understand that practicing his mental fitness skills is as important as taking grounders or batting practice.

John

John frequently found himself worried and anxious about his performance as a wrestler whenever his father or an important group of friends were in attendance. I taught him to use their presence as a cue to refocus his energy and attention and move it inside. John began to see that by practicing his breathing along with progressive muscle relaxation training he could quickly bring his anxiety down to the level he needed in order to perform at his best. John came to understand when he was and was not in his zone and began to feel a sense of mastery in his ability to get and keep himself there. It did not always work, but like the acquisition of any skill, because he practiced it regularly, he became increasingly effective at centering himself and bringing his talents to what mattered in those moments: being the best wrestler he could.

✦ Goal Setting ✦

It may sound strange to think of the ability to set goals as a skill, but as you will see it is a very important component of mental fitness training. In order for our boys to get where they want to go as athletes they have to have a goal. To say this is of course a matter of common sense, but establishing a plan that will ensure that the goal is reached is no small matter. When a boy becomes proficient at the skill of goal setting, he becomes adept at articulating the very specific things he wants to achieve *and* the very specific things that he must do to ensure that he will achieve his goals. The former are known as *content goals* and the latter are known as *process goals*.

Content goals spell out what we want to achieve and when we want to achieve them. Content goals are specific and measurable. Some examples are: to win a championship, to win by pins in fifty percent of my wrestling matches, to bench-press a certain weight, to improve my rate of catching a football to a certain percentage, in swimming to bring my time in the hundred-meter fly down to a specific number, and to increase my batting average to a certain percent. Content goals can also refer to attitudes and behaviors brought to a sport that can enhance performance. Examples of these are: always take practice seriously, bring a winning attitude into every match or game, pull myself back together whenever I become unfocused. In contrast, process goals detail the specific means of achieving my content goals. Examples of process goals are: to weight-train three times per week, to practice fifty tennis serves per workout, to catch five balls from each of seven different pass plays twice per week, to run sprints twice per week, to conduct a distance run once per week, to practice meditative breathing and affirmations twice per day, and to use imagery three times per week. I encourage the boys I work with to write out their goal-setting strategy and to get input from their coaches. This is how a strategy frequently looks.

A goal-setting strategy is a dynamic process that can be adjusted as the young man engages in the process. He may move up more quickly with some process goals while others may take a little more time than he had planned. I find detailing only two months' worth of process-goal activities at a time to make sense. This way adjustments can be made as time goes on. Content goals are likely to be achieved if they are reality based and are guided by a concrete set of process goals. Midpoint content goals are also very helpful in serving as benchmarks on the way toward the ultimate goals.

While at first glance such a detailed plan of content and process goals may seem overwhelming, many young men who have availed themselves of this goal-setting strategy are frequently liberated by it. For instance, it can be enormously gratifying for a boy to know that *he* has taken some very specific action, according to *his* plan to meet *his* goal. Fostering this sort of self-efficacy increases a tendency to be more internally directed and guided rather than to seek approval and direction from others outside. Many boys find it liberating to not have to decide on a daily basis what to do in order to move toward a desired goal. Because it has already been decided, he can save a lot of suffering, indecision, procrastination, negative feelings about himself, and wasted energy by merely following the plan for each day.

Coaches and parents can not only be very helpful in formulating the process and content goals that best serve a boy's interests, but are an absolutely necessary part of the process. The knowledge, experience, and perspective that these men and women possess can be extremely valuable sources of guidance for the boy. However, it is imperative to listen intently to what the boy wishes to accomplish in order to establish goals that he can really buy into. Unless this is done you may be creating a wonderful plan of action, but it will be of little use if it is *your* plan for him, rather than *his* plan. If the goal-setting strategy accurately reflects his interests, then it will be easier for him to follow through, especially during difficult moments.

John

Given the variety of issues that John was wrestling with, the following content and process goals were established in consultation *with* him as his goal-setting plan:

JOHN'S SPORTS PSYCHOLOGY PLAN

Athletic Content Goals
  1. To pin fifty percent of his wrestling opponents
  2. To make it to the district tournament

3. To be fully present in mind and body in practice and in matches
4. To carry a winning attitude into every match
5. To wrestle for himself
6. To "surrender" to being a wrestler and to be fully present in the moment
7. To follow through with incorporating his mental fitness skills into his regular in-season and off-season practice routine
8. To meet sit-up targets of 60, 80, and 100 three times per day five times per week at four-month intervals
9. To meet push-up targets of 30, 50, and 75 three times per day five times per week at four-month intervals
10. To meet bench-press targets of 165, 175, and 185 three times per week at four-month intervals

Athletic Process Goals
1. To attend all practices
2. To consciously choose to be fully present in body and mind in all practice sessions and matches
3. To consciously choose to bring a winning attitude to every match
4. To choose to remove his ego from the match, leave self-worth issues on the bench along with the desire to please others, and in so doing just be the wrestler in the moment
5. To complete twice-weekly distance runs and sprints in the off-season
6. To do push-ups and sit-ups at least four times per week year-round
7. To weight-train twice per week throughout the year
8. To visualize successfully completing difficult wrestling moves
9. To reframe adverse situations (e.g., wrestling against a renowned opponent or in an away match with a hostile, partisan crowd) as opportunities to excel
10. To reframe adverse circumstances in a particular match in order to find his advantage
11. To practice his meditative breathing and progressive muscle

relaxation and repeat his positive affirmations related to wrestling and personal confidence twice per day
12. To make daily entries in his personal journal of his thoughts and feelings so as to maintain and increase his awareness of himself

John was able to bring a winning attitude into the vast majority of his wrestling matches. He ended the season with a record of twenty victories versus nine defeats. Included in that victory total were nine pins of opponents. He made it to the district tournament, lost in the second round, but wrestled well. His approach to wrestling and his accomplishments were well beyond what he had previously done and were among the things he previously had only dreamed about.

John is a hardworking and courageous young man and he followed through with his plan because he really believed in it. He met with a great deal of success and he made it happen. The increase in his self-esteem as a result of his success in both sticking with his plan and moving toward accomplishing his goals had considerable ramifications for his life outside of sports.

✦ Visualization ✦

Once a boy has established clearly defined goals and an effective plan of action in order to reach them, he is in a position to literally "see" where he wants to go. This "seeing" is an application of the mental fitness skill of visualization. Just as the word suggests, visualization allows us to create a mental picture of where we would like to go, what we would like to accomplish, and what it would look like to do so. It builds directly upon the skill of goal setting in that having a specific target in mind is necessary in order to create the mental images associated with heading toward the target and actually hitting it.

The movie *Space Jam* starring Michael Jordan and Bugs Bunny sends a positive motivational message to kids that is every bit as meaningful as the movie is entertaining. A line from the theme song "I Believe I Can Fly" goes, "If I can see it, then I can be it. If I can believe it, then I can do it. I believe I can fly." Not only does this song underscore the story of a boy's determination to see his dream to fruition, but it also accurately attests to the powerful tool that visualization can be.

There are two primary uses of visualization. The first has to do with what we have just referred to, creating a mental image of success in its various forms and employing those images along with the other mental skills to move our boys toward their goals. This application of visualization is broad and overarching in that a boy "sees" a mental image of success as a guide and theme that consistently gives him an overall positive direction. It is his North Star serving as a fixed point that consistently keeps him on his path. The second application of visualization is very specific and has direct application to particular aspects of a boy's performance as well as particular circumstances in which he might find himself.

Keep Your Eye on the Prize

This saying was one of the guiding principles of the civil rights movement. Its purpose was to remind people not to be distracted by the forces of resistance, but to keep focused on what was most important: acquiring equal rights. Participants in the civil rights movement were advised by Dr. Martin Luther King to practice nonviolence, for he feared that the momentum and virtue of the movement would be diminished if acts of aggression were responded to with aggression. Needless to say, sports does not have the same meaning as the noble cause of bringing justice to the oppressed. It really doesn't matter if Army beats Navy or who has the most home runs. What does matter is using sports to develop a sound and virtuous character in a young man and that is a prize worth keeping our eyes focused upon. A boy who is helped to stay focused and follow through with a prescribed plan to achieve certain goals is laying the groundwork for the development of a strong character.

In the broad use of visualization we need to teach our boys to focus on the particulars of their sport that require discipline and hard work. Keeping their prize in focus, be it winning a championship or lowering their time in a race, will greatly help our boys to maintain their momentum. One of the benefits that many boys receive in addition to meeting the sports objectives written into their goal-setting plan is strength of character. It is not easy to be a young man, pulled by all the temptations that abound, and still follow through with the hard work that is called for by a goal-setting plan. When a young man does in fact follow through, regardless of meeting the sports goal, he can be proud to know he did so. When part of the plan includes fair play and good sportsmanship we help develop a young man with a virtuous strength of character, and that is indeed a noble prize. Coaches are sometimes quite direct in addressing character and sportsmanship issues, while at other times they model the importance of fair play and integrity. Regardless of whether the message is sent explicitly by our direct words or implicitly through personal actions, it is a message we must get to our boys. We will talk more about building this kind of character and integrity in the next chapter.

The primary utility of the first function of visualization is helping our boys to stay focused on their long-term goals and on their plan for achieving them. As coaches and parents we do this by guiding and sometimes reminding them when they begin to stray. The passive reminders of the value of working hard are ever present with the images on the positive affirmation posters and signs hanging in a locker room or in a boy's bedroom. In short, every thing and every effort is focused on the target.

Applying Visualization

There are a number of ways to utilize visualization techniques to improve sports performance, including:

- Analysis of a bad habit or error
- Correcting a bad habit or error
- Recovery from injury
- Transfer to game situations

Each of these applications of visualization is based upon the neuromuscular connection that is automatically wired into human beings. What does this mean? It means that the body and the mind are intricately connected. What is in the mind in terms of thought, belief, and mental image has a direct impact on our physical actions. What are the implications for helping our boys improve their mental and physical games? It means that not only do we tend to act out what we believe, but *that we tend to actually play out what we see in our mind's eye.* This "thinking" and "seeing" can be thought of as constituting a person's personal construct. These constructs are maps that guide him as he navigates through the world. Whether they know it or not, all people create their own maps. Because our boys will follow whatever is on the map, it is very important that we do our best to make sure that these images are self-enhancing rather than self-defeating.

A boy can use the mental image of himself successfully kicking, hitting, or catching a ball, powering effortlessly through the water, or jumping and completing two full revolutions in the air before touching his skate to the ice to enhance his performance when he is actually in the water, on the field, or on the ice. The only proviso to the use of mental imagery is that the boy has the ability and the proper training to perform the tasks he is picturing. Visualization is not last-minute wishful thinking or seeing. Rather, in order for a boy to use visualization to improve his performance he must include practice of this mental fitness skill as a regular part of his training.

There has been a great deal of research in this area of sports psychology and the results clearly demonstrate the positive effects of developing the mental fitness skill of visualization. It is the neuromuscular connection that accounts for this success. For instance, some research has shown that when an athlete pictures performing a certain task in his mind's eye, the specific muscles responsible for that activity become activated along with the areas of the brain responsible for their movement. I once worked with an eighteen-year-old named Scotty who was gifted with a very powerful body and remarkable physical skills. He was a fine pitcher on his high school team, and had designs on pitching in college and beyond. He was so tall and strong that he could pitch with great success at the high school level despite poor mechanics. He utilized little of his lower body and could get away with pitching mostly from his arm. To his credit Scotty took his coaches' counsel to heart and knew that he would not be able to so easily handle batters on the college level. By underutilizing the leverage of his legs Scotty would not get enough power on the ball to put it past a disciplined collegiate batter. Furthermore, he was bound to eventually injure himself and ruin his arm by making it do all the work.

The first use of visualization was in analyzing the incorrect mechanics in the way he was used to pitching. By visualizing himself in his pitching motion he could "see" where he was going wrong. In fact, he could use a freeze-frame technique to isolate specific mental images so as to get the most accurate picture of this ineffective pitching style. He used visualization to understand and analyze the errors he was making. This helped him see the limitations that resulted from this bad habit.

With the insight gained from the analysis of his errors, Scotty was in a better position to utilize his coach's instructions. Scotty learned the right way to pitch and his challenge was to discipline himself enough to use it both in practice and game situations. Through our work together he learned to use progressive muscle relaxation and focused breathing to relax. After he put himself in a calm state, Scotty began to create a mental image of pitching the right way. With his eyes closed he saw himself getting set, winding up, and extending his body and arm forward as driven by the power coming from his legs. He repeated this a number of times, each time feeling the movement of his body, feeling the power originating in his lower leg and exploding out of his hand as he released the ball. Every time he practiced this visualization he was actually training his body and mind to work together in a new way. Every time he saw the image of "Scotty pitching the right way" he was activating the center in his brain responsible for these movements *and* the actual muscles that would do the physical work. He was applying visualization to correct his bad habit. Although it was very hard to break, Scotty eventually transformed his pitching style. He is now pitching in college.

Visualization can also be very helpful in assisting an athlete recover from an injury and prepare to return to play. Needless to say, athletes are not happy when they have an injury. They are excited to play, are mentally ready to play, they love to play, but if they're injured their bodies will not allow them. Depending on the type of injury and the length of time for healing, it is not unusual for an athlete to feel pretty down. Sitting on the bench is no fun, but what is worse is the feeling that he is losing his edge. This can be compounded by calculating how long it will take for him to return to the level of play he achieved before the injury.

Because of all the above, injured athletes are frequently chomping at the bit to do *something, anything.* Fortunately they can utilize their time out of play to great advantage through the use of visualization. Studies have shown that athletes who have regularly practiced creating mental images of their particular athletic event resume play, after recovery, at their previous level much more quickly than they would have otherwise. Using visualization can help an injured athlete to not skip a practice. It gives him something to do and is enormously constructive. One of the great things about the use of visualization is that every time a boy creates the mental image of his particular athletic performance, he is actually practicing that particular set of skills. This allows an athlete in any condition to practice over and over again, without the negative effects of fatigue or limitations due to injury. This sort of mental rehearsal can also utilize other senses.

Although there are endless uses of visualization, the last one I will mention here is to help an athlete transfer skills and mental preparations to actual game situations. Practice is practice and a game situation can frequently be quite different. For instance, a football team practicing its offense when it starts on its own five-yard line is far different from actually playing an away game when the players are stuck in the closed end of a very noisy and hostile stadium. Sports psychology pioneer Dr. Dick Suinn once told of helping to prepare the Team USA women's track and field team to anticipate and deal effectively with possible disruptive influences at the 1980 Olympics in Moscow. As it turned out, the United States boycotted those Olympic games, but Suinn was helping the women prepare for external conditions designed to knock them off their rhythm, such as hostile crowds and transportation services that might get them to their events in only the nick of time. Visualization accompanied by having a positive mental attitude can increase levels of confidence and increase levels of self-efficacy. It can help to reinforce the notion that "I will be able to perform at my level regardless of the conditions or the opponents."

Another way of using visualization to help transfer skill sets to actual game situations is for an athlete to work on a particular physical skill, such throwing a runner out at first base, and then imagining performing that task in a stadium where an upcoming important game will be played. This can be further reinforced by actually visiting the stadium prior to the game. Many athletes are known to come out to a stadium by themselves hours or days before they are to play there. Actually being there and creating the image of successfully performing there helps set the stage for optimizing their performance. The same holds true for practicing mental fitness skills. For instance, actually visiting the site of a future competition and visualizing situations which might call for energy regulation techniques and bringing the arousal level down into the performance zone can be very helpful in preparing for the actual competition.

John

John was able to create a mental image of each element of his content goals. He saw himself pinning his opponents, making it to the districts, bringing a winning attitude to each match, surrendering to being a wrestler in the moment, and he visualized wrestling moves that his coach advised that he include in his repertoire. He was comfortable with the use of focused breathing and progressive muscle relaxation and that set the stage for him to include his positive visual images once he was relaxed.

Kids, Don't Try This at Home

A note of caution must be offered if you are considering the use of visualization in youth sports. Using visualization to enhance their perception of themselves is absolutely appropriate. Helping boys to see themselves work hard and follow through in making a sincere effort is just fine. However, because children at this level are just learning a sport and are at very different places in terms of their social, psychological, and physical development, the application of visualization to specific behaviors is not advised. Because their cognitive development does not allow for more "adult" processing of mental concepts, you cannot be sure as a coach if they really have the correct image of the physical skill you wish them to learn. It is possible that the wrong image could inadvertently be reinforced. Although some boys will be able to utilize this skill earlier, it is best to wait to use visualization until they approach adolescence. Not only will they be more mature, but they will more likely have acquired the foundation skills of their sport. For younger boys it is best to focus on the mental fitness skill of developing and maintaining a positive mental attitude as the primary message. Your encouragement and praise for their hard work and for the importance of having fun is exactly what is needed in the entry levels of sport.

✦ Optimal Performance Psychology ✦

When we teach our boys to be mentally fit, we equip them with a skill set that goes well beyond sports. The mental fitness skills can be applied toward *any* meaningful goal or activity outside of the arena of sport. When we do this we call it optimal performance psychology.

By teaching our boys the same five mental fitness skills, we can help them to optimize their efforts in a variety of areas. Among the important ones are: academics, dealing with girls, interacting with other boys, enhancing communication with parents, finances, losing weight, public speaking, searching for a college or a job, and many others. Let's look at John's nonsports-related goals. Besides his desire to increase the number of victories and the number of pins in his wrestling season, and to bring a winning attitude into every match, John had several other important personal goals.

As you might recall, John's father had withdrawn from active involvement with him ever since his parents divorced. Consequently, the contact between father and son, while precious to John, was infrequent. As a young man, John was discovering his feelings of hurt and resentment toward his father and did not know what to do with them. He feared further rejection if he were to approach his father; consequently he was stuck with these feelings boiling inside of him. It was probably no coincidence that John had on occasion found himself in the midst of various conflicts and skirmishes with other young men at school. He also found himself feeling resentful toward some of his coaches and teachers for "slighting" him. His perception was probably skewed by his relationship with his father. At the same time he deeply longed for his coaches' (and his father's) approval. He was caught in a tough spot.

As a highly anxious young man, John had frequently underperformed academically. Just as it had manifested in his wrestling, John's combination of wanting to please and being concerned about how he appeared to others served to place a great deal of pressure on him in his relationship with girls and in the classroom. His relationship with his girlfriend was punctuated by her occasional disloyalty and lack of honesty with him, yet he felt obliged to stay with her. In the classroom his high levels of anxiety led to errors of underinclusion. He felt overwhelmed both when the content was initially presented in class and later when he had to demonstrate his mastery of it. As a result he frequently found it difficult to focus in testing situations and found it difficult to generate answers that he knew. His anxiety and self-consciousness also hampered his ability to learn new or difficult material. It seemed that it wasn't bad enough that the subject matter was challenging, but feeling as if his self-worth was always riding on his performance hampered his efforts to do his best. Included along with John's sports psychology goal-setting plan were the following nonsports content and process goals:

JOHN'S OPTIMAL PERFORMANCE PLAN

Academic Content Goals:
1. To make the honor role in each academic quarter
2. To follow through and complete his study time even if he has completed his homework
3. To maintain a positive attitude toward his academics
4. To "surrender" to being a student
5. To be present in the classroom

Academic Process Goals:
1. To complete his required summer reading
2. To establish the following out-of-wrestling-season Monday-to-Friday study plan:
   45 minutes—study
   break (snack, phone calls, computer, etc.)
   45 minutes—study
   break
   30 minutes—study
   fun (snack, phone calls, computer, favorite television program, etc.)
3. To establish the following in-wrestling-season Monday-to-Friday study plan:
   45 minutes—study
   break
   45 minutes—study
   fun (snack, phone calls, computer, favorite television program, etc.)
4. To use the entire study time to complete homework and use remaining time to work on projects due later, or to outline chapters in preparation for future examinations
5. To seek help from teachers whenever he is unsure about a subject
6. To have each teacher complete a weekly progress report which assesses his performance to date, acknowledges things done

well, points out areas of deficiency, and makes recommenda-
tions for improvement
7. To attend all his classes

Social Content Goals
1. Keep relationship with girlfriend in perspective (i.e., put academics and wrestling as first priority, not give in to the drama
   of the neediness, jealousy, break-up and make-up cycle
2. Have a more genuine relationship with father
3. Feel more confident in general
4. Be more internally driven

Social Process Goals
1. Limit contact with girlfriend to in-school and weekend time
   only
2. Be as honest and clear as possible when communicating his
   thoughts and feelings with girlfriend
3. Seek father out for assistance in his life and to spend more
   time in general with him
4. Tell father clearly what he wants from him (occasional financial assistance, equal treatment among siblings, fair treatment
   toward mother, to come to see his wrestling matches, and to
   want to come see his wrestling matches, and to feel like a priority in father's life)
5. To practice his meditative breathing and progressive muscle
   relaxation and repeat his positive affirmations related to social
   and personal matters twice per day
6. To make daily entries in his personal journal of his thoughts
   and feelings so as to maintain and increase his awareness of
   himself

John followed through with his plan. He went from a boy who did
not study, or did so only in the few minutes that homeroom provided,
to a young man who consistently used his specified study times on a
daily basis. He also frequently practiced his focused breathing and imagery and was able to call it up as needed in the classroom. Whenever
he was anxious in class he used a "cleansing breath" to bring his anxiety
down and "surrender" to being a student. Whenever he found his mind
drifting or daydreaming in class he actively chose to bring himself to be

"present" by focusing on the class discussion or lecture. John went from a C and D student to making the honor role in each quarter of his last two years of high school.

As for his relationship issues, he was able to set clearer limits with his girlfriend and become better able to see when she was being unreasonable. Toward the end of the school year he was even able to break up with her and stick to it without succumbing to either his feelings of guilt or neediness. His dealings with his father are still a work in progress. He is becoming clearer as to what he feels toward his father (both longing and resentment) and now feels entitled to have the feelings. He is currently preparing to have a heart-to-heart talk with his father. He is getting ready to acknowledge the (few) things his father did for him and the many ways he has felt let down by him. To his credit John is continuing to struggle with his feelings in reaction to this important and most difficult relationship. He is a young man doing the things that young men must do to find themselves.

One of the nice things about teaching boys to employ the skills of mental fitness is that if they are dedicated and put a sincere effort into following through, they almost always succeed. That does not mean that a boy will necessarily always achieve the specific goal that he is shooting for, especially when it is a particularly lofty one. However, it is almost guaranteed that they will be much further along toward accomplishing it, and that is something for which to feel proud. That said, a great many boys are highly likely to meet goals if they are practical and reasonable, given their own personal resources. One of our roles as part of the coaching process is to help them develop challenging yet achievable goals. This holds equally true in sports and nonsports applications. A simple, yet effective tool to help our boys in all these areas is the Mental Preparation Checklist in appendix 2. It was constructed by Olympic performance coach Peter Jensen and presented in his fine book *The Inside Edge*.

✦ Keeping it Positive ✦

It must be noted that attempts can be made to employ mental fitness skills and other tricks of the trade in order to try to psych out an opponent. The staring down of fellow pugilists at the beginning of a boxing match is but one example. Words exchanged by opposing linemen in the seconds before the football is snapped is another. This sort of "trashing talk" may involve references to one's sister or mother, other derogatory comments, or sometimes even racial slurs. These methods can frequently be useful in getting the opposition to "get out of their rhythm" or "off their game." A player enraged by such insults may loose his focus, and in doing so, his anger can be used to his own detriment. In these cases he might be so interested in "payback" that he might miss his assignment or be called for a penalty. However, there is always the risk that employing such methods can backfire, for there is much to be reckoned with when a fired-up opponent maintains his focus and channels it into his play, but that is another story.

If we are going to employ dirty tricks such as in the above examples, why stop there? Why not trip people, or throw an elbow when the referee is not looking? It is true that we can gain certain advantages over opponents by orchestrating to work against them by various devious means. The point is, however, that the victory tastes sweetest when it is honorable and is hardly worth having when it is tainted. We need to encourage our boys to focus on preparing themselves for sound play rather than worrying about the opposition. Because a player can only directly effect a positive change in himself, it is not only dishonorable to "play dirty" or to otherwise attempt to distract the opponent, but it can also be distracting to one's own effort to perform optimally. Our boys need to be directed away from the goal of tearing down the opponent, and toward building themselves up in order to do their best.

The skills of mental fitness that comprise sports psychology clearly are effective in assisting our boys to optimize their athletic performance. Mental skills training must be accompanied by an understanding of the personal responsibility that goes with it, just as teaching a boy to drive requires much more than merely tossing him the keys. The mental fitness skills will help him become more accomplished as an athlete and to receive the acclaim and status that are heaped upon athletes at all levels. We need to help them remain grounded and centered throughout all this. Imparting these tools in athletics is, in essence, using sports as a medium to develop a sense of personal mastery in the world. When a boy applies this found competence in a spirit of fair play and honor he goes a long way toward developing a personal belief system that is governed by integrity.

In this chapter I have presented an overview of sports psychology as well as its application to other important areas of our boys' lives using optimal performance psychology. I do want to encourage you to refer to the bibliography provided in appendix 1 if you would like to acquire a more thorough knowledge of sports and optimal performance psychology. It really works and it is worth knowing about. In the next chapter we explore some specific ways in which we as coaches and parents can foster the development of character and integrity while encouraging the mastery of sports psychology and sport.

5

Coaching for Performance and Fostering Integrity

THE PRIMARY REASON this book is focusing on sports is that boys tend to already be interested and participating in sports. If they are not already doing so, they soon will be because they are naturally drawn to it. Most boys are interested in competitive, group activities in which they are provided an opportunity to develop and show their sense of mastery through the manipulation of objects (typically spherical) through space. Because they love playing various ball games we have a chance to teach them to be the best boys and young men they can be when we participate with them. The fact that they are already interested provides a great opportunity for us.

In the previous chapter we discussed the use of the five skills of mental fitness as tools to help our boys optimize their performance in sports or in other meaningful activities. Because these powerful techniques can be life-changing it is probably wise to assess the potential negative consequences of their use. Boys who have been helped to develop their athletic prowess have the potential to run amuck if they are not provided a sound and healthy structure in which to operate. The Glen Ridge, New Jersey, rape case in which five star high school athletes stood trial for sexually assaulting a mentally handicapped female classmate is but one example. Many in their bucolic and affluent community found it inconceivable that well-liked and handsome young men could be accused of such a vile act. The first chapter of *Really Winning* abounds with other acts of boys directed by their shadows.

Fortunately we have an opportunity as coaches and parents to create the external standards and conditions that can teach our boys not only right from wrong, but the importance of why we want them to do the right thing: honor. By honor, I am not referring to fame or glory, but rather to the esteem one carries when he is guided by integrity and an allegiance to high principles. There is nothing wrong with fame or glory or for that matter being esteemed by others. In fact, others frequently look upon a principled person with esteem. However, a principled or honorable person's behavior is not driven by a desire for such fame and status, rather it is driven by the desire to simply do the right thing. If fame or status comes, it does so on its own. If a young man is not grounded by a principled intent, he will be subject to the temptation to feed off his fame and glory and thus lose his way. The negative consequences that follow wayward actions can be thought of as generated by the darker, shadow aspects of his personality.

The major way coaches and parents can help our boys eventually develop the type of sound character that reflects this sense of honor and integrity is *by our own behavior*. It is an established fact that this sort of modeling is one of the strongest, if not *the* strongest, method of teaching. When we show them the way through words, but more importantly through our own actions, our boys gradually incorporate the importance of honor and integrity as part of their own value system. Our boys will literally take all of this in as part of the process of developing their own code of honor.

The psychological process by which this is done is called introjection. Our boys are preprogrammed and biologically hardwired to receive the sound teachings of coaches and parents through the introjection process. Similar to what is required when the space shuttle and a cargo ship dock in space, all that's needed are the right supplies (sound values and principles) and patiently maneuvering the payload into position (repeatedly modeling sound principles over time) so the docking (introjection) can occur. When the payload is received in our boys' "cargo bay" they are supplied with what is necessary to become fine young men. When this occurs there is no going back. Because their consciousness has been transformed into the thinking employed by mature and healthy young men, we can say with confidence that they have become young men with sound character. The personalities of such young men can now be thought of as in their more permanent form and we can safely say that the values and principles of honor and integrity will endure throughout their years. This is in marked contrast to boys who have not been provided with this sort of "values mentoring." Those boys who are helped to develop sound values and an internalized sense of integrity will not be unduly influenced by fame, glory, the crowd, the media, or MTV. Rather, they will be guided by their own personal code of conduct. These are boys with character. This is the prize we are after. This is really winning.

✦ The Challenge ✦

It is abundantly clear that effective mental fitness skills can dramatically increase the performance of any athlete regardless of his level of skill or whether he competes at the professional level, in high school, or in youth sports. Given that we have the ability to crank out more effective and better skilled athletes, I believe we are confronted by several responsibilities that many coaches and parents frequently overlook:

- Our work with athletes is not limited to the specific skills training in that particular sport or to merely winning.
- Our mission is only partially accomplished when they become accomplished athletically.
- We have a duty to be interested in how they conduct themselves in and out of sport.
- Part of our job is to help them manage the hubris that can frequently accompany athletic success.
- We need to help them manage the elevation in status, confidence, power, and prestige that the community tends to bestow on athletes by teaching them to give back to the community.

Helping a young boy, an adolescent, or a young man to become proficient in a sport can give him a boost in life. However, given what we have discussed in chapters 2 and 3 about the psychology of boys, it is imperative that we consider the acquisition of athletic skills and the accompanying success to be only one half of the building block that serves as the foundation for the development of sound character. Given the potential negative impact of our boys' shadows, it is especially important to be mindful of the danger of giving them access to the power of their bodies without a sense of responsibility and humility. When we teach them how to run, shoot, pass, and catch our job is only half done. In fact, even when they have successfully incorporated the value of hard work, our job is still only half done. The other half of the building block of character development is comprised of integrity, sportsmanship, and honor. Until our boys have fully integrated these qualities into their personality, they will not become psychologically mature boys and men.

At this point it is reasonable to ask what it is that we have to do in order to foster the development of their character and when we would begin this process. Character development is not an easy process, but it is a simple one. It does not occur overnight and is the result of countless "training" sessions. Ninety-nine percent of these sessions are of the informal variety. When our boys observe you giving change back when the cashier at McDonald's mistakenly gave you too much or acknowledging that you made a mistake or did not know something (but then went and sought out the answer), or following through with a commitment, or treating the boys you coach with respect while calling for them to do their very best, you are providing the most effective training in how to be an honorable person.

The development of sound character in our boys is grounded in common sense and in the willingness to put our own character on the line for our boys. The time to work on the development of character is now. As a coach or parent you must consider the development of character to be *at least* of equal value to skill acquisition, regardless of the age or level of sport in which your boy is involved. That means that we hold the same principles regarding the importance of honor, sportsmanship, and integrity with our eight-year-olds as we do with our eighteen-year-olds. At the risk of being redundant I want to reiterate that in order to develop sound character in our boys, the use of sports psychology, sound

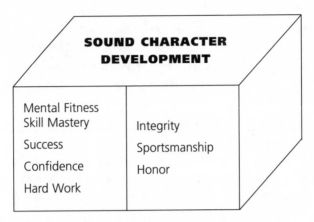

Figure 5–1 The Building Block of Character Development

coaching for skill acquisition and proficiency *must be simultaneously* accompanied by fostering the development of integrity. This is illustrated in figure 5-1.

There is no time like the present to begin to create the environment that fosters good character development. However old our boys are when we first encounter them is the right age to begin. Intervening in order to teach a three-year-old to share with a friend is on par with encouraging a college senior who is an accomplished athlete to take a self-conscious freshman under his wing. In short, whenever we get access to our boys is the time to work with them with an eye toward the development of sound character. However, in order to do this we must be guided by the principle that the sport is merely a medium to foster character and integrity and that skill acquisition and winning must never come at the expense of honor and good sportsmanship. In a way this complex task which takes so long to accomplish is quite simple, not easy, but simple.

✦ Integrity ✦

I devote about half of my work as a psychologist to assisting athletes to improve their level of performance. In doing so, I pay particular attention to how the young man approaches that sport. Invariably the psychological makeup and self-concept of the boy are manifested in his athletic endeavors. This makes sense, of course, because how he feels about himself will naturally be reflected in who he is in the sport. In the process of working with a boy I frequently discover ways in which he approaches the sport that hinder his performance. I once worked with a hockey goalie who did well as long as the other team did not score. Once one goal went in the floodgates opened. What I learned was that his sense of himself as a competent person was tentative at best; consequently panic ensued when the first goal hit the back of the net. In the spirit of the old saying "wherever you go there you are" this young man got in his own way. This is not particularly surprising as most of us are prone to occasionally do this. The nice thing about working with boys to improve their athletic performance is that because they are motivated to do better, they are also usually open to the feedback that can help them do better in ways that may positively impact their lives outside of sports.

While the athlete's psychological approach is the primary area of our attention, we also discover, through our discussions, ways in which he physically performs that are in need of attention and correction. This frequently involves consultations with coaches for their informed input in regard to areas that need improvement due to flaws in a boy's technique. It is interesting to note that when given an opportunity to talk about one of their boys, many coaches bring up what they perceive as "attitude" problems. All of this information goes into the mix of helping boys do better and it is very gratifying when I see the work that we put in come to fruition. But if my sole involvement were limited to simply helping Johnny throw a ball harder and with more accuracy, I would not be so interested. The personal meaning that I derive from my work with our boys comes through using the sport as a medium to increase their self-esteem and self-confidence while building character. I happen to enjoy sports as an amateur and as a fan and that helps to make this work fun for me, but I know it would ring hollow were I to omit the other half of the building block of character development: *integrity*.

If we were to go through several dictionaries, the consensus definition of "integrity" could be boiled down to four key components: *soundness, incorruptibility, completeness,* and *honesty.* It logically follows then that if our involvement with boys were guided by these components, we might do a good job of developing young men who have sound character. So let's examine each.

1. Soundness has to do with helping our boys to have unimpaired mental and physical conditioning. In particular, when it comes to integrity soundness refers to guiding them to take a very grounded and ethically correct approach to sport and to all other aspects of their lives.

2. Incorruptibility refers to the ability to take a clear stand and having a firm adherence to a code of conduct. When our boys are able to develop a strong work ethic along with an untainted sense of fair play and sportsmanship, we can be assured that they are on their way to becoming fine and trustworthy young men.

2. Completeness refers to a condition or state toward which we are helping to move our boys wherein they have all the necessary elements for success, both in the arena of sport and in all other arenas of life. This is not simply about teaching them to perform effectively at external things such as a sport or a job; it also includes being effective in having honorable relations with others and in being true to themselves. It is also about learning to work hard and follow through.

4. Honesty is not merely the absence of lying, cheating, or stealing. It is having a solid sense of trustworthiness. As our boys grow to become sincere men who lack pretensions, they will quite naturally conduct themselves with a sense of grace and honor in all their endeavors. On and off the field these will be genuinely good guys.

It is probably safe to say that how our young men go, so goes our culture. And because of this, it is imperative that we create the conditions for developing good, decent, and capable men. It may surprise some readers to know that Plato also spoke of this very issue over two thousand years ago. In his writings, he considered men to be the guardians of the culture. He recognized their need for personal integrity because they carried the mantle of responsibility for protecting the community from internal and external threats. He wrote of the need to train the guardians to be willing to sacrifice for the greater good. It is noteworthy that he also recognized the place of sports by stating that boys needed to be raised with education in physical skills. But of equal importance was the need to raise them with a cultural education. Furthermore, he cautioned society to be vigilant in making sure the guardians, as youth, are not corrupted by untrue or unvirtuous influences. In the *Republic* Plato described the need for the sort of character education that would produce men "in whom the poles of aggressiveness and gentleness have been adequately trained." We might say that Plato is talking about helping boys to manage their shadows so that they might become sound and balanced young men. The great coaches of our time have echoed the same theme. Vince Lombardi and John Wooden, for instance, are also known for encouraging individuals to sacrifice for a greater good and to live with a sense of integrity.

✦ Fostering Strength of ✦ Character and Integrity

Raising boys we could all be proud of is clearly something worth striving for. *Really Winning* is written for particular use within organized sports settings. But let us make no mistake, fostering the character and integrity of our boys can be done in every environment. There are opportunities to develop character in boys in settings that range from urban community centers, the Boy Scouts, high school chess club, or a college debate team.

The great news in *Really Winning* is that common sense and common decency are making a comeback. There is a groundswell of activity wherein people have, as individuals, been dissatisfied long enough and they are now moving as an organized force to change our approach to youth athletics. We will discuss this in detail in chapter 8, but for now let us discuss a method of involvement with our boys that I refer to as the integrity method.

I did not invent it. It has been with us all along and is used by good men and women who are effective coaches and mentors for boys. Because it is rooted in common sense it comes naturally to coaches who have a clear sense of why they are involved with our boys: *for the sake of our boys.* There is no one way to apply the integrity method because each coach and parent has his or her own personal style. However, there is one particular condition that must exist in order for it to occur: the approach to coaching must be boy-centered.

Boy-centered

A boy-centered approach to coaching, parenting, and mentoring takes into consideration the experience and perceptions of the particular boy we are coaching as we engage with him. Furthermore, a boy-centered coach has a sense and knowledge of the psychological and social development of boys, and can factor this into his decisions on how to address the boy or young man.

Let us recall six-year-old Patrick from chapter 2. You might remember him as coming from what we could describe as a shame-based family. Given what we learned in that chapter of Erikson's theory of psychosocial development, you are aware that Patrick is in the process of forming his self-concept around whether he can come to see himself as capable of showing initiative as opposed to being timid. A boy-centered coach would take particular care to let Patrick know that he appreciates his efforts and that he is a good player, while at the same time addressing with him his tendency to barrel over a fellow teammate in the dugout on the way to get his baseball glove. A boy-centered coach would know that he owes it to both boys to address this dugout behavior.

Let me tell you about Eric, a high school senior, and his football coach, Cliff, who took a boy-centered approach to his duties. Eric was tall, blond, and handsome. Standing six feet three inches tall, with his full beard and muscular build Eric looked more like a man than a boy of seventeen years. His good looks and athletic success provided considerable status among his peers. He was the star of the team.

An incident occurred during a football practice session where players were taking turns holding a heavy body bag while other players practiced slamming into them. When it was Eric's turn he ran up and quite intentionally directed his shoulder into the face of his teammate holding the bag. Immediately afterward he grinned. Fortunately Coach Cliff saw what transpired and immediately confronted Eric. In his own style Cliff barked at him, "What the hell are you doing? He's on your own goddamn team." He then went right to the other boy and asked him if he was okay and directed him to take a water break. At the end of practice Cliff held Eric back from the locker room and explained why he was going to bench him in the next game. Without knowing the psychological terms, Cliff had a sense that Eric was directed by his shadow in the form of a bullying exploiter and he wanted to impress upon him the importance of having honor and a sense of fair play. Because it was important that he center on what was best for Eric, the boy in a man's body, Cliff took the time to do the right thing.

Coaching the Whole Boy

It follows quite naturally that when a coach takes a boy-centered approach he would be interested in all aspects of the boy's life. These would include: how he does in school, how he gets along with peers, the way he communicates with peers, the nature of his involvement with females, how things are going in his family, his possible use of alcohol or other drugs, what plans he has for his future, along with his commitment to practice and to his teammates. I am not suggesting that coaches become intrusive or nosy, but that they care about the boy as more than just a player, as a person worth knowing.

A coach who is secure enough in his abilities tends to be comfortable with his players using the mental fitness skills we discussed in the previous chapter. In fact such a coach would encourage the use of these skills with his players, at the very least because he wants them to be more aware of themselves. This can be very fortunate for the players because the mental fitness skills can be applied in the other important areas of our boys' lives.

For instance, a boy or young man who wishes to make the honor roll can make this a content goal and develop the specific process goals necessary to accomplish it, just as he did when he decreased his time in running the forty-yard dash. A young man who feels timid in his dealings with the opposite sex can also develop specific strategies in the form of process goals that can eventually lead to asking a young woman on a date or to a formal dance. There is almost no end to the application of mental fitness skills in helping our boys to become more effective in their lives outside of sport. I will provide a brief list that is the tip of the iceberg of possibilities:

1. Helping to research a paper
2. Helping to follow through with a difficult project
3. Helping to save money
4. Helping to talk to an estranged parent
5. Helping to prepare for college admissions

6. Helping to prepare for entering a career
7. Helping to lose weight
8. Helping to learn how to talk with females
9. Helping to regulate intake of alcohol or other drugs
10. Helping to manage test anxiety
11. Helping to eliminate irrational negative attitudes toward himself
12. Helping to manage anger
13. Helping to become more effective at emotional and physical intimacy

As we coach the whole boy we move toward developing a young man with a solid character who conducts himself with a sense of integrity in all his dealings. He will have many areas of success in his life and as a result his self-esteem will be high. Because he knows the value of hard work and is not taken with himself, he will also possess a sense of humility.

Having the Right Values

When we take a boy-centered approach to coaching the whole boy, we are not only guided by the building block for the development of character, but we also extol values specific to being honorable boys and men. The following values help move our boys toward becoming mature men whose shadows are known, but do not in any way run the show.

✦ **Hard Work** helps to give him an appreciation for things, consideration for other people, and a sense of humility.

✦ **Personal Commitment** helps him to take a stand in life for himself and for his teammates. It teaches him to listen and respect his inner voice and to use it as a guide. It also helps him to become a true loyal teammate, to trust, and be trusted.

✦ **Following Through** is an extension of having a capacity for personal commitment in that he has the conviction to not give up, but to persevere and see the mission through to the end, be it to make the team, to break the tackle and make the touchdown, or study as planned every night despite the temptation to party or otherwise avoid a difficult subject.

✦ **Sense of Fair Play** is integrated when a boy comes to see that winning without fair, sportsmanshiplike behavior is not only pointless, but unattractive and unappealing and is something he has no interest in being a part of.

These values apply to sports as well as to every other aspect of our boys' lives. They produce success in whatever area of endeavor in which he finds himself and they are the mainstay of a young man who possesses character and integrity.

Honoring the Opponent

A value that is specific to the area of sport is to honor the opponent we face in combat. This is something that great generals and commanders have known. When we respect what the other is capable of, we help to raise our level of play. We can all cite examples from professional sports in which an underdog is not taken seriously enough by the team favored to win. Or when a boastful player on the favored team makes an arrogant prediction of victory or otherwise trash-talks the opponent. By giving honor and respect to the person or team we are about to meet in the competition of sport we are also giving honor to sport itself as a means of human encounter, and honor to ourselves as worthy opponents. The result of giving honor is twofold. We play to the best of our abilities and we promote good sportsmanship and a sense of fair play. When we do this we create the best conditions for a healthy and lively competition.

When our approach to coaching, fathering, and mentoring is informed by the four components of integrity in addition to the use of the mental fitness skills, we will increase the likelihood of developing boys with sound character. The reason for this is quite simple: we will be addressing the whole boy in providing fully the elements comprising each half of the building block of sound character. We will be giving our boys access to their greatness as masters of their bodies, equipping them with a set of skills specific to a given sport, and giving them access to their greatness as men. We will more likely be successful in our work with them when our actions toward them are further informed by our knowledge of boy psychology. As we discussed in chapter 4, a reasonable degree of insight into our own thoughts, feelings, and motives is also necessary for us to be sufficiently grounded as a coach. The following common-sense formula will ensure that our boys will really win in the only game that really counts: life.

Caring Men Who Are Cognizant of Their Own Shadows

+

Knowledge of Boy Psychology

+

Boy-centered Coaching

+

Mental Fitness Skills

+

Integrity Training

=

Boys Who Play Up to Their Abilities

+

Good, Decent, and Capable Men

✦ Integrity Sessions ✦

One structured way of promoting the development of character and integrity in our boys is the use of what I call Integrity Sessions. I have found them to be enormously effective not only in promoting integrity and good sportsmanship, but in building a sense of team. Here's how they work.

Our boys are first given whatever training is necessary to support their involvement with the sport. It may be comprised of combinations of working with the strength coach, speed coach, the trainer, nutritionist, or with a sports psychologist to develop the skills of mental fitness in order to transform weaknesses into strengths. With that foundation under way our boys are provided with several lecture and discussion sessions that introduce the five skills of mental fitness, teach the value of hard work, commitment to themselves and each other, never giving up, a sense of fair play, and honoring the opponent. These sessions conclude with particular emphasis placed upon the notion of becoming a noble warrior, along with the value of commitment to themselves and their teammates.

The players are also presented with motivational quotes from famous athletes accompanied by stories of their own personal struggles to overcome hardships. Among these athletes are Michael Jordan, Lou Brook, Carl Lewis, and Tiger Woods. In addition, the work ethic and keys to success used by legendary coaches such as Phil Jackson, John Wooden, Vince Lombardi, and George Allen are presented. In order to get the point across that we are working on developing the whole person, not just the athlete, fascinating stories and quotes from great historical figures such as Nelson Mandela and Plato are provided. By doing this, the stage is being set for our boys to begin to comprehend that it is our mission to help them find their greatness.

The concept of the Integrity Session is then introduced to the players. They are told that for a specific number of weeks or throughout the season, depending on scheduling opportunities, they will meet on a weekly basis. They are also told that in these sessions they will learn a new way of talking to each other so that they can communicate honestly and effectively. During these sessions athletes are encouraged to:

1. honestly assess their performance during the game and in practice;
2. commit to certain behaviors for the coming week;
3. honestly assess their peers' performance in following through with personal goals and commitments;
4. practice a style of communication in which each person takes responsibility for his own thoughts and feelings and conveys his perceptions of a teammate's behavior in an honest and respectful manner;
5. bring a sense of integrity into all aspects of their game: practice and game situations;
6. extend the standard of integrity to all nonsport activities, including academics and relationships with women.

Players are provided with specific instruction in how to communicate more effectively with each other and are given handouts that explain the process of communicating in specific detail. You will find a copy of the Integrity Sessions for Athletes: Goals and Ground Rules in appendix 2.

These handouts, lectures and discussion materials are intended for use with high school and university athletes. More basic and easy-to-read versions can be adapted from them for use with boys who are younger. Because the concept of good sportsmanship and being a team player is understandable at any age, a modified Integrity Session can be held with eight-year-olds or ten-year-olds. Regular Integrity Sessions in which teammates are encouraged to make commitments and give feedback to each other can be introduced to boys as young as twelve, depending on the group's level of maturity. Common sense dictates that the younger the group, the less formal and more brief the meeting. In fact, we need not tell the young boys that we're having an Integrity Session. To them it might appear to be an impromptu two-minute discussion with the coach in the dugout or locker room. I want to remind you that we are guided by our knowledge of boy psychology and the developmental stage they are in when planning such a discussion. A boy-centered approach is always sure to hit the mark.

I consistently found in using Integrity Sessions that not only did performance in sports improve, but the players' character also seemed to strengthen and mature. Improvement in sports was measured by content goals such as number of wins, completion rate, batting average, earned-run average, goals against average, speed, etc., while evidence of characterological improvement can be inferred by a combination of academic performance, disciplinary actions, relationships with women, development of humility, receptivity to feedback, and in leadership qualities. Plato spoke of this internalization of integrity in saying that "good men, with an understanding of principle will not need endless rules to guide their lives." What follows are examples of using Integrity Sessions with teams and with individual boys.

Team Integrity Sessions

One of the most dramatic cases for the use of Integrity Sessions came when I spent one fall several years ago working with a Division I college football team. The team had gone without a victory the previous year and was ranked dead last in the top two college football preseason rankings. Because desperate times call for desperate measures the head coach, who was generally not particularly partial to the idea of sports psychology, nevertheless directed his wide receiver coach to have me work with his players.

When I arrived I found an atmosphere characterized by frustration and a sense of powerlessness among the coaches. Although it would not be voiced, there was a general feeling that they just did not have the right kind of personnel to compete with the other major college football programs. Fortunately I found the wide receiver coach to be quite bright and very curious about the impact one's mental state can have on athletic performance. We agreed that I would lead two sessions in the spring in which the players would be introduced to the concept of sports psychology and the five skills of mental fitness. These sessions went well. Although the players were still somewhat shell-shocked from the disastrous previous season, they were generally curious about sports psychology. It must be noted that several players expressed a skepticism about the subject matter, and one player in particular expressed the belief that sports psychology was a lot of baloney and that he doubted he needed it or could be benefited by it. I conveyed a respect for his position and expressed a wish that he remain open to the idea. I told him that although he knew himself already to be a fine athlete, perhaps he might learn some ways to be even better. We settled our difference of opinions, with his affirmative nod that I took to mean that he heard me. We both staked out territorial positions that seemed to foster a sense of mutual respect.

Throughout the sessions I gave many specific examples of athletes using each of the skills of mental fitness and the young men expressed their eagerness by asking numerous questions. I made sure to emphasize that learning to use these skills did not mean that they had a problem or were otherwise at a deficit; rather, it meant using an additional tool to help them do their job. I also conveyed the message that asking for and receiving help is a sign of strength, rather than a sign of weakness. I ended each session by shaking each of the ten wide receivers' hands.

Over the rest of the spring and summer I met individually with each of the players in this unit and tailored a sports psychology program that fit their individual needs. One inexperienced player would freeze on the line of scrimmage and forget the plays he knew so well in practice. Another would get down on himself whenever he dropped a pass, which made it even more difficult for him to catch subsequent balls. Another would get disgusted when the defensive unit gave up lots of points. As a result he would mentally take himself out of the game and only go through the motions of running out his patterns. Another needed to develop the mental and physical preparation to help him "explode" off the line with the hike. As needed, the wide receiver coach or a strength or speed coach was consulted to help round out the specific content and process goals for each player. To their credit most of the players followed through with the process goals throughout the spring and summer leading into the regular fall playing schedule.

Several weeks before the first game of the season the players were introduced to the concept of Integrity Sessions at a meeting of the entire wide receiver unit led by their coach and myself. Each player was provided with a copy of the Integrity Sessions for Athletes: Goals and Ground Rules, provided for you in appendix 2. They were told that every Monday afternoon throughout the season we would meet for a fifty-minute Integrity Session. The players learned that these sessions would provide the unit a chance to assess their performance in the previous game, and an opportunity to make plans and commitments as to what they were going to do in the week of practice before the next game. Players were encouraged to declare how they were going to approach the next game and their mid-week practices and assess themselves and their teammates in regard to whether or not they followed through with their commitments.

Having been both a college student and a college professor, I knew not to count on most of the group reading the details of the handout, so I described the salient points to them. For instance, I explained the difference between an "I-statement" and a "You-statement" and why people were much less defensive when addressed with the former rather than the latter. We discussed the importance of listening respectfully to each other and in making commitments to each other. I also discussed how we owe it to ourselves and each other to be honest even if it means respectfully confronting someone for not having followed through with a commitment. The young men seemed understandably cautious about the prospect of engaging each other in this new language. But although they were tentative, they seemed subtly excited and open to it.

So we began to meet. Although I had a lot to say in the first few

Integrity Sessions, as the season wore on, the players had more and more to say as they began the process of claiming ownership over *their* Integrity Sessions. In the first session I initiated a discussion about Vince Lombardi and his notions about the work ethic and about the importance of striving to win. I ended the session by asking each player to make a public commitment for the coming week. Most made specific commitments as to how they were going to practice the following week. I again shook their hands at the end of the session.

I opened the second Integrity Session with a discussion about the philosophy of John Wooden and segued into a review of the difference between I-statements and You-statements and of listening and respecting each other. I then asked how they did in following through with their commitments from last session. The young men generally said they followed through. However, two of the players acknowledged not having done all they had planned, but resolved to do so the next week. I saw this to be a very good sign. They were comfortable enough to own up to it and made a further commitment. Then toward the end of the session one of these two players respectfully confronted a third player for having made a commitment to practice hard every day, and instead taking it easy one day. This was another good sign. However, in recognizing it as the first major pivotal moment in the Integrity Sessions I knew that the resolution of this "confrontation" would either move the players forward as a team or fragment them in disunity. The young man called on the carpet happened to be the most athletically accomplished player in the unit and he courageously acknowledged that his teammate assessed his behavior accurately. Fortunately both players "played" by the rules and the team-building function of the Integrity Sessions really took off from this point.

Constructive confrontations like this one do not happen merely as a matter of luck. Rather, if you have relatively emotionally healthy players they will first confront someone who is capable of dealing with it. It is important that you as the coach work to create the conditions where such a constructive engagement can take place. Through your own words and actions you can create an atmosphere characterized by safety and trust. You might find it helpful, as I do, to convey important messages to players through storytelling. I encourage you to use any metaphors and motivational quotes you are comfortable with or those that are best suited for your team.

In subsequent sessions with this team I talked about Ghandi's notion of finding satisfaction in the struggle, Nelson Mandela's will to resist, along with the belief of George Allen and other famous sports figures that fostering a positive mental attitude has an important place in sports . . . and in academics and in dealing with women. We talked about their lives outside of football and how they owed it to each other to confront a teammate about how he might be treating a girlfriend or about drinking in the week before a game. In one session I introduced the notion of being a noble warrior; of having a cause and giving oneself fully to it. We even talked about feeling afraid. I told them that being a real man did not mean not having fear. Rather, it means acknowledging the fear and learning from it. In this particular session, which occurred just after the midpoint of the season, I asked them if any of them ever felt afraid in a game. After an awkward silence the player who had expressed the most direct skepticism during the introduction to the sports psychology lectures raised his hand and said, "I feel afraid from the moment the whistle blows to begin the game until the moment the whistle blows to end the game." This was a courageous act of openness, from a young man who tended to be considerably closed and who was even said to be "uncoachable" by some of the coaches. Because of his status as the best player in the unit, the younger players' eyes were visibly widened during this demonstration of personal strength and self-acceptance.

Seemingly serendipitous events such as this one will occur if you allow yourself to be open to them . . . to be pleasantly surprised when a transformation occurs. If we mentally pigeonhole a young man into being only a certain way, we block a change from occurring. By being open to players such as this one to be their best, we pave the way for him to do so. Regardless of whether it was the time for him to blossom, we would have at least created the external conditions necessary for him to emerge as a more complete person, one who was increasingly accepting of himself.

Over the course of the season, the players became more and more comfortable with using the Integrity Sessions to make commitments and assess their own and others' behavior. Younger players asked for help and the older players agreed to look out for them during games. They agreed to pick each other up after a tackle. They agreed to "finish off" their runs after catching a ball, rather than merely running out of bounds. The players became more of a team as they regularly complimented and confronted each other. In an Integrity Session after a late-season win, the players were shocked to learn that their unit coach and I, quite independent from each other, felt angry and disappointed in how they had played. They seemed to have let their success go to their heads and did not follow through with many of their commitments, such as to run all the plays out even if they were not the primary or secondary receiver. By session's end they came to appreciate our honesty. It was not about winning; they were confronted for not striving.

By the end of the season the team had gone from 0–11 the year before to 6–5. There were significant gains in the percentage of passes completed, the amount of yardage gained through the air, and the amount of yardage gained after a completed pass, in contrast to the previous year. No doubt having an additional year of life and football experience influenced this success, but the combination of mental fitness training and use of Integrity Sessions clearly had had an impact. It is noteworthy that this unit had no disciplinary actions during the season, increased its grade-point average over the previous year, and had no cuts from class, study hall, or appointments with their academic advisors. Most important, these young men seemed to grow toward being dignified and honorable men.

Individual Integrity Training

When I conduct training sessions with supervisors and other professional managers, I readily acknowledge up front that *they* are the experts at what they do . . . and I mean it. My purpose is to help them to sharpen their thinking and give them some additional tools to use. The same holds true in applying the concept of integrity training in youth sports. When it comes to doing individual integrity training, good coaches have always approached their charges with an eye toward addressing the whole boy. They have not needed psychologists or other academic types to tell them what their boys required; they knew it intuitively. However, it is my hope that regardless of your degree of experience as a coach or parent you will utilize the fundamental points in *Really Winning* to help keep you focused on what is most important in dealing with our boys. Because most of your contact with them will take place in the countless encounters of everyday life, it is especially important that you see each of these moments as opportunities for Integrity Training.

Unlike the more formal structure of group Integrity Sessions, individual Integrity Sessions are much less structured and are tailored to the unique needs of the athlete. What is required on the part of the coach, parent, mentor, or counselor is to be mindful of what comprises the building blocks of character. On the one hand our boys' self-esteem and sense of confidence increase with the success that comes from hard work and skill acquisition. However, they are only able to stay grounded through the sense of humility and perspective that is derived from the practice of good sportsmanship, being an honorable warrior, and the integrity that these engender.

Opportunities abound for conducting individual Integrity Training. It is obviously easiest when a coach, parent, or counselor is sought out for assistance with a particular dilemma. In these cases the boy is directly requesting input. But because boys are less likely to be so forthright about their troubles and questions, we must be prepared to intervene when we perceive the timing is correct. Fortunately, already being a coach, parent, or counselor provides the infrastructure and credibility to make such a move. It is particularly advantageous when we are already working with a boy within the context of a sport in which *he* has chosen to participate. Let's use the situation with John as an example.

John at Sixteen

As you recall, John was a wrestler. He never cheated and never had any interest in sneaking in a move that would hurt an opponent to gain the advantage. He clearly had a sense of good sportsmanship and he could be thought of as an honorable warrior. John needed Integrity Training not so much in terms of how he was dealing with others, but how he was dealing with himself.

He worked so hard to please others and he frequently tried to be what he perceived them as wanting him to be. He did this with his mother, father, teachers, girlfriend, friends, coach, and counselor. Because his actions were so externally focused, he all too often felt confused as to what was the correct thing for him to do. It is not surprising that feelings of frustration, resentment, and anger were familiar to him. Because he did not listen to his inner voice for direction it could be said that John was not honoring himself.

John sought me out for help with academics and wrestling, and eventually experienced success in these areas. Because of this success *and because I conveyed a sense of respect for him* he trusted me. It was this trust that paved the way for John really hearing what I had to say. I told him that both of us needed to listen to the inside of him for what was the right thing for him to do. Though he tried hard, it was very difficult for John to begin to move away from tuning in to what others wanted of him instead of honoring his own inner direction. He resisted telling his girlfriend how he wanted to be treated because he did not want her to feel hurt. John resisted telling his coach he did not want to wrestle in a lower weight class because he did not want to let him down. He also resisted telling his father that he wanted to be treated fairly for fear of being rejected altogether. Ironically he even spent a considerable amount of time trying to figure out what I wanted him to do so that he could please me. All I wanted was for him to listen to himself and be himself.

Through both words and actions, I established with John that:

- I saw his habit of seeking direction from others as a vestige from the uncertain days of his early life in which his security was in doubt;
- I respected him as a young man;
- I truly believed that he was the expert on what was best for himself;
- I was skilled at listening to his inner voice and that he could learn to hear it also;
- the only sure way to increase the probability of being successful in all aspects of his life was learning to trust his inner voice.

It is noteworthy that what appeared to be the most helpful agent of change for John was the relationship between us. For instance, after he talked for a while about how his girlfriend's actions demonstrated that she was untrustworthy, and I commented as such, John would say, "I know you want me to break up with her." I insisted that I was just commenting on what *he* was saying and that he was in charge of his life. I only wanted him to be happy. While it was true that I saw their relationship as a dysfunctional one, I knew that, unless John gave voice to his true thoughts and feelings he would likely not have his needs met in relationships with other young women, either.

Throughout his relationship with his girlfriend, I insisted that he listen to himself. Regardless of whether he was disappointed in something she had done or whether he really wanted to ask her to the prom, I encouraged him to listen to what he was feeling and to understand what those feelings were about. I told him that we both needed to understand and respect his inner voice.

Individual Integrity Training with John also centered on confronting him about following through with the commitments he made to himself. Although he was unwavering in following through with his preparations for wrestling, he was less resolute in the early days about implementing his schoolwork plan. As you know, John already had a clearly established set of process goals that guided him toward his ultimate academic success. In the beginning, however, John found it difficult sometimes to choose between studying and spending time with his friends. Fortunately, because he was an honest person he told me when he went out with friends on a school night instead of completing one of his study sessions. As per his style, John expressed a concern that he did not want to let his mother or me down. I insisted that was not the real issue, it was *his* content goal of making the honor roll and *his* process goal of completing his study sessions that were up for discussion. If he still wanted to pursue these goals, he would be letting himself down by not following through. When he asked me what he should do, I truly meant it when I told him it was entirely his choice. Many more times than not he chose to stay with his plan because he really did want to do well academically.

John's individualized Integrity Training involved encouraging him to listen to his inner voice and learning that he was the best source for decision making. It also involved confronting him when he did not follow through with his plan. This kind of confrontation was in no way hostile; it conveyed a genuine respect for John as well as for his thoughts, feelings, and dreams.

What follows is Integrity Training that called for a different kind of intervention.

Tommy and Kenny at Six

Tommy and Kenny are two boys I coached in a soccer league for six- and seven-year-olds. After a practice session I overheard them talking about how good one of their teammates was. We had conducted an intrasquad scrimmage that day and Bobby had been assigned to the other team. As usual he was masterful in his control of the ball and in his ability to excel regardless of whether I put him in goal, on defense, or as a forward. Bobby's squad won 3–0. On and on I heard Tommy and Kenny praise the virtues of Bobby, but as they did I detected a "woe is me" in their voices.

COACH: Yeah, he's got a lot of good soccer skills. You guys did a good job working hard out there.

BOYS: All the good players were on Bobby's team.

COACH: That's not true, you guys are good soccer players.

BOYS: No we're not. Bobby and his guys are the best.

COACH: Bobby's really good. You guys can learn from him because he's on our team.

BOYS: Yeah, it's great he's on our team. We'll be great.

COACH: The team will do great because you guys are on the team, too.

BOYS: What are you talking about?

COACH: You are both fast and you are not afraid to work hard and that means a lot!

BOYS: Yeah, but we can't win without him.

COACH: I know you feel that way, but that is simply not true. Do you know about the Seattle Mariners? They had the best record in baseball in 2001 and one of the best of all time. Do you know how they did it?

BOYS: No.

COACH: For years they had superstars like Ken Griffey Jr. and Alex Rodriguez but they were never able to make it to the World Series. They traded both of them and the team has never played so well. Do you know why? Because now they are a team. You don't need a superstar to win as long as everyone plays together as a team. You guys are the kind of players that can help make a team win. Just don't give up when you have to cover a guy like Bobby. Let yourself have fun at the challenge!

BOYS: [Said nothing, but they were listening intently.]

I was concerned that the boys not be so discouraged as to underperform in future practice sessions with Bobby and or in actual game situations when they encounter particularly talented players from another team. Consistent with the mental fitness skill of energy regulation I knew they needed to bring their energy up in order to do their very best against such good players. I also knew that if they got too down and could not get up for the game they would enter the following vicious circle: underperform> feeling discouraged> feeling down on themselves> underperform.

There are many ways to have fun in the context of a game and it is imperative that these boys have fun. Fun is the driving force in youth sports and without it the experience would be pointless. The tendency of boys of this age is to link fun solely to winning. It is important to help them have fun while playing the game within the game. Much like basketball players faced with the challenge of covering Michael Jordan, it is important to equate success with more than just stopping him from scoring. It could be fun to strive to meet the challenge of holding him under a certain number of points, or to make a steal, or to not let him go baseline to the basket, and so forth. In short Tommy and Kenny could learn that if they do their very best and Bobby still scores, they can tip their hat in respect for his skills and hold their own heads high for hanging in there. Their experience in soccer could provide an important lesson for not giving up and for the satisfaction that can be gained by doing their best regardless of the outcome.

Because of their age, it was not necessary to talk specifically about energy regulation or reframing in order to have a positive mental attitude, but through my words I was introducing them to these mental fitness skills. Over time as their coaches take advantage of opportunities to reinforce these concepts Tommy and Kenny will develop inner strength and determination. Their coaches have to be willing to listen for these teachable moments and take the time to engage with our boys.

Lloyd at Twenty-one

I knew Lloyd as an acquaintance and over the years we had become quite friendly. He was very bright and met with considerable academic success in high school and at the Ivy League college he attended. It was there he developed quite a reputation for his prowess on the lacrosse fields; he had led his team to victory many times. On the field and off, his friends and fellow classmates would chant his name over and over. He confessed once that this made him feel like a Greek god.

Like most young men of twenty-one years, he seemed to have godlike powers. Because he was handsome and quite charming he also developed a considerable reputation for his prowess in the field of love. It is not surprising that young women were drawn to him and he had the time of his life playing the field. He told me that he had begun to date a mutual friend and eventually their relationship became quite serious. The couple agreed to forgo opportunities to date others and to make a commitment to be with each other exclusively. The only problem was that Lloyd's commitment to Jennifer lasted only about three days.

Lloyd found it very difficult to pass up the many offers that were presented to such a handsome young man. That would have been fine if he had told Jennifer that he realized he was not ready for such a serious relationship, but he didn't. He even began to have phone sex on a frequent basis through one of the 900 services. I mentioned to him that Jennifer needed to be treated better and he agreed, yet his various betrayals of their relationship continued. I ultimately came to confront him much more firmly as I thought he was being dishonorable to his girlfriend and in addition he was disrespecting himself by acting in such an unethical manner.

It took a long time for Lloyd to clean up his act. But the important thing was taking the risk to tell him to do the right thing. To have just looked the other way would have been to indirectly condone his actions. It would have been a disservice to both of these young people.

As coaches, parents, and mentors we have a constant stream of opportunities to support and lovingly confront our boys. We have to be willing to see them and we have to be willing to not turn away, but to intervene. We do this because our boys need us and we care about them.

✦ Touchstones for Integrity ✦

Most people who seek to employ Integrity Sessions will not have the benefit of a trained sports psychologist to assist them. This is a simple fact of limited resources. However, a professional can be consulted to help guide you in this process. Furthermore, because of the great interest among the public that something be done to help our boys and to help clean up youth sports, a sports psychologist or other counselor may be willing to volunteer their services.

Let's assume however, that you are on your own. Here are some important things to keep in mind:

1. Don't go beyond your own comfort level. If what you are trying to do seems over your head don't do it. Stay within your area of expertise and your own style of leadership.

2. Keep appropriate boundaries with the boys whom you are coaching. A well-trained counselor is never intrusive and neither should you be. For example, do not pry into the romantic life of your players, but if it becomes obvious that a player is involved in either dangerous sexual behavior or unethical interpersonal behavior it is important that you do not turn your back to it.

3. Adjust your use of the Integrity Session concept to the level of the boys on your team.

4. Consider using age twelve as the entry level for beginning to teach the concept of effective communication, commitments, and confrontation as detailed in the Integrity Sessions for Athletes: Goals and Ground Rules handout. If a handout is provided with this age group, it should be tailored to them by using language that will make sense for them. Such a handout is not necessarily required.

5. Keep the Building Block for Character Development in mind as a reference point (see figure 5–1).

6. Be the model. Remember, it is not about technique, it's more about substance. Practice using "I-statements" versus "You-statements." An "I-statement" tells the other about yourself along with your thoughts, feelings, and perceptions. It demonstrates your willingness to be open and honorable in your encounter with the other. On the other hand, a "You-statement" reveals nothing about yourself except perhaps your judgment of the other. The tendency of the other to react by being closed and defensive is understandable.

7. Practice being respectful.

8. Remind the boys to practice good sportsmanship and to have fun.

I stated in the previous chapter that a victory tastes sweeter when it comes by honorable means. This holds true for grand events as well as seemingly insignificant daily acts of honor. This applies in and out of the arena of sport. Returning an extra dollar we were given as change for a purchase is one such meaningful act of integrity and honor. So are holding the door open for the next in line, allowing someone to merge in front of you in heavy traffic, and conveying a sense of respect to another regardless of that person's station in life.

Ghandi once stated that he gained considerable satisfaction, not so much in the ultimate victory, but in the struggle toward that end. When we encourage our boys to savor the hard work involved in playing their sports honorably, we teach them a lesson that they can apply in their lives long after the crowd noise of youth, high school, and college sports fades into the distance.

6

The Role of Administrators, Parents, and Coaches

BOB AND STAN are volunteer coaches in their town's youth soccer program. Like many coaches they are doing it because their children are interested in participating in sports. In addition to their coaching activities, both of these well-educated professionals contribute money and their time in other positive ways for various local causes and activities. Both men have good intentions of doing good work for their family and neighbors. They are the kind of fellows that help solidify the fabric of the community.

However, some notable differences in style were revealed when the teams that Stan and Bob coach recently played each other. The players are six and seven years old and at this level one coach from each team is allowed on the field in order to teach, encourage, and actively coach the players. It was obvious by their intensity and excitement that both coaches wanted their team to do well and to win. One of the ways this was revealed was in how they encouraged their players to run when they were on the field and in the game. Stan would call out to his team, saying things like, "Run, run, run . . . if you are wearing blue you need to be running!" and "Run to the ball, go take that ball!" If one of his players was finding it hard to run Stan would go to the player and have a quick private discussion about whether he was tired and needed to rest while a teammate with fresh legs came in for him. The message was "we need you to run, but if you're tired it's no problem, just let me know and we'll switch you with a rested player." Stan was encouraging and supportive while simultaneously conveying an expectation that his players keep moving while on the field.

Bob would also call out to his players and encourage them to run; however, his tone was markedly admonishing as he barked, "I told you to run, you gotta run out here!" In a not so private moment he, like Stan, addressed one of his players who was not running hard, but did so by saying in a severe and threatening tone, "If you don't run, I'm taking you right off the field! I told you before!" Bob was conveying the same expectation as Stan that his players keep running, but he was doing so in a way that hinged his sense of acceptance and support of his players to their performance on the field. Although he believed he had the best interests of his players in mind, in actuality Bob was being abusive to the six-and seven-year-olds in his care.

It is reasonable for coaches to demand that their players keep running if they are out on the field. In fact, sports can be a positive and transforming experience because of a coach "raising the bar" and having faith in a player's ability to perform at a higher level. When their coaches help them to stretch in order to be greater than they are, our boys can learn to be more confident and to have faith in their ability to overcome obstacles in and out of sports. But *how* we convey these demands and expectations to our boys makes all the difference between being a positive influence or having our good intentions inadvertently influenced by our shadows, as was the case with Bob.

✦ Boy-centered Coaching ✦

In the previous chapter we briefly introduced the concept of being boy-centered. Because the successful accomplishment of our duties as parents, coaches, and administrators hinges so much on being boy-centered, it is worth going into more detail about what it means. When we are oriented in a boy-centered manner our encounters with our boys are informed by three factors: (1) an awareness and an appreciation of the phenomenological experience of the particular boy with whom we are interacting (2) a general appreciation of the progressive nature of the psychological and social development of boys, and (3) an intent to be boy-centered and that all interactions serve the boy.

Phenomenological Experience

All boys are individuals and thus it is reasonable to expect that no two boys are the same. Not only do they differ by age, maturity, and experience, but they differ by temperament and personality as well. This is not rocket science; rather it is simple common sense. Why then do some coaches and parents tend to take such a blanket approach to our boys? When they are treated as a group or class, rather than the individuals that they are, our boys are actually being treated as if they were objects. An object is an "it" rather than a "who."

If we treat a boy as an object how can we possibly say we know who that boy really is? The most we can honestly say is, "This is how this particular boy acts under these conditions when we treat him like an object." An extreme example of objectifying boys happened several years ago during two incidents in a junior high school gym class. On each occasion the gym teachers were reacting to mundane male teenage matters; either several boys were fooling around and not paying attention or not enough of the young men were wearing their mandatory white socks. In both circumstances the entire class was directed to strip naked and march single file through the showers over and over for the entire double gym class. Even if those teachers had had any chance of getting to know those young men, the Auschwitz-style group treatment that they employed as a "teachable moment" would have forced the boys to not reveal their real selves. Not only did these teachers treat all their students as objects but they also taught the boys to behave as objects and to hide their true feelings, which included feelings of fright and contempt for male authority figures who could find satisfaction and even humor in such a dehumanizing act.

In order to help bring out the best in a boy we need to convey a sense of acceptance for the person who is the boy. A description of the most healthy and ideal forms of the four components within the psychology of boys was first introduced in chapter 3. Logic and common sense dictate that in order to foster the emergence of these ideal archetypes in our boys we must first receive them for the boys and young men that they know themselves to be. If we genuinely accept and respect them for who they are, we put ourselves in a much better position to bring out the leader, the hero, the strategist, and the loyal teammate. Boy-centered coaching does not mean letting boys run wild or not calling them on misbehaving or not listening, it means taking care to not crush or injure their egos in the process. In a fashion similar to that of putting oneself in another's shoes, trying to appreciate the unique phenomenological experience of a boy includes consideration for *how* he sees and experiences us as coach, father, or mentor. This kind of empathic understanding is a necessary prerequisite to foster the better self within our boys.

Ironically, while it is certainly important to be able to have an empathic appreciation of the phenomenological experience of our boys, no special expertise or training is necessary. Nothing fancy is required, just an appreciation for where the boys or young men are coming from. Consider the following simple examples from coaching at different levels of male sports in which a crucial attitude that is essential for winning is addressed.

Coaches seek to instill in their players a sense of entitlement while in the area of competition. By this I mean to feel equal to anyone else on the field and to not let fear or intimidation, whether or not intentionally conveyed by the opponent, result in a boy's not playing up to his ability. Sometimes the mere presence of a clearly gifted athlete on the other team elicits a fear reaction in average players. Players need to be coached to learn from the fear and harness its energy, otherwise they are at risk to underperform and play below their natural and developed abilities. No doubt you recognize this as the specific technique we referred to in chapter 5 as reframing, which is part of the mental fitness skill of developing and maintaining a positive mental attitude. Obviously with a gifted athlete on the other side of the ball our boys can ill afford to not be fully present in body and mind. Regardless of the opponent, the sense of entitlement that naturally resides in our boys varies with age, personality, physical ability, and temperament. Consequently, coaches who work in beginner T-ball leagues as well as those whose charges are college-level football players make sure this important mental attitude is aimed in the right direction. The degree of success that coaches have is in part due to the extent that they are able to understand, really understand, who their players are.

A young man in his early sixties recently shared some observations he made from his vantage point behind the wheel of a bus hired to transport high school players and their coaches to away games. Wally has a master's degree in health and physical education from Penn State and spent a number of years coaching at the high school and college level. Perhaps his most important credential is that he is an honorable man who is also a people person. His work as a bus driver serves to supplement his retirement income and also enables him to interact with people of all ages, something he particularly enjoys. He has observed coaches who are genuine role models of boy-centered coaching. Several of them do not allow certain kinds of music on the bus because the words or messages are deemed inappropriate. Instead they create an atmosphere more conducive to the message of integrity and character-building they want to provide. They use the time on the bus to engage with the boys about their sport, and in the relaxed setting they give feedback that really seems to impact their boys in positive ways. Furthermore, they are willing to extend their engagement with their boys beyond the particular sports they are coaching. This is evidenced by discussions about college plans, how they are doing in school, and occasionally even about girlfriends. On the other hand, our fly-on-the-wall behind the wheel of the bus has witnessed the actions of shadow-driven coaches. They frequently spend the vast majority of their time talking with another coach instead of engaging with their players. When they do engage it is by yelling occasional threats at the young men to keep the noise down. Inevitably, in the unstructured and unsupervised atmosphere on the bus, boys being boys, their shadows emerge and they get out of hand, which requires more yelling. There is no learning, no reviewing, and little teaching of anything positive in this time spent together. Sometimes after the team has lost a freshman football game these coaches deem it wise to make all the players ride home in silence. What is it like for these boys? Losing hurts, but what a waste of an opportunity to learn from it! A boy-centered coach could use the loss to help this group of young men assess both their strengths and areas in need of strengthening. He could help his fourteen-year-olds to put the loss into perspective so that they could all grow personally and as players from it. In order to do this, however, he has to know and respect the experience of the young men who are his players.

Consider working with a different age group. A coach working with six- and seven-year-olds in a soccer league might explain in a quiet and playful moment how he loves eating meatballs. He asks the players if they love meatballs and they join in with the silliness by saying they do also, regardless of whether they really like meatballs or not. Then the coach explains that he wants the players to see the soccer ball as a meatball and that even if someone from the other team is dribbling with it, "It's still your meatball, so you gotta go get it." This then sets the stage for game-time coaching in which the coach calls out; "It's your meatball, Zachary, go get it!" "I know you're hungry for that meatball, Devin!" It is amazing how the kids turn on their afterburners when reminded that they are entitled to their meatball, and in the full fun of the game, they go right after it. High motivation, hard work, lots of fun, and nothing but supportive coaching is exactly what coaching on this level calls for. More important, this sort of coaching with a silly edge reaches the kids right where they live.

Common sense dictates that a coach working with fifteen-and sixteen-year-old high school soccer players might lose them if he followed this same method. He would have to apply more age-appropriate imagery. For example, he might teach that when the other team has the ball and crosses the midfield line his players should see them as "trying to steal your girlfriend and you gotta go get her back." With boys of this age he could freely use military analogies that are well suited for planning a line of attack and in securing territory and ultimately the ball. In the hands of a right-minded coach either of these examples could certainly produce the sense of entitlement necessary for winning, while maintaining their status as honorable warriors. However, in the hands of a coach under the influence of his shadows either of these examples could get out of hand. I recently learned of a college football coach who employed a rather foul method for psyching up his players' sense of entitlement. They were apparently preparing to play a team whose mascot was a rooster. The coach then arranged for several real roosters to be let loose on the practice field, only to have his players work themselves up into a frenzy, and having quite a ball, while chasing after and kicking the birds. This no doubt is yet another example of an individual's astounding blindness to his own dark side. Nevertheless, he may have reached his players, but not in the place that would in any way foster the notion of a noble warrior. It is a safe bet that there is no character or integrity being developed in that football program.

Having a sense of empathy for the boy, as well as for his emerging sense of self, will go a long way in terms of reaching him. When this is fine tuned and adjusted for the particular group of boys we are working with and when it is grounded in a boy-centered coaching philosophy, we are all sure to really win.

Serving Our Boys

Because our ultimate goal is to foster character and integrity in our boys all our words and actions must be guided by the question, How does this serve the boy? Unless we can say with confidence that a comment, interaction, or intervention with one of our boys serves him, it is reasonable to consider that we may have missed the mark. Caring about our boys is fine and in fact it is necessary. However, as the scenario with coach Bob indicated, caring is necessary, but not sufficient. In order to be truly boy-centered, all our engagements with our boys must serve them. If we are not serving them, then we are attempting to serve our adult egos and ourselves.

President Bush stated soon after the terrorist attacks on September 11, 2001, toppled the Twin Towers that either people or countries actively commit to standing with the democratic world against terrorism or be considered as aligned with the terrorists. While of course I am not attempting to equate the actions of an adult-centered coach with the actions of a hateful terrorist, I clearly believe that a very strong commitment is required in order to be a boy-centered coach. If you are not going to make the active commitment to be centered on serving them, you will be hurting our boys. This hurt may be inadvertent, but harm will be caused just the same. This is especially the case when we consider that the atmosphere that fosters adult-centered, shadow-influenced coaching continues to exist. The litmus test for determining whether we are serving our boys requires us to answer several questions including:

- Why have we chosen to be a coach?
- For whom do we want them to win?
- How do we feel when they lose?

- Why were we disappointed that they lost the shutout?
- What is our internal experience just before we get angry with them?

It is reasonable to speculate that one of the reasons Bob was so aggressive with the players on his team was because he was caught in being adult-centered. Bob is a competitive person. He runs a profitable and successful business and he likes to do well. While there is certainly nothing wrong with that approach to his entrepreneurial dealings, there is everything wrong with bringing that attitude into his coaching. Bob was being adult-centered. He was specifically being Bob-centered. In doing so his attitudes, beliefs, and ego investments from his adult life spilled over into an area where they had no business being.

Ten year-old Ronnie's experience as a Pop Warner football player is another example of encountering an adult-centered, me-centered coach. Ronnie has played for the same team for several years. He has always worked hard and always made the practice sessions. He is also a genuinely skilled quarterback. Objective observers have speculated that he has the best arm and the coolest head on the team, yet he is not the starting quarterback. In fact, he rarely gets in the game on offense. Although he has been continually disappointed by this, Ronnie maintains a good attitude. Even in situations when the team had been winning in convincing fashion and also when the tide had turned against them, the head coach refused to put him in the game. Sometimes spectators even call out for Ronnie to be put in the game, mostly to no avail. Who is the starting quarterback the head coach stands firmly behind? His own son.

It is reasonable to ask the question, Whom was the coach serving in not starting the better player? Whom was he serving in not giving him a chance at some action even in lopsided games? Was it for Ronnie's own good? Obviously it was not. Was it for the good of his own son beyond the superficial level? This is doubtful, for that boy knows all too well the skills that Ronnie possesses. He also must know in his heart that his reign as exclusive heir to the quarterback position is illegitimate. The head coach is not serving either boy or their teammates. His actions, rather, are transparent attempts to aggrandize himself through his son. How unfortunate for everyone.

When coaching a team on which our son is a member, we must rein in our desire for ego gratification and for favoring our own son, while simultaneously being appropriate and fair to the other players on the team. It is important to not go overboard in either direction in striking the balance. It is an unfortunate state of affairs in youth sports that so many coaches step way over the line in favoring their own kin. These coaches are not boy-centered, they are me-centered. Whatever their intentions, because they are partly directed by their more negative, shadow forms, any attempts to foster sound character and integrity in their boys will be undermined. Even the best-intentioned parents and coaches among us need to do their very best to keep the basic tenets of boy-centered coaching in mind. For instance, it is all too easy in the midst of a competitive game to feel the urge to go for the win, even if it means not playing all the boys on your team. However, having the impulse to override what is best for our boys is very different than acting on it. A boy-centered coach is often engaged in the art of coaching so that the team that is currently on the field includes weaker players balanced out by stronger ones. When everyone plays, the entire team can work toward the win, and when the win comes the entire team can share in the satisfaction. If in the heat of battle a coach errs on the side of keeping the stars on the field, he is nonetheless capable of making the necessary adjustments once he realizes that his original actions may not really serve his boys.

Content and Process in Communication

By now you are familiar with these terms as they pertain to the goals our boys may desire to achieve (content goals) and the means by which they actually do so (process goals). These terms have a similarly useful application in understanding how best to communicate as coaches and parents with these boys and young men. In order to be boy-centered we must be mindful of the nature of the communication to and from the boys we encounter. Differentiating between the content and process of that communication is a helpful touchstone for this purpose. As you will see, this is especially important because whether we know it or not, we simultaneously send messages along these two dimensions of communication whenever we have a dialogue with our boys.

As a coach or parent we want to convey some very specific information that can help in the development of skills necessary to achieve success in a sport. A boy who wishes to be a good shortstop would be encouraged to stand with knees slightly bent and leaning slightly forward on his toes, rather than back on his heels; a midfielder in soccer would be encouraged to anticipate the spaces that open so as to effectively pass to a striker moving into them; and a wide receiver in football would be taught how to explode off the line with the hike of the ball. All of these are special skills and parts of skill sets that with practice and proper guidance will become more refined and help to elevate the level of a player's performance. The specific input, information decimated, and feedback regarding a player's actions in performing the skill in question are the *content* of communication.

In addition to imparting information about the acquisition of a physical skill, the content of our communication may also include discussing a player's mental attitude toward an upcoming game or his attitude and beliefs with regard to a particular skill that has yet to be acquired. An example of the former is when a coach takes a player aside to caution him about his overconfident attitude. The danger of taking an opponent too lightly is that it could lead to a player or team experiencing a real letdown and consequently performing considerably below their ability. An example of the latter is when a player's self-doubts and irrational beliefs interfere with his acquiring the skill in question. For instance, boys who are first beginning to learn how to effectively shoot on the goal in soccer tend to kick the ball toward the goal from a considerable distance out and also to direct the ball toward or in the vicinity of the goal tender. These tactics usually prove fruitless and frustrating for the player, thus reinforcing an I-can't-do-it attitude. This sort of neophyte soccer player behavior usually results from a combination of simply not knowing what to do in order to increase the probability of successfully scoring a goal and a disbelief that they can actually score a goal. Because a player's mind-set conceives goal scoring as something that is more of a fantasy than a real possibility, they are less inclined to actually do the things that would work, such as moving the ball in a little closer to the goal and shooting for the corners. Helping our boys to overcome these attitudes and beliefs is important content for communication for coaches and parents to initiate a discussion around. In doing so they might evoke the words of legendary UCLA basketball coach John Wooden who said, "Don't let the things you can't do interfere with the things you can do."

The long and the short of it is that the content of our communication with our boys spans specific corrective information regarding their actual physical movements along with feedback and assistance in addressing the attitudes and beliefs that may inhibit those movements. Content is the stuff we want to talk to our players about.

In contrast to content is process. While content has to do with the specific things we want to impart to our boys, process has to do with the infrastructure that actually conveys the content message to them. Process has to do with *how* the information actually gets there. Let's take a look at the communication differences between Bob and Stan from the beginning of the chapter. They were virtually identical when it came to the *content* of communication in that they both wanted their players to be working hard and running when they were in the game. However, they were worlds apart when it came to the *process* of *how* they conveyed this information. Because of this difference in process they were sending very different signals. Through Stan's process communication he was sending messages that included:

> I want you to work hard, but I respect you if you need a rest. I support you and I accept you as a worthwhile and decent person, even if you are tired. Regardless of whether or not you are a star player with lots of stamina, you are an equal and valued member of this team.

In contrast Bob's process communication sent messages that conveyed:

> My acceptance of you as a person and as a valued member of this team is contingent upon your complying with my demand that you run. If you are tired and do not run I will be disappointed and angry that you let me down. I only value the stars and players with stamina.

As I said before there is nothing at all wrong with creating a reasonable expectation that players run when on the field. In fact there is everything right with elevating such a standard of performance. However, the other messages that we send through the process of communicating with our boys make all the difference between whether we are coaching from a boy-centered perspective or not.

We are practicing boy-centered coaching when we consider the personality of the particular boy with whom we are communicating. One-size-fits-all coaching is not boy-centered and thus causes us to miss our target of developing character and integrity in our boys. Just as every parent knows that all kids are different and thus have to be dealt with a little differently, a good coach is mindful of the differences in the boys on his team. It does take a lot more time and effort in understanding the psychology and personality of each player, but that really is part of the job as a coach. Coaching is not just about getting the wins.

We are also practicing boy-centered coaching when we consider the age of the boys we are coaching. What was Bob thinking when he was barking out his ultimatums to his players? These kids were six and seven years old, yet the process of his communication suggested that they were considerably older. Perhaps he was not thinking. He certainly was not being boy-centered. Bob is a decent guy with good family and community values. There are a lot of Bobs out there and we are all capable of having a little Bob inside of us. In this sense he represents our less than enlightened form. Bob represents our shadow.

Dual Dimensions of Communication

Coaches and parents must become mindful that communication always occurs along the dual dimensions of content and process. Because of this, whenever we are talking with our young charges, we are always sending two messages to them. Therefore it behooves us to do our best to make sure that

- The messages are compatible and consistent with each other
- The messages are the ones we actually want to send

Without a conscious intent to be boy-centered in our coaching and parenting we may inadvertently send the wrong message and in doing so we might not be acting like the adult mentor that would be our ideal. For instance, a coach's process communication might convey a message to a player that "you are an idiot because you have failed to preserve the shutout I really wanted us to achieve."

Or he might convey a process communication to another coach or fan that "you are a _____ idiot and I ought to kill you."

In both examples the coach is taking a me-centered versus a boy-centered approach. How do we know this? Simply by asking the question: Whom does this serve? Both process statements appear to be self-focused around the ego gratification of the coach and do not seem to be in the best interests of his players. If the boy tried hard but the other team scored, the boy-centered coach would have to agree with Vince Lombardi that "striving to win is everything." If the boy did not put out a reasonable effort and the other team scored, the boy-centered coach would have to address the boy's underperformance in a way *appropriate to the age of the boy*. If a fan or the opposing coach did something outrageous to infuriate the coach, a boy-centered approach would dictate that he gather himself and act in a way that modeled sound character and integrity. This might mean talking in a dignified fashion to a referee, or afterward to a league official, or—depending on the circumstance— pulling the team off the field so as not to subject them to abuse.

We know that no one is perfect; neither the boys who are our sons and players, nor we as their parents and coaches. We do not have to be perfect in order to do a good job. We just want to keep from making gross errors and to take corrective action when we do so. We must strive to stay boy-centered in order keep ourselves on target.

There may not be a clear demarcation line as to when it is all right to bark out orders to a team and when it is not appropriate. Similarly there may well be a point when it is legitimate for a coach's approval of a player to be conditional upon his effort and performance. However, it is a matter of common sense that barking out conditional, judgmental, and admonishing statements is just not appropriate in the early levels of youth sports. A basic understanding of the psychology of boys and of the formation of a healthy self-concept informs us of this. At the other end of the male sports continuum it seems reasonable to expect that young men who are professional athletes can expect their financial rewards and personal approval from a coach to be solely conditional upon their performance. Between entry-level youth sports and entry-level professional athletics there is a whole range of boys and young men that need their coaches to center upon them in healthy ways. They need this to become better athletes. They also need this in order to foster the self-esteem that is necessary for the development of sound character and integrity. However, regardless of the age or level of play it is reasonable for us to demand and expect coaching personnel to convey a sense of respect for the individuals who are their players. In order to do this, they themselves must be persons of character.

Modeling

There is an old saying that children may forget what you say, but they will not forget how you make them feel. In a similar fashion you can talk a good game regarding values and what is best for our boys, but if your actions are not consistent with your words, they will mean very little. Not only that, but you will lose esteem and the respect that is conferred upon men who are perceived to have sound character.

One of the best ways to teach a boy something is to model it for him. You might be demonstrating how to perform a corner kick in soccer, a takedown in wrestling, or a proper batting stance in baseball. As he watches, a mental picture is created that is imprinted in his memory. When he gets the chance to try the maneuver your feedback is especially helpful for him to refine his technique. If you are supportive and encouraging in the process, you will make it easier for him to get it right. This is the reason modeling is such an effective teaching mechanism. The kids really get it . . . and they get it because it gets inside of them.

Given that modeling is such a powerful teaching technique it is imperative that as parents, coaches, and administrators we are mindful of what we are really teaching our boys. I think we have to consider that every encounter we have with our boys is a teachable moment. They are not only learning whenever we preface a conversation with, "Son, I want to show you something"; they are continually soaking up the atmosphere around them and incorporating it. What you say, how you behave in general, how you react to adversity or the unexpected, and the values you hold are all reflected in your actions. Because you are an adult and because you hold a position of authority as parent, coach, or administrator, all your words and actions are meaningful to your boys. Because of this you must do your best to model the right way of thinking and behaving.

We all screw up on occasion. We do this because of our personal weaknesses, our shadows, and simply because we are human. Because we are all imperfect people, it is important that we not give up when we mess up. We might curse, we might yell, and we might act as if winning was all-important. Our boys need us to try hard to do our best. In fact we can't bail out in reaction to our frustration in making mistakes because that would teach them the negative values of not following through and reinforce the poor character traits we're trying to overcome in ourselves! So what's the solution? I think it's important to keep it simple. Try your best. When you mess up by not living up to your own expectations of how you want to behave, acknowledge your mistake (at least to yourself) and move on as a good role model. Remember, Charles Barkley was wrong when he said he was not a role model; we all are.

✦ Lead ✦

A coach once shared with me his perception of what it was like to be at the sidelines of a college football game. He said it was like a war going on. Although I was not in Vietnam, there is a consistent image that friends and clients who were there have imparted to me. It is a picture of chaos, noise, and stimuli that come at you from everywhere all at once. Therefore, coaches at all levels of sports, even in entry-level youth sports, could benefit from a reminder to keep their priorities in order. In this regard I offer LEAD.

LEAD by name alone serves as a reminder of the important leadership position coaches and parents hold by virtue of their status in relation to our boys. It also serves to keep us focused on the reason we are involved with boys and young men in sports: to have fun while teaching skills and fostering character and integrity.

> **L** is a reminder for parents and coaches to LISTEN to what their boys are trying to say through their actions or their words;
> **E** is to encourage adults to try to imagine what it would be like to EXPERIENCE the world and us through *their* eyes;
> **A** is there to keep us mindful to ACT in a manner consistent with a model of integrity; and
> **D** reminds us to DIRECT our boys with a clear and firm yet respectful voice.

Only when we have the best interests of our boys in the forefront of our mind can we be assured of doing the right thing. Boy-centered coaching requires that we be conscious of for whom we are doing all this coaching and fan supporting. LEAD serves to keep us focused on the specifics that underpin our efforts at being boy-centered, for if we do not listen or have an empathic appreciation for where our boys are coming from, we will surely misread them and be unsuccessful in sending messages to them. Furthermore our authority as coach, teacher, parent, and mentor is ensconced with honor when our actions model the behavior of a person with integrity and when we convey a sense of respect to our sons and players. LEAD can help us all keep focused.

✦ The Role of Administrators ✦

Make no mistake about it. Principals, athletic directors, athletic department heads, and league officials are the ones in charge. Regardless of whether they act like leaders, they occupy the positions of influence and power. They are the patriarchs and matriarchs of our youth sports programs and academic athletic programs. How they go, so goes the program. As I have said previously, in order for a sense of respect and honor to be conferred upon our boys, the coaches responsible for sending these affirmative messages need themselves to be sufficiently enlightened. They need to be guided by the principles of boy-centered coaching and they also need to make sure the kids work hard, develop some skills, feel good about themselves, and have fun. However, in order for this to occur, administrators have to take a much more active role in the athletic programs for which they are ultimately responsible.

Those who administer or who are responsible for athletic programs need to take a the-buck-stops-here attitude. They need to take their heads out of the sand (if they happen to be there) and get actively involved. They need to not let business as usual take place; rather they need to make waves if necessary in order to ensure that youth sports programs are emphasizing the right values. For instance, administrators of community soccer, football, hockey, basketball, and baseball programs need to take a proactive role in making sure that coaches and parents understand the expectation that in the course of teaching athletic skills the emphasis should be on making the activity fun, while at the same time fostering sound character and integrity. There also needs to be a strong message from the top down as to what behavior is acceptable and what is not at all appropriate. Running up the scores, not allowing all the kids to play, and placing an inordinate emphasis on winning need to be confronted as unacceptable and outmoded methods of operating. In addition, hostile, aggressive, and abusive methods of motivation need to be placed in the trash heap. Principals from elementary through high school must step up to the plate and make sure that the day-in-day-out teaching and coaching in athletics is boy-centered. They need to feel not only entitled but obligated to directly monitor and direct *how* gym teachers teach and *how* coaches coach. They need to introduce and integrate Integrity Sessions or modified forms of them into the regular practice of coaching and teaching. They need to set the standard and follow up to make sure it is not just being paid lip service to.

There are three specific areas to which administrators must attend. First of all, they must forever be focused on the boys and young men who will participate in these programs. The primary emphasis must be on providing a forum where our boys can have fun while learning some skills. This must be done against a backdrop that makes it clear to players, coaches, officials, and parents that the purpose of this activity is to develop character and integrity in these children. Secondly, administrators who run programs that rely on volunteer coaches must not settle for taking just anyone they can get to help out. They must make sure that all volunteers thoroughly know the rules of the game and have an understanding of the skills necessary to play it. Significant and active steps must be taken to ensure that coaching staffs, volunteer and paid alike, must understand and practice a code of ethics and good sportsmanship. And last but certainly not least, all referees and officials must have a thorough understanding of the rules of the game. They must be trained to learn how to comport themselves with a sense of dignity and convey a sense of respect to all players and coaches. They must learn to understand that through their actions they help to create the type of atmosphere in which our boys will play. They must be helped to develop a sense of responsibility for producing a positive setting. And that also includes learning to deal with inappropriate coaches, players, and parents.

Administrators and principals alike need to act as the head of a household and convey clear and direct messages as to what kind of behavior they want from teachers, coaches, and parents. If their constituents and employees are not yet with them in this vision, they need to take on the mission of educating and enlightening them. Not only are the potential gains in producing boys who are comfortable with themselves and who will grow to be fine young men well worth the effort, but administrators and principals are those in the key positions to bring about these changes.

✦ A Return to Goal Setting ✦

In chapter 4 the concept of sports and optimal performance psychology was introduced along with the five skills of mental fitness. While all these skills are useful, the one that has the most overall impact is goal setting. The reason for this is simply that without having a clear vision of where we want to go there is no telling where we will end up. Similarly, without a clear plan of how to get there we decrease the likelihood of our success. It is imperative to make use of this mental fitness skill in our efforts to be successful and effective in our roles as parents, coaches, and administrators. I offer the following sets of content and process goals for each:

Content Goals for Parents
1. Provide a positive and fun sports experience for their son.
2. Have him acquire specific individual and team sport skills.
3. Have him integrate good sportsmanship into his approach to sports.
4. Have his experience reinforce the foundation of his character and integrity.

Process Goals for Parents
1. Make sure that it is your son's choice to play the particular sport.
2. Attend practice sessions and games to monitor the proceedings and possibly to assist in some capacity.
3. Practice playing the sport at home.
4. Be encouraging and strike a balance between being corrective and just having fun.
5. When you hear him speak in the extremes of either being too boastful or too self-depreciative offer him the necessary balance of humility and encouragement.

6. Discuss with the coach or league officials, after the game, any matters regarding unfairness, unsportsmanlike behavior, or verbal abuse by fans or coaches.
7. Regularly practice LEAD.

Content Goals for Coaches
1. Make sure all your players feel included and are having fun.
2. Create an atmosphere in which the boys perceive a sense of respect from you while respecting your authority.
3. Impart instruction and feedback on specific skills in an age-appropriate manner.
4. Convey a consistent expectation that all players work hard and practice good sportsmanship.
5. Impart a winning "can do it" attitude about each boy and the team.

Process Goals for Coaches
1. Model fairness and integrity in all your words and actions.
2. Take the playing time of players very seriously. At the younger ages make sure all players have fairly equal playing time regardless of ability. At older ages give all players consideration, respect, and at least some playing time.
3. Be consistent and follow through with commitments you make to the players, including timeliness and routines for warm-ups and practice.
4. Be boy-centered in how you instruct and coach your players.
5. Have your actions reflect the mind-set that winning is not the only thing, but that striving to win is.
6. Be courageous enough to confront your own shadows when you see them creep into the mix.
7. Be secure enough to employ mental fitness skills, consultations with sports psychologists, and/or Integrity Sessions for appropriately aged boys and young men.
8. In a dignified manner stand up for the values of sound character and integrity in the face of behavior counter to that by other coaches and league officials.
9. Consistently employ LEAD in communicating to our boys.

Content Goals for Administrators

1. Make sure all programs under your authority operate consistently with the values of hard work, good sportsmanship, and integrity.
2. Do your best to ensure that all participants in your programs enjoy the experience and emerge as better boys and young men.
3. Ensure that the atmosphere around your programs, including fan and parent behavior, is consistent with your programs' principles.

Process Goals for Administrators

1. Issue clear directives to coaches in regard to your expectations that their behavior and coaching style be consistent with the value of fair play and fostering character and integrity in our boys.
2. Follow through and observe and make sure that these principles of boy-centered coaching are carried out. Directly address efforts to undermine these goals and point out coaches' blind spots.
3. Model directness and respect for the other in communication, and strength in your convictions.
4. Encourage coaching personnel to elevate coaching standards to include values education. Patiently but consistently bring them along so that old dogs are taught new tricks.
5. Do not shrink away from challenges to your authority that stem from the "we've always done it this way" sort of thinking.
6. Convey the expectation that coaches use the LEAD model.
7. Implement a form of integrity training and sportsmanship programs for the boys and young men in your programs and their coaches and parents.
8. Employ LEAD when communicating with our boys.

✦ Never Leave Our Boys ✦

All of what we would like to teach our boys in order for them to become young men with solid character will fall to the wayside if we don't demonstrate it ourselves. We must be mindful of ourselves as role models. Furthermore, unless we see ourselves as fathers to the boys in our extended community we are abdicating our role as the ones who are charged to guide our boys and young men into adult life.

It can be said with a degree of certainty that the younger the youth sports the greater the emphasis on supporting the self-esteem of the child. Sports psychology research along with common sense has borne out the value of solidifying the child's sense of self as a prerequisite to the successful acquisition of sports-specific skills. It can also be said that the emphasis on the refinement of specific sports skills would naturally increase the older our boys become. The difference between boy-centered coaching and shadow coaching is that with the former our boys never get left behind. That does not mean that a coach does not occasionally yell or get tough and demanding with a boy or team, it means the coach is always mindful of *acting in ways that serve our boys*. Perhaps we can learn from the ancient Greeks who developed the original model of the gymnasium as a place for the full development of the bodies and minds of boys.

Our actions within our roles as administrators, coaches, and parents need to be governed by an intention to be boy-centered and thus we need occasionally to ask ourselves, *For whom am I taking this action?* We also need to actively foster an empathic understanding for the kids with whom we are involved. Using the LEAD model can keep our communication with our boys clear, direct, and helpful. Lastly, we need to be willing to stand up for what we believe. For some that might mean coaching, for others being on the governing board of an athletic program, or speaking up with regard to inappropriate behavior on the part of another parent, fan, player, or coach. If it requires us to ruffle a few feathers for the sake of our boys, then so be it. Ruffling the feathers of the entrenched youth-sports establishment for the purpose of insuring a more positive experience in which the development of sound character is the governing principle is the subject of the last chapter of *Really Winning*. But first let's look in the next chapter at some of the challenges our boys are likely to present to us in our day-to-day dealings with them.

7

Handling the Curveballs
Your Boys Send You:
Unexpected Challenges

A S WE MOVE toward the conclusion of *Really Winning* let us remember one of the central principles of working with boys. Boys will be boys. That is a simple fact. This fact does not condone or make excuses for the actions they take that are governed by their shadows. Rather, it is an acknowledgment that boys are unique unto themselves. Consequently they are likely to present some unique problems and challenges to those who care about them. Further compounding the issue are the two particular ways in which they differ from girls. First, boys tend to take action, and problems frequently result when these actions are ungrounded, extreme, or confrontational. Second, boys and young men tend to not express their thoughts and feelings directly. They very well may not even understand them, much less know what feelings and thoughts they are wrestling with. Thus we face quite a challenge.

It is a simple fact that we cannot anticipate all the curveballs our boys will send us. People experienced with raising or coaching boys know all too well that just when you think you understand where a boy is with himself, he soon enters a new phase of development. Our ability to know with confidence what is in store for us as parents and coaches is frequently all too fleeting. Given that change is the constant it is important to keep the following in mind:

- Be flexible and quick on your feet so that your response fits the situation. I used to work with a former Golden Gloves boxer who frequently reminded me through the metaphor of boxing to "always keep moving, keep your feeling moving, you're dead if you stop moving." Frequently when we take a rigid stance with our boys what we are really trying to do is to force the boys into our conception of what is right for them. We may be absolutely correct in terms of wanting them, for instance, to be honest and forthright, but if our presentation is too stiff and authoritarian we may only get the message across that they have messed up and have disappointed us rather than our successfully conveying the virtue of honesty. There is a place for coming down on our boys when they run too far afield, but how we do it makes all the difference in the world if we are interested in also fostering character and integrity.
- Remember to use LEAD in communication with our boys. We need to listen to the message our boys are trying to send and attempt to see the world from their eyes. We also need to have our response informed by our interest in modeling the very behavior we wish our boys to incorporate within themselves. Lastly, we need to make sure that our message is clear, direct, firm, yet conveyed in a voice that is respectful of the persons who reside inside our boys.
- Remember to be guided by a boy-centered approach that always keeps its eye on the prize in regard to the building block of character. As you might recall from chapter 5, I presented the concept of sound character development as being comprised of two clusters of equal importance. One concerns what are essentially content-related items. These action-oriented functions include mastery of the five skills of mental fitness and the development of a strong work ethic. Also included in this half are the products of such mastery, namely success and confidence. The other cluster is comprised of process-oriented functions. I

am referring to the manner in which a boy or young man goes about the business of his life and sport, specifically that he carry within himself a sense of integrity, honor, and sportsmanship.

With these things in mind, let us consider some of what is in store for our boys and ourselves. Remember to keep your feet moving.

✦ Unexpected Challenges ✦ Within the Game

Whenever a group of boys gets together there is bound to be competition, rivalry, and various attempts to affirm themselves. Sometimes these natural impulses get acted out in ways that negatively impact on others. Fortunately within the context of a sport there is an actual set of rules that in essence provides a code of conduct. The rules of the game are really a social contract for defining how our boys are permitted to interact with each other. There are coaches on hand who may guide our young troops toward the more balanced, healthy, and ethical ways of behaving toward each other. What follows are but a few of the encounters that are bound to occur.

The Bully and the Star

It is inevitable that when a group of boys gets together sooner or later each will find a role that for better or worse will be his. This tendency is a natural function of what all people do when forming groups. Anyone who has taught a class or who has managed a work team knows this all too well. For that matter anyone who has ever had a family intuitively knows how each person tends to gravitate to particular roles as leader, joker, lost child, bad boy, et cetera. This also holds true for boys who join together on a team to play a sport. You cannot stop it from happening and in fact there is nothing inherently wrong with it, provided the boys play within bounds and are not cruel, abusive, or exclusionary in some way. In order to prevent this sort of *Lord of the Flies* syndrome from occurring it is imperative that the adults involved with them take a very active role in managing their youthful exuberance.

Two of the roles that coaches invariably must come to manage are those of bully and star. Sometimes the same person holds these roles and sometimes two different boys hold them. Bullies tend to emerge as a function of either one of two conditions. The first is the lack of close supervision by adults. Without a proactive and involved coach present to help a boy keep his shadows in check, they are at risk to be acted out, with the bully being a frequent example. The second condition is the result of a boy or young man emerging as a more confident and capable individual. Sometimes along the way toward becoming boys with a sense of mastery our boys may attempt to manage feelings of uncertainty and apprehension by walking with a little too much swagger and carrying too much of a me-centered point of view. This is sometimes expressed by literally showing up other boys and intimidating those who are lower on the food chain, so to speak. Boys who do this are not necessarily "bad" boys or lost causes; they too need help from the adults in their lives. They need to be "reined in" and there are a variety of ways to do this.

I know of an old-school college coach who used to bench his star players as a method of getting his message across to them, saying, "One of the best assets in basketball was an ass set on the bench." Depending on who the particular player is, an unexpected benching can be a very effective wake-up call, motivating the boy to develop a more positive attitude, increasing his level of play, or helping him to become more of a team player. However, because some of our boys can feel very deflated by a benching it is important that a coach really know how best to motivate each individual player. If a coach observes that a player is egocentric and bullying weaker teammates he may choose to have a quiet one-on-one conversation with the young man. In such a talk the coach can impress upon the boy his belief in the boy's capabilities as an athlete and a team leader and can also convey how he would like him to behave toward teammates. He might even charge the young man with responsibility for mentoring younger players. For example, instead of teasing and busting the chops of freshmen, the upper classman might mentor his "younger brothers" and help bring them along in terms of learning the plays, developing their skills, and in general helping them to develop a feeling that they belong on the team.

Because of a boy's natural ability and a refined set of skills, he may be able to run fast and catch, kick, or shoot a ball. When our boy does these things well considerable status and accolades are heaped upon him.

Parents, fans, coaches, girls, and teammates all join in to offer him praise. It can feel like a fantastic dream, but it is not easy to manage the status as a star of the team. Unless a boy is naturally mature and gracious, he may not necessarily know how to manage his success. If he is not helped to foster the mature and balanced components of boy psychology such as the leader, the hero, or the strategist, our boy might manifest behavior driven by his shadow forms. The three corresponding darker forms are the exploiter, hot dog, and wanna-be and we all know how ugly they can be. The solution once again is the willingness on the part of coaches and parents to get involved and stay involved. Therefore parents and coaches must guard against the impulse, which may be generated by their own shadow, to feed off the team star. When we remember to ask ourselves the question, For whom am I doing this? it is likely to become clearer whether that extra heaping of praise or that overlooking of poor sportsmanship serves our boy or not.

The Bench Jockey

Given the competitive nature of sports not everyone wins and not everyone can be the star. The question in this case for the boy-centered coach is how to find a place for all of our boys on the team. A coach's benevolence in this regard will vary, of course, depending on the age of the boys and the level of competition. For instance, it would be hard to imagine Penn State's Joe Paterno or Alabama's Bear Bryant putting in a player in the middle of a very competitive Division I college football game just for the sake of making him feel better. With such an emphasis on winning at that level of play, coaches typically approach game situations as a general would approach a battle, in that you do what you have to do to win in terms of utilizing players in the best interests of the team. This is not to say that coaches even at this level cannot make some accommodations for a hardworking but not particularly gifted player. Taking the player aside and praising his work ethic can be a very meaningful encounter for such a young man. Similarly, giving some consideration to putting this sort of B-level player into a game at an appropriate time can benefit everyone.

While the matter of giving a player reasonable playing time impacts our boys at all levels of sports, common sense suggests that the younger the age of the boy, the greater the potential for a negative impact on him if he doesn't get enough. I recently encountered a mother who still found herself harboring a resentment toward a baseball coach who kept her son on the bench virtually the entire season . . . and that was over fifteen years ago. She knew as only a mother could how bad it made her son feel to be excluded so regularly. As she put it, "I know he wasn't the best player, but he was a member of the team who always came to practice. I think his coach could have found times to put him in, really!" Her sentiments are of course biased by motherhood, yet her point is well taken. A boy-centered coach is not just interested in always putting the best team on the field. While it may be necessary to field the most effective defense in crucial games and at crucial moments, not all moments are crucial. This type of exclusionary action on the part of coaches in youth sports can turn a boy who may be a late bloomer off to sports. Furthermore, it can unnecessarily reinforce negative self-esteem and a social stratification that tells him and his peers that he does not measure up. This insensitivity is just not necessary.

Another matter of concern to a boy-centered coach is handling the negative attitude that can develop in a boy who spends a lot of time on the bench. Just as our boys must come to terms with losing, how they adjust to being a bench player reveals the degree to which they will have their balanced and healthy self emerge, or whether their shadow becomes reinforced instead. As parents and coaches we must be mindful of helping our boys find their place. All boys need a place and unless they are blessed with a sound and balanced temperament, they will need us to guide them toward a right place. By that I mean coming to see the role one plays as part of the overall team, seeing the value in that role, and becoming comfortable with it. Take professional baseball. It is safe to say that all players at this level want to be on the field and playing every day, yet there is only room for the starters. Former New York Yankee utility infielder and pinch hitter Luis Sojo provides a fine example of a player who, while he wanted to start every day, adjusted well to his bench role. In fact his playoff and World Series heroics have led to Sojo carving out a very valued and honorable niche for himself. Because he accepted his role, he became comfortable with it and as a result his performance was optimized.

Since not every boy who spends a considerable amount of time on the bench is likely to have the grace of Luis Sojo, we must be vigilant to guard against the boy's shadows being acted out. For instance, learning to come through in the clutch can really reinforce the hero archetype in a boy, but such performance will not be possible if our boy becomes too down on himself or afraid of seizing the moment. Similarly, instead of having the loyal teammate reinforced as a valued and balanced expression of boy psychology, its shadow form of the dreamer can further undermine the boy's interest in being an equal member of the team. We might consider the manifestation of the dreamer as a form of psychological withdrawal. Coaches and parents have to be prepared to help a boy through his fear and also to find his place as a worthwhile member of the team. We have to keep in mind that for almost all boys shame and ridicule are not the most effective methods to help him through this difficult time. A boy-centered coach who is guided by the question How does this serve the boy? will know this quite clearly.

Losing

Like many people who enjoy engaging in sports, I really like to win. I do not like to lose and it is my preference that I do not lose. However, as long as I work hard and do the best I can, I'm pretty comfortable if a loss comes. I also know that if I am competing at a level appropriate to my ability I will win a fair number of times because of my willingness to work hard. If I'm on my game and do my best and my opponent plays better, I can tip my hat to him for a job well done. As much as I love winning, I get the most satisfaction out of being fully immersed in the act of doing. Being totally into the rhythm of a tennis match, making a crisp pass on the soccer field, or unleashing a throw to the plate from the outfield are acts that I have found to be enormously satisfying. The Zen-like experience of being one with the ball, and in the moment *really* being the outfielder, the tennis player, or the soccer player, helps me do well and to some extent also helps me moderate my investment in having to win. Don't get me wrong, unless I am playing a game with my young sons, I always want to win. But when I am working hard and fully engaged in the act of being an amateur athlete, if the ultimate outcome doesn't go my way, I'm less troubled by it. Because I know I have given it my all and that I have done my best, my ego seems less invested in whether I've won or lost. Our boys frequently have a more difficult time in coming to terms with losing. This is an area that needs much involvement and wise counsel from a coach.

When we are able to keep sports in perspective as the game it is, we are better able to not sweat the small stuff. After all, losing a game is not life or death. Maturity can definitely help manage a loss, just as having had some victories can help moderate the sting of a loss. Our challenge is to help get our boys prepared so that they experience the satisfaction and good feeling that comes with winning while helping them cope when things don't go their way.

Sometimes, when behind in mid-contest, our boys give up on themselves out of a belief that they cannot win. This results in a self-fulfilling prophecy. A demoralized team tends to implode, making the experience of the loss so much harder to swallow. Not only did the other team win, but also irrational beliefs, such as not being good enough or of being ultimately doomed to fail, are reinforced. Self-esteem can be further eroded from this sort of collapse. Sports and life itself have been so full of unexpected comebacks of the David-beats-Goliath type that we can never really be sure that a team is doomed to fail. As the old football saying goes, "On any given Sunday any team can beat another." Almost anything is possible when a boy or team has the right attitude. The 1969 Mets certainly proved the value in the motto "You gotta believe!" Therefore one of our jobs is to help boys face adversity so that they don't give up on themselves. If we can encourage our boys to, as John Wooden said, "Don't let the things you can't do stand in the way of the things you can do" then we've taught them how to persevere through difficult times and do the best they can.

Sometimes losses occur. If we had the power to script the moral and character-building education of our boys we would probably try to include some difficult tests as well as some losses. As adults who care about our boys we do not wish them pain or disappointment, but we also know part of growing up as a well-balanced young man is to learn not to be thwarted by loss and to handle it honorably when it does come. Our boys need us to show them the way to handle loss.

They might be crushed with disappointment. When this happens they might use the loss to validate whatever notions they might have of not being good enough. They might cry foul by blaming the referee or the dirty play of the other team. They might act out aggressively by showing poor sportsmanship toward their opponents. National Hockey League teams have a long-standing dishonorable tradition of sometimes sending out their goons at the end of games for this purpose. Our boys might commit the divisive act of attributing blame among fellow team-mates for the team's loss. When this occurs feelings are hurt by the unfair accusations and a team's unity begins to disintegrate, making future success even more difficult. This negativity can snowball out of control. As parents and coaches we must be prepared for all of these reactions because some of them are likely to occur in at least a few of our boys.

We need to remember that regardless of their ages our boys are young. The do not have a lot of life experience and these games of sport *are their world.* They need us, therefore, to have the capacity to understand their disappointment. They need us to acknowledge it. But they also need us to show them the way beyond the disappointment. They need to be guided by our words and our example to learn from loss and to be accepting of it. This does not mean being complacent, rolling over and playing dead, or being a quitter; it means learning to hold one's head high and feeling comfortable with oneself regardless of the loss.

Coaches and parents can be assisted in their mission by utilizing some of the techniques of the mental fitness skill of developing and maintaining a positive mental attitude. For instance, we need to help them to reframe the loss as an opportunity to make them stronger and more determined. We can even help them examine their areas of weakness and deficit so that they might compensate and work to make themselves better in these areas. In the spirit of Michael Jordan's advice to "make your weakness your strength," we need to help our boys examine their performance without being excessively critical. However, the moments immediately following the end of the game are a time for support and congratulations for having fought the hard fight. A conversation assessing the team's performance or a one-on-one talk regarding an individual's performance would be much better suited to quiet moments later on that day, or in the next practice session. Helping the boys to see whatever positive can be gleaned from a loss can really go a long way toward making the loss more tolerable and enabling them to learn from the experience. New York Yankee manager Joe Torre's comments after his team lost the 2001 World Series to the Arizona Diamondbacks serve as a model for grounded coaching in dealing with a loss: "I'm disappointed with the results, but I'm not disappointed with the effort." It is reminiscent of Vince Lombardi's emphasis on striving instead of exclusively on winning.

That said, there is a place for directly addressing what went wrong on the field. Obviously, the older the boy the greater his ability to benefit from a critical and honest examination of his performance. However, regardless of their age, if a coach's attitude, behavior, and words primarily convey admonishment, then our boys are guaranteed to feel bad about themselves and alienated from their coach. Even if the team was mentally absent and played as if they had already lost the game, a team and its individual players can handle the inevitable confrontation if the coach does so in a way that is respectful toward them. Not only can players take a verbal tongue-lashing from a coach who they know really cares about them, but they can really benefit from it. Being boy-centered does not in any way have to mean being wimpy. Being caring and firm go together quite nicely.

Coaching Our Boys When They Really Are Our Boys

Many men are initially drawn to coaching because one of their own children is interested in playing a sport. Coaching is one of the meaningful ways for a father to lend himself to his son. Frequently this sort of involvement can deepen the father-son bond. Having an activity in which they can engage together will create a "we" feeling, and give them a constructive avenue for mutual play. The father-as-coach can also create the framework for the ritual of an elder male passing on knowledge to a young man in training. Depending on how each handles such a father-as-coach relationship, it has the potential for creating a medium through which both sport and life lessons can be taught.

Fathers are also sometimes inclined to be a coach out of a protective instinct for their sons. Mothers and fathers who have heard about incidents of unfairness or insensitivity on the part of some men who are associated with youth sports are rightfully concerned about who will be coaching their son. Many parents decide that having a father volunteer to coach might be the best insurance policy. However, as with most things in life, this arrangement can also have its challenges. The first course of business for the father-as-coach is to deal with his son in the context of coaching as he would with any boy who is not listening, not following direction, or otherwise being disrespectful. In the next few paragraphs we will discuss some general guidelines for dealing with boys who are disruptive.

The coach must firmly convey what is expected of all the players and must intervene if a boy is beginning to drift. Some things he might require of the boys are to listen, to follow through with instructions regarding physical form or position on the field, and to be coachable and do what is asked of him. In the event of noncompliance, we need to act promptly so as to reinforce the boys' understanding of what is appropriate behavior as a member of the team. However, we must consider the age of our boys and thus our response must be similarly measured. For instance, having a four-or five-year-old in microsoccer who finds it difficult to follow directions is not particularly unusual. In this setting we can only expect to do our reasonable best and then turn to his parents if he becomes too disruptive. If he happens to be your son, turning to the other parent is an option you should consider. That parent might be in a better position to reach the boy by taking him aside and addressing the issue at hand in a manner that may result in a less reactive response from the child. Because the other parent is *not* his coach, he or she might be in a better position to elicit a reasonable response that is less driven by the boy's shadow.

Similar behavior on the part of a ten- or fifteen-year-old is either a sign of disrespectful acting out or an indication that the child has emotional or cognitive deficits. Regardless of the cause for the disruptive behavior, the coach must act to manage the child's actions, for to not do so would negatively affect the entire team. If the boy is acting out, a one-on-one talk with the boy may do the trick. Frequently children prone to act out in these ways come from families that are less then ideally functional. One of the characteristics of these families is the tendency to swing between extremes in child rearing. Some parents may be quite severe, physical disciplinarians who also employ emotional admonishment as a means of controlling the child's behavior. Some children from these families are apt to break out whenever the cats are away, so to speak. However, they may be quite cooperative when a reasonably fair and caring adult makes an effort to relate to them. A boy-centered coach is ideally suited for this purpose.

It has been my experience that most dysfunctional families err on the side of not making enough appropriate limits for their children and are inconsistent in the enforcement of what limits they do make. Boys of almost any age from these families frequently respond quite well to a coach who sets reasonable limits and has a clear as well as a fair set of expectations regarding their players' behavior. The boys and young men who are on these teams can even be said to appreciate it when the coach follows through with consequences in response to violations of these rules. Not only is the consistency reassuring to our boys, but the fact that the coach's reaction is reasonable is genuinely appreciated. It is a different matter in the case of a child who is impaired in the regulation of his own thoughts or feelings. Depending on the level of the sport the coach may very well need a family member nearby to intervene if necessary.

I knew a very generous man who agreed to coach an autistic six-year-old on a T-ball team. When he managed to help the boy successfully swing the bat and hit the ball, he couldn't tell if he would run to first base, third base, or even the pitcher's mound. Sometimes he would make it to first base and keep on running down the right field line. Sometimes on the way to first base he would dive into the foul line and sit in the dirt and run it through his fingers. Coach Wink and his assistants were very patient in their attempts to help this unfortunate boy integrate as a member of the team. Thanks to their role modeling, the other kids on the team were able to accept him without any complaints. This of course is a highly exceptional situation.

In contrast to the situation above, a common complaint among parents who are youth sports coaches is that they sometimes experience their own quite normal children as the most difficult to coach. Unlike most or all of the other children on the team, their own son is sometimes the least receptive to tips, counsel, and other acts of mentoring. On teams such as baseball or football that have a number of coaches available, fathers can work around this problem by occasionally asking other coaches to reinforce a behavior or skill that their own son is resisting hearing from themselves. This can be a source of enormous frustration to parents who really want to teach their son something, have a positive experience with them, and at the same time convey a sense of authority and leadership to the other children on the team. If a coach is teaching the team the proper way to stretch, but his son is reluctant to go along, his authority with both his son and the rest of his team is undermined. For example, a coach may direct the team to always clap after finishing each set of exercises in a particular sport. He may intend this as a means of psyching up the team as well as to develop a ritual show of unity. If his son refuses to clap along with the others or only makes a halfhearted attempt, the team energy will be drained by the boy's divisiveness. The coach is then faced with yet another unexpected challenge. Ignoring such behavior would inadvertently reinforce the shadow form of the strategist that we referred to in chapter 3 as the wanna-be. Therefore the boy-centered father-as-coach must take constructive action. There are two strategies to employ in this case. The first is to treat the son as any other child. This would entail directing and encouraging him to join in with the rest of the team. If the child refuses or balks indirectly then the coach might tell him his playing time is going to be restricted because of his noncompliance. Letting him know this in advance so that he has a chance to avoid this negative consequence would be preferable.

The most effective course of action is likely to be a heart-to-heart conversation between father and son. It would be best for such a discussion to take place at a relaxed time away from the sport. The son probably does not understand the ramifications of his intransigence on his team and his father's role as coach. Consequently the father-as-coach would need to explain this to him. Furthermore, having a father who is a coach may be a somewhat confusing experience for the boy, especially early in youth sports and then again in the teenage years. In the former there may simply be disorientation regarding roles and boundaries, while in the latter the young man may be feeling reactive to his father as part of his movement toward developing a separate sense of identity. In both cases it can be particularly helpful if a calm conversation takes place in which the father asks his son whether in fact he wants him to be his coach. It can sometimes take this very basic examination to help a boy choose to continue to have his father be coach. When the boy or young man reconfirms his preference that his father serve as his coach, he is now in the position to allow himself to be coachable. Everyone benefits when this happens.

We must recognize, however, that the boy might actually choose for his father to no longer serve as his coach. He may be feeling too crowded and may feel there isn't enough room for him to be himself. Teenage boys sometimes prefer to not have their fathers telling them what to do, and would rather receive the benefits that go with having a father who is a loyal fan. The challenge for the father in this case is to manage any feelings of hurt or disappointment that might arise. It is quite normal to have this sort of emotional reaction, but it is important to not act on these feelings, for to do so might produce some hurtful, angry, or guilt-producing statements that might otherwise be directed by the father's own shadow. When a son chooses to not have his father be his coach, and the father feels a normal but upsetting emotional reaction, he needs to remind himself why he was interested in coaching in the first place: to lend himself to his son. If for whatever reason his son feels the need for his space, then the father should do his best to respect his son's preference. The father can be aided by remembering to ask, How can I best serve my son?

Parents

Regardless of whether you are a parent who is involved with your son's team as coach, team parent, or a regular garden-variety interested parent, other parents can sometimes be a serious problem. They may be the parents of one of your son's teammates or they may have a child on the other team. There are many manifestations of parental lunacy in youth sports. It is all too common for parents to yell at the referee or other league officials, coaches, or even at players on the other team. They might argue calls the umpire has made or not made and openly challenge a coach to give their child more game time. These actions, of course, undermine the very sort of respect for authority and rules that sports can help our boys to develop. Furthermore, public criticism of a coach regarding strategy or playing time for a child can put the boy in a very awkward position. It can negatively impact his relationships with both teammates and coach and can cause him to feel very embarrassed as a result of his own parent's actions.

It can also be uncomfortable for a parent-as-coach or a parent on the sideline to deal with a fellow parent's actions. For example, it can be very distracting for a coach to be heckled by one of his player's parents. It can also result in a strong impulse to react in anger. A friend who coaches soccer at the high school level told me of an incident recently in which a parent approached him at halftime to share his displeasure about the playing time his son was getting. Even though the boy was an average player, the coach had made sure that he received a fairly equal amount of time on the field. This was consistent with his coaching philosophy. Nonetheless the boy's father got right in the coach's face and called him a derogatory name and told him that he didn't know what the hell he was doing. Being a rather mild-mannered fellow, the coach was more amazed at the parent's behavior than he was angry, but another coach might have had a more difficult time managing his reaction.

The same holds true for parents on the sidelines. It can be quite a challenge to bite one's tongue in the heat of a sporting event when another "fan" acts in an offensive manner, especially at the expense of our boy's team. It is only natural for parents to identify with their son's team and to feel protective of its players and coaches. Consequently they might react strongly to another parent crossing the line. At the very least it is simply uncomfortable to be in the presence of others who are acting inappropriately and who do not have their own shadows in check.

Although this offers no solace, it is all too frequently the case that the focus of parents who are to some degree under the influence of their shadow is their own child. There are three main manifestations of their actions and they are all usually conveyed by yelling. In the first case they are attempting to improve their child's performance in the sport by coaching him from the sidelines during the actual game. This once occurred in a soccer game in which I was an on-field coach. The play at that point happened to be right in front of the parents and the mother yelled out, "Kick the ball, Joseph. Kick the ball! Pass it! Pass it!" Being positioned right there, I called out in a light manner to the mother as I went by, "Okay, I've got it, mom!" I wanted to let her know that I was handling the coaching, but I also did not want to alienate her or make a big deal about it. I also know how confusing and overwhelming it can be for a seven-year-old to hear this sort of "cheering." It frequently results in underperformance because the boy is overstimulated. You might recall the mental fitness skill of energy regulation from chapter 5 and the inverted U. The athletic performance of our boys is enhanced only by moderate levels of arousal, but is undermined by higher levels. The shouted directions and coaching from the sidelines will more than likely increase the level of arousal in our boys, thus creating a self-defeating exercise for all concerned.

In the second case parents show their dark side by admonishing their child from the sidelines. This sort of public reproach and shaming usually undermines the child's level of play. Some of our boys, however, will respond by trying even harder and may even perform at a higher level in an attempt to seek the validation and approval they desire from their critical and withholding parents. The problem with this is that it teaches the child to be outer directed and as such to be driven by the never attainable carrot that dangles in front of him. Even if these boys were to do well, they would be doing it for the wrong reasons. It is a matter of common sense that their self-esteem will also suffer from this kind of treatment. It is frequently the case that the boys who need us most as coaches do not get the support they need at home. A boy-centered coach who becomes aware of a boy's longing for approval from the people who matter to him most is in a unique position to support him and provide some of the recognition he needs. A coach always retains the option of speaking directly to the boy's parents; however, this can become somewhat of a slippery slope. On the one hand, an otherwise well-intentioned parent could respond very well to the advice offered by his or her son's coach. On the other hand, it is just as likely that the parent may be offended by the intrusion of the coach into family matters and react defensively. Because the last thing we want is for the child to pay a further price, it is imperative that the coach take the time to become very measured in his actions. More often it is best to take the conservative approach and focus on what offers the highest probability of having a positive impact: fostering a positive relationship with the boy. It would also be wise for a coach to consider taking a proactive approach with parents by telling them of any expectations held both for parents and for their children.

The third case reveals a manifestation of another particularly dark shadow. In this circumstance parents attempt to live and play vicariously through their child. Their child's successes are their successes and they drink it all in with the relish of a drunk at an open bar. They simply cannot contain their glee and are all too willing to tell us about it. What I am talking about are the actions of those we might refer to as "good ol' boys." They might shout out to their boy things like, "You show 'em, Joey! That's my boy kicking some ass!" with all the sophistication and decorum of Bob Ewell in *To Kill a Mockingbird*. As is frequently the case with people of this ilk, confronting them will tend to inflame the situation rather than correct their behavior; consequently the matter is best left to league officials.

The Coach as a Problem

When your son is playing against a team whose coach is particularly aggressive or offensive it is natural to want to protect your child and his teammates from him. Fortunately, you will likely have the support of the other team parents with whom you can commiserate. If your son's coach is on the ball you can also feel assured that he will do what he can to control the situation and handle the damage. But you also have the option of bringing your concerns to the attention of league officials and administrators. It is a much more complicated and difficult matter, however, when the man who is coaching your own son is a problem.

As we have discussed throughout *Really Winning,* coaches may sometimes be guided by their own shadows. They may be coach-centered rather than boy-centered and they might also seek too much of a sense of personal fulfillment through the performance of their boys. Coaches may not give some boys a chance to prove themselves or improve their skills, and some coaches may play favorites, who may sometimes even be their own sons. They may be insensitive to your child and may also be gruff and unapproachable. There is, of course, no one way to address these circumstances. As parents you must trust your gut instincts when it comes to what seems fair and what does not. If you are confused regarding protocol for getting playing time, it is absolutely appropriate to ask a coach for clarification. Generally speaking, boys from about ninth grade and above need to be mentored in how to approach their coach in regard to matters of their concern. It can be a good learning experience for the boy to approach such an authority in a respectful manner while speaking up for himself. Of course, if the problems persist and are of a serious nature you should feel free to discuss the matter with the coach, athletic administrator, or principal. Parents of boys below that age should feel free to intervene by respectfully making requests and asking questions of coaches.

Occasionally, addressing a concern with a coach will result in the problem being ameliorated. It is likely that little headway will be made, however, in circumstances in which there is a clash of personalities or of values between the coach and parent. Depending on the circumstance parents have the option to take the matter up with a higher official or to bide their time and seek an alternative coach in the next season. In the next chapter we will explore some of the ways parents have been organizing to initiate more lasting institutional changes that attempt to address some of the more serious root problems in youth sports.

In chapter 8 we will also discuss specific ways in which caring people, like yourselves, are dealing with circumstances that have been described above. However, it is important to remember some of the basic principles of communication that have already been discussed. If you ever plan to address the actions of other parents or coaches, *how* you approach the individual can greatly influence whether the interaction will be positive and productive or negative and frustrating. In the spirit of content and process remember that people first respond to the process through which we are sending a message and then to the content. Consequently we need to do our best to send the message that really serves our cause: serving our boys. Although there can be a place for a firm and direct confrontation with an out-of-line parent, for the most part we all are far better served by sending an initial message that says in essence, "I come in peace." It will produce less of a defensive reaction and that is a good first step. Unless you have a chance of developing rapport, any confrontation will more likely serve your need to get your frustration off your chest, rather than serving our boys by providing good role modeling. Similarly, by demonstrating respect toward the person who holds the position of coach for our son we might help that individual rise to a level of dignity and reasonableness that he might not otherwise achieve. *How* we approach these people who so affect the world of our boys can make a great deal of difference in the outcome we desire.

✦ Unexpected Challenges ✦ Outside the Game

Boys will be boys. At every age they are curious and adventurous and this is in part why we find them so fascinating. But because they are boys, even the ones who are young men are sometimes bound to step over the line. Although it may feel like the end of the world, depending on which line they have crossed, it is usually not. When our boys venture into uncharted waters they can frequently end up over their heads. Therefore we need to set the groundwork so that they might turn to us when this happens. We also have to be prepared to reach out to them regardless of whether they appear receptive or not; after all, they are only boys. We will touch on a few of the more typical pitfalls that may unexpectedly snare our boys.

✦ Sex, Drugs, and Rock 'n' Roll ✦

Young men and women seem to be getting involved romantically at ages considerably earlier than in the past. There is also evidence that the initial use of alcohol and other substances is also occurring at earlier ages, sometimes even in elementary school. We would be kidding ourselves if we were to think that our boys could be immune to the effects of these social influences if only they donned a pair of Air Jordans. The fact is that our boys bring the rest of their world with them into the locker room, gymnasium, and arena, and their world includes girls, alcohol, and other drugs, and various beliefs about sex and drugs. To think you can be a caring parent and a boy-centered coach without making some contact with these worldly matters is delusional. If we really try to stay in tune with our boys, then we will catch wind of romance and experimentation with various substances. The question is what to do when this occurs.

Some parents and coaches adopt the approach employed by Sergeant Schultz in the *Hogan's Heroes* television show. You might recall that when Schultz stumbled upon things that troubled him, he would say to himself, "I see nothing! I see nothing!" When parents and coaches follow the Schultz guide to dealing with our boys they turn a blind eye to the signals our boys are sending that indicate that they are treading on increasingly thin ice. When these important adults do this, they skate over the surface of our boys' lives and forgo the opportunity to really make a meaningful impact. Some parents deny to themselves the need to even discuss issues of sex and alcohol and other substances with their boys. In my work as a psychologist I have come across parents who permit their high-school-aged children to use marijuana and rationalize their decision based upon their own drug use as teenagers. The liberal guilt from which these parenting decisions are frequently derived may be a well-intentioned attempt to treat their children fairly, but such thinking does not in any way serve their children. It is the rare child who would not take this permissiveness as an invitation to use or experiment with LSD, ecstasy, cocaine, or even heroin. The teenage years are difficult enough without complicating matters by the addition of such substances. Therefore we need to be willingly vigilant to intervene *for their sakes*.

Sexuality, on the other hand, is not a matter of choice. Unlike forgoing the use of alcohol or other drugs, our boys can only forgo acting on their sexuality, but they still have it. What are they to do with it? It is wonderful being wanted by someone, especially as a young man fraught with the insecurities and uncertainties so common during that period of life. Having a girl who is willing to be kissed, or is even receptive to sexual advances, can be very affirming. The potential emotional and physical pleasures can be considerable. The same is true regarding the potential pain, shame, disappointment, and heartbreak.

The biologically driven impulse to procreate and the longing for social acceptance are understandable reasons why young people are drawn to each other. Remembering back to chapter 2 we know that boys go through stages, some of which have to do with developing a sense of themselves as separate from parents, so that they can prepare for eventually successfully partnering with a significant other. The tasks associated with these stages are also directing much of that action at this point in life. Nevertheless, coaches and parents need not merely stand back and take on the role as onlookers. When as coaches or parents we learn that one of our boys is crossing a dangerous line by being promiscuous, exploiting young women, or getting too wrapped up in the drama of a roller-coaster teenage relationship, we have to care enough to intervene. I am not suggesting butting into the normal lives of young people. I am also not suggesting doing a whole lot of moralizing. Rather I am talking about stepping in when it makes sense to do so and in a manner that is respectful of the boy in question. Again, we can be guided by asking ourselves, How does this serve our boy?

When we are willing to not turn a blind eye to the trouble in our boys' lives we are truly attempting to serve them as mentors. A coach who does not settle for a star halfback averaging one hundred yards running per game, but rather takes him aside and inquires about what he has heard of the young man being rough with his girlfriend is serving the boy. This is similar to a college coach reaching out to counsel a player he would love to have as a backup quarterback so that the young man might consider transferring to a school where he may be a starter. Both of these coaches have the boys' best interest in mind and this thinking guides all their interactions with them.

We would be remiss if we did not mention rock and roll while we are already talking about sex and drugs. I am specifically referring to the lyrics of some rock and rap songs that are particularly misogynistic, racist, or violent. Regardless of the spin Hollywood and the music industry put on it, the words and messages young people hear over and over again in their music impacts upon them. We cannot in good conscience take a passive stance on this matter, either.

I am not talking about being a stiff, uptight, moralizing prude. We simply have to be willing to stand up and not take for granted the negative brainwashing that some of this music begets. It is important that we not treat it as normal. Rather, we need to sit with our boys either as a group or individually and remind them how to live their lives consistent with being young men of good character and integrity. I believe that most of the time our boys know what is the right thing to do; we need to remind them of this. To not do this is to inadvertently condone and reinforce our boys' shadows.

Obviously a thorough examination of how sex, drugs, and rock and roll impact our boys is beyond the scope of *Really Winning*. However, I would be remiss if I did not acknowledge the influence of sexuality and popular culture on the boys we are coaching and otherwise parenting. If you want to learn more about this subject I encourage you to look through the books listed in appendix 1.

✦ Loss in the Shadow of ✦ the World Trade Center Tragedy

There are losses on the field and there are losses off the field. A friend could die from the use of drugs. A parent may be suddenly stricken with a fatal illness. Boys can lose in the world of love. Their parents may divorce and they may lose the sense of family that was previously a given. A parent's employer may require that the family move to an entirely foreign community, thus losing the continuity and roots that tend to ground all people, especially young ones.

All of these losses can tend to create a sense of alienation within a boy. Alienation can easily lead to some negative acting out. Boys and young men are at risk for substance abuse, sexual acting out, violence, dropping out of sports, giving up on academics, and also depression. The terrorist events that began on September 11, 2001 have also set in motion a new sense of loss. The finishing touches were being put on *Really Winning* just as these transforming events took place. Consequently I have come to know some young people who lost friends and relatives in the bombings that occurred that day. The loss for countless other young people has been more indirect. They lost some of the innocence of youth and the sense of absolute safety and invulnerability that was synonymous with America. As a consequence many of our boys have had their normal anxieties exacerbated in ways that they might not even be able to articulate.

As in the case of any other hazards that might befall our boys, we need to get involved with them. Regardless of the loss, as parents and coaches we need to be proactive and say the things they need to hear from us. We needn't wait for either a ten-year-old or an eighteen-year-old to ask us a direct question. We should offer a response to a question that has yet to be asked. For instance, it is reasonable to assume that for so many of the losses mentioned above our boys need assurances that they will be all right. Tell them so. Depending on the age it is also reasonable to assume that they may have other, more specific questions regarding divorce, death, worries, and fear. It is important that we normalize their experience by talking directly about these events and feelings. As we demonstrate through our actions, for instance, that a boy can feel a little worried and still be no less of a real boy, we will really be serving him. When we reach out to our boys in this way we help to ensure that any tendency toward alienation will be minimized.

Whether we serve our boys as a teacher, parent, neighbor, or coach, when a loss occurs we must not ignore it. This does not mean making a big deal out of everything, rather it means taking the loss into consideration as we interact with the boy. In some cases it will mean talking directly about it with him. In other cases, we may acknowledge the loss indirectly by reaching out to the boy and having meaningful and respectful contact with him. Knowing what to do requires that we be flexible and keep our feet moving, so to speak; after all, reaching out to make meaningful contact with our boys is somewhat of a mixture of science along with a large component of art. We need not be perfect, but we do need to be boy-centered.

In the next chapter we will explore some ways in which you can maximize your impact on the lives of your boys. We will discuss what others have already done and how you can join in to ensure that character and integrity become a foundation for youth sports.

8

A Call to Action:
What You Can Do

A FRIEND TOLD ME of his experience in coaching several of his son's teams. Because Don did not have a father who was involved with him, he was particularly intent on being a positive presence for his own son. Consequently, Don found himself coaching Jason in basketball, football, and soccer. It was in the midst of a soccer game when Don observed the man coaching the other team berating one of his players and saying among other things, "Listen to me, you asshole, when I tell you to do something, do it!" Don quickly went over to the other coach and told him, "Listen, asshole, I better not hear you ever talking that way to a kid." The man backed right off, although it is not known whether he did so because he knew he was wrong or because Don was a particularly muscular individual. It may have been both.

This incident took place during the mid-1980s and now several years into the new millennium we are increasingly aware of more constructive ways to intervene that would not necessarily provoke an additional negative response. Nevertheless, the encounters between the coach and his player and the one between the two coaches are quite telling. Common sense and common decency tell that there is absolutely no place for the kind of derogatory and abusive talk that was displayed by this man under the guise of "coaching" boys and young men of any age. The fact that these players were a collection of eight- and nine-year-olds makes his actions all the more appalling, yet their coach felt perfectly entitled to say what he did. Don's verbally aggressive encounter with the other coach served the purpose of protecting the boy from further abuse while simultaneously serving notice to the coach that this sort of behavior was unacceptable. Although Don's intervention was the better of two evils, it clearly was an over-the-top response. However, in the context of the coaching atmosphere in youth sports at that time his actions could be considered heroic. Nonetheless, we don't want our heroes to model aggressive behavior or to use abusive language. Furthermore, we don't know whether the other coach took his embarrassment for being shown up by Don out on that boy or another player behind the scenes. There must be a better way to stop such abuse from going on while ensuring that a more positive climate is created so that the behavior and attitudes that give rise to abuse will no longer have a place in youth sports.

As was evidenced in *The Lord of the Flies*, boys and young men need the grounding presence of adults, particularly men, in order to rein in what can frequently be a truly unbridled enthusiasm. Hopefully it is clear to you by now how the biological and psychological package that comes wrapped up in our boys can easily lead to arrogance, acts of aggression, and insensitivity. If not for caring parents and other adult caregivers and coaches who can be there to model, nurture, and teach our boys to regulate their impulses, in-your-face attitudes and other acts of poor sportsmanship are likely to overshadow the mission of creating noble, hardworking warriors.

However, problems in youth sports are of course not limited to coaches and players being directed by their shadow to cross the line in terms of a reasonable code of conduct. We discussed in the first chapter how parents as fans and team "supporters" step way out of bounds not only in terms of role modeling, but also in terms of public decency. Some of the incidence of parental sideline rage we discussed led to ugly confrontations with very serious consequences. While violence and death have occurred in the "interest" of youth sports, the more frequent problem is the creation of a very unpleasant atmosphere and poor role modeling on the sidelines. A nonconfrontational response is often the best course of action when these same parents are yelling at referees, umpires, or their own kids. I am not suggesting ignoring them and being passive; rather, I am suggesting moving in a direction that will ultimately get at the root of the problem. By the end of this chapter you will be equipped with the resources necessary to do so.

✦ Enough Is Enough ✦

One of the famous lines from the early black-and-white *Popeye* cartoons has our hero beaten up pretty badly by Bluto before he finally utters, "I've taken all I can stands and I can't stands no more!" Popeye of course goes on, with the help of a can of spinach, to rally against Bluto in yet another episode in which good ultimately triumphs over evil. There is currently a similar process going on in youth sports. People all over the United States and Canada are fed up with so much of the negativity, poor behavior, bad sportsmanship, poor role modeling, and primitive thinking associated with sports in which boys from first grade through college participate.

There is a revolution going on in youth sports and it has a good chance of taking hold. One of the major indicators of its viability is that the sense of being fed up with business as usual has spontaneously grown as a grass roots movement in communities all over North America. Just as with other evolutionary processes, this revolution in youth sports seems to be organically derived in that a significantly large number of people seem to have awakened, independently of each other, at about the same time. They have awakened to the need to do something about the behavior of coaches, players, and parents. Who has awakened? It is the many coaches, players, and parents who have a sense of what is right and who see what is wrong and no longer want to sit on the sidelines and walk away frustrated. It is the volunteer and paid coaches who shake their heads in amazement at the stubborn resistance on the part of some of their colleagues who cling so tightly to the old ways of doing things. It is the parents who have been tempted to keep their boys out of organized sports in an attempt to avoid the hostile, winner-take-all atmosphere that so often encourages coaches and players to turn a blind eye to poor sportsmanship while being singularly focused on "the win." In that same vein it is also the parents who really want to reinforce the building of sound character and integrity in their boys and simply do not want them to play in any atmosphere that would undermine this intent. It is the older players who retrospectively regret not having coaches who took the time to explain things and teach technique, rather than merely conveying disapproval or barking at them. Some of these boys and young men look back in amazement at the way some coaches display patience in instructing boys who are not naturally gifted or who are late bloomers. Many of the boys who dropped out of youth sports because it did not seem to have a place for them might otherwise be inclined to lend their voices to this chorus for change. However, many have become so alienated they now resent jocks and hate anything related to sports.

With the revolution in youth sports making rumblings for change in numbers that have not been seen before it will soon not be necessary for men like Don to go it alone. The reality is that we don't need to change a single coach, we need to change the whole system. We need to create an expectation that behavior that runs counter to that which fosters character and integrity in our boys is simply not done. Furthermore, we need to have the infrastructure in place in each youth sports program that would dramatically reduce such incidents. If this was the case, were such an incident to take place as Don faced, all the procedures for addressing it would be well known by all coaches, parents, and children. This can only happen if each of us as individuals continues to demand a higher standard from administrators, coaches, other parents, and players. Furthermore, this can only happen if the organizational infrastructure to promote good sportsmanship becomes entrenched in each sports system, be it recreational league or part of a school or college sports program, at all ages of our boys.

✦ Grass Roots Interventions ✦

Communities have come together in a variety of ways to address the problems inherent in youth sports. Invariably the focus has been on the issue of poor sportsmanship and its impact on the children. These efforts and the programs that have resulted have direct ramifications for our interest in fostering character and integrity in our boys. What follows is a description of several of these programs that are a good representation of those which are particularly promising. Please note that while there are differences in how each approaches the issue of sportsmanship the common theme is comprised of three elements:

- To set a clear standard for defining appropriate behavior
- To make individual parents, coaches, and players take responsibility for their actions
- To keep focused on the goal of helping kids to have fun

I encourage you to think creatively as to which program or which parts of each program may work for you in your community. Because the movement to revolutionize youth sports is relatively new, no single program has emerged as the one every middle and secondary school, college and university, and community recreational league must implement. It is basically a matter of tailoring a program to fit the individual needs of the community or organization it serves. It is also a matter of timing. Many organizations are not quite ready for a full implementation of such programs. Experience tells us that there must be enough of a groundswell of interested constituents in order to generate the political will among the leadership within schools, recreational leagues, and communities for a major overhaul of an established sports system. When this is the case a slow, determined, and subtly relentless push can eventually pay off in the form of big changes. In the following section I will highlight some specific programs and organizations that are particularly relevant in terms of promoting good sportsmanship, and in the process helping to foster character and integrity in our boys. As you read about them it is important that you recognize the general understanding among the people who are putting forth these efforts. There is a common sense of humility that no one program or organization has the answer, but rather there is a respect for input from the experience of others. There is also a genuine appreciation that in the process of developing and implementing more effective efforts to promote sportsmanship and create an atmosphere where young people can have fun while learning important lessons for life, change is the only constant.

Parents for Youth Sports Education Program

Paula Jo Powell had a career in the military before she came to be the sports operations supervisor for the El Paso Parks and Recreation Department. It was there that she, along with a willing community and administration, developed and implemented the Parents for Youth Sports Education Program. As in so many communities this program was developed after many brutal and abusive incidents that involved parents, coaches, and players in their youth sports programs. Powell and the El Paso community were faced with many incidents that went beyond poor sportsmanship and included stabbings, brandishing of guns, and other acts of violence and aggression in the stands. The program was first implemented in the fall of 2000 and has since garnered a considerable amount of attention from the national print media, including *Sports Illustrated for Kids, USA Today,* and the Associated Press; from the national television media, including *Oprah Winfrey 20/20,* ESPN, and CBS News; and was a finalist for the Livability Award by the U.S. Conference of Mayors. Here is how it works.

The Parents for Youth Sports Education Program states as its goal: "To restore balance to the teaching situation that youth sports offers: to eliminate violence, negative talking and taunting on the sidelines; to improve communication between coaches, officials, parents and children; and to return to the fun and learning inherent in youth sports." It was decided that the medium for accomplishing this mission would be two three-hour seminars that would operate simultaneously, one for parents and one for their athlete children. The children's session is a fun interactive session wherein issues related to good sportsmanship are discussed and explored within an entertaining format. It is structured so that children as young as four years of age as well as those through the high school years can find things to interest them.

The session for the parents has a much more serious tone and is comprised of six different components. In the introductory section parents view actual footage of other parents from their community as fans at various youth sporting events. It can be enlightening to observe from this perspective people one can identify with acting in a less than desirable manner. They are also shown artwork and essays completed by children in an attempt to increase parents' awareness of what they really want out of their own sports experience, which is primarily to have a good time. The second component is entitled "Sports Parenting" and is presented by a psychologist. This presentation focuses on problematic behaviors that are exhibited on the sidelines. Parents are taught how to overcome these negative impulses and actions and to focus instead on helping to create a healthy youth sports environment.

If the parents' attention has not yet been activated, the third component is bound to deliver. Counselors from the El Paso Child Crisis Center direct the group to consider specific forms and examples of child abuse as they are manifested in youth sports. In the fourth component, "Rules of the Sport," the parents are broken down into subgroups related to the particular sport their child is going to play. They are then taught the rules for that sport. In this component parents learn the ways in which youth sports rules are different from high school, college, and professional sports. Rules that address consequences for unacceptable behavior are emphasized. There is a good deal of interaction in this component, with parents asking many questions as they come to learn what is expected of them on the sidelines during games as well as what they can expect from the sports administrators. In the fifth section a local police officer addresses the parents. Specific, documented sidelines incidents of poor parental behavior that have occurred in their community are presented. All of these incidents required police intervention. The officer then educates parents about the possible consequences of their actions. In the last component the Parents Association of Youth Sports (PAYS) video is shown. Parents view other parents engaged in a constructive discussion of the importance of sportsmanship. Before the conclusion of this section parents are asked to sign a Parents' Code of Ethics in which they pledge to act in compliance with good sportsmanship and sound ethics.

Unless parents attend this three-hour session and sign the Parents' Code of Ethics their child is not allowed to participate in any sports administered by the El Paso Department of Parks and Recreation. Efforts are made to facilitate parental attendance by administering three different sessions for each sport; and for those unable to fit any of these sessions into their schedule they may make arrangements to watch a video of one these live sessions. The policy is very firm, with no exceptions given. All patents have to attend a session and sign the ethics pledge in order for their child to play.

The Parents for Youth Sports Education Program is a massive program with at least five thousand parents trained during each sports season, totaling over twenty thousand for 2001. The sports administered are football, soccer, basketball, cheerleading, baseball, T-ball, softball, swimming, and in-line hockey. If you hail from a community that you might consider to be ethically primitive, take heart, for this program had a trial by fire in the beginning. As it began to take shape in 1999 Ms. Powell was physically assaulted by an angry parent, attempts were made to have her employment terminated, several bomb threats were received, and an actual device was found in the Parks and Recreation facility. Please note that while the parent involved in the assault mentioned above was banned from all sporting events, his child was not punished for her father's behavior and continued to play in the softball league. The father was permitted only to drop the daughter off in the parking lot.

The results from 2000, the first full year of program implementation, are impressive. A dramatic change occurred in the behavior of parents of young athletes. Unlike past years, there were no acts of violence among the parents and there were very few suspensions. Parents' consciousness seems to have been raised. It is generally understood in this program that parents are not the problem, but rather they are the solution in helping to create a healthy atmosphere of trust and cooperation among other parents, coaches, and officials. When they do this parents can see their positive impact on their child and their child's team. Coaches are no longer distracted by sideline nonsense and referees are better able to concentrate on calling a good game. The bottom line is that space has been made for the kids to have fun.

Sage

Another piece of evidence of the evolutionary nature of the revolution in youth sports is the development of the Set a Good Example sportsmanship program, otherwise known as SAGE. Although the seeds were sown in the early 1990s, the Mid-New Jersey Youth Soccer Association (MNJYSA) formally introduced SAGE in 2000. This association provides an organizational framework for more than 70 soccer clubs, which in turn sponsor their own teams. There are about 750 teams in the fall and about 900 teams in the spring that participate in the MNJYSA, totaling about 12,000 players. The motto presented to this massive audience is "Kids Come First" and this reveals a lot of what SAGE is all about.

SAGE was created to deal with the all too common lapses in behavior that can lead to the sad and troubling incidents involving parents, coaches, and players. The association recognizes that although relatively few individuals act inappropriately, their impact on children who participate in sports can be considerable. The ultimate goal of SAGE is to create the conditions in which children have fun and feel good about themselves. Its mission is "to remind us that the game is for the kids, that respect for others is a lesson we can help teach, and that setting a good example is more important than winning."

There are three main components to the SAGE program. The first involves a preseason meeting with parents away from the soccer field. At this meeting parents are educated as to how to increase the fun and the learning process for their soccer-playing children. Emphasis is placed upon encouraging parents to be mindful of their behavior and to remember that the things their child may learn through participation in sports can have significant and hopefully positive ramifications for the rest of their lives, outside of sports. Three brief films are shown. The first is entitled *Sideline Rage* and was originally shown on the Nickelodeon childrens' television network. The second film is *What Kids Wish Their Parents Knew About Sportsmanship* and was produced by the Michigan High School Athletic Association. While the first two films are applicable to any sports program, the third film, *Myths of the Game* by the United States Soccer Federation, details some rules specific to soccer of which many parents are frequently unaware. Misinterpretation of the rules is the origin of many sideline incidents among parents.

The second component pertains to the signing of sportsmanship pledge forms. A separate pledge is provided for coaches, players, and parents and participation in the league is contingent upon all signing. As with the El Paso Parents for Youth Sports Education Program, unless a parent attends the preseason meeting and signs the Parent Sportsmanship Pledge, their child is not permitted to participate in league play.

The last component is the selection of two parent SAGE representatives from each team. They are given SAGE T-shirts and attend a special seminar on sportsmanship. Twice during the season they and/or club officials will hold two-minute meetings on the sidelines reminding attendees about good sportsmanship, what comprises appropriate behavior, and to keep the game fun for the children. They may give out SAGE literature, buttons, or bumper stickers at these times as well. SAGE buttons are encouraged to be worn when on the sidelines. Colorful "Set a Good Example" signs are also visible at every game. It must be noted that SAGE representatives are not enforcers of the SAGE program, rather they remain on the sidelines as visual reminders of good role modeling. In fact they are strongly discouraged from any sort of confrontation on the sidelines. The worst time to talk about sportsmanship to people is when they are loud and negative. SAGE representatives and any parent, coach, player, or referee can inform the club or league about examples of either good or poor sportsmanship. Clubs may then take any action they deem appropriate in response. Actions may include a conversation at a later time with the individual(s) involved, suggesting or mandating that they attend a sportsmanship seminar, or a suspension from attending matches.

Similarly to the El Paso program, the MNJYSA is more than willing to share its materials with anyone interested. Other individuals, leagues, or organizations are encouraged to use any SAGE materials and to modify them to fit their particular needs. The MNJYSA's only request is that others share any innovative ideas or insights so that everyone might learn from each other. In that spirit neither the SAGE program nor any of its materials are copyrighted or protected in any way. The attractive SAGE logo is also available to be downloaded and used by any interested person. Copies of all three sportsmanship pledge forms are provided in appendix 2 for your perusal and use, along with the Web address for the MNJYSA and other similar programs.

Good Sports Are Winners Award

The Michigan High School Athletic Association (MHSAA) has consistently taken a progressive and proactive approach to impacting positively on youth sports. One of their efforts at promoting good sportsmanship is the Good Sports Are Winners Award. The MHSAA took advantage of the fact that it regulates postseason tournaments by integrating the Good Sports Are Winners Award into the tournament system. At each stage of the tournament—district, regional, quarterfinal, semifinal— teams are recognized for their sense of fair play and sportsmanship. Any number of teams may receive this award. It is possible that every team participating in a particular tournament may be given this recognition. It is also possible that no team wins it. In other words it is never awarded by default; it must be earned. While prior to the finals any number of teams may receive the Goods Sports Are Winners Award, by the end of tournament play only one team is chosen. Tournament management, coaches, and MHSAA officials are among those who give input to determine the winners throughout the process. They employ a check-off sheet on which they rate each team from 1 to 10 on a number of sportsmanship criteria. The high school represented by the winner of the Good Sports Are Winners Award in the final round is given a check for one thousand dollars.

Other efforts to promote good sportsmanship by the MHSAA include its Program for Athletic Coaches' Education, the Sportsmanship Summit Conference, which is held every other year in the fall, and the Chance Clinic, which is open to students, faculty, coaches, and media. In this clinic, individuals are divided into groups in order to discuss in depth specific issues related to sportsmanship. Mostly people from Michigan attend, but anyone who is interested is welcome. The MHSAA has also produced two fine films that are available for use in your sportsmanship training efforts: *Sportsmanship in the Home* and *What Kids Wish Their Parents Knew About Sportsmanship*, which was mentioned earlier.

National Alliance for Youth Sports

Among the bowl games in college football the Rose Bowl is considered "the granddaddy of them all." The same can be said for the National Alliance for Youth Sports (known as the Alliance or NAYS) among programs that promote sportsmanship. Although it was originally founded in 1981 as the National Youth Sports Coaches Association (NYSCA), this nonprofit organization now provides the organizational structure for the NYSCA, the Academy for Youth Sports Administrators, the National Youth Sports Administrators Association, the National Youth Sports Officials Association, the Start Smart Sports Development Program, and the Parents Association for Youth Sports (PAYS). You might recall that the PAYS video comprised the sixth component used in the Parents for Youth Sports Education Program from El Paso that was discussed earlier.

The goal of the National Alliance for Youth Sports is to make sports safe and positive for America's youth. It believes that this can only happen if:

- We provide children with a positive introduction to youth sports;
- administrators, coaches, and game officials are well trained;
- parents complete an orientation to understand the important impact sports have on their child's development; and
- youth sports are implemented in accordance with the National Standards for Youth Sports.

In moving toward this goal, the work of the Alliance is divided into the Youth Development Division and the Education Division. One of the programs offered in the Youth Development Division is the Start Smart Sports Development Program, which is an instructional program that prepares children for the world of organized sports without the threat of competition or the fear of getting hurt. Currently there is a Start Smart program for baseball, soccer, and golf. In these programs parents work together with their children in a supportive environment to learn all of the basic skills such as throwing, catching, kicking, hitting, and batting. As a result parents spend quality time with their child while learning how to properly teach them and support them in sports. Another important Alliance program in the youth division is Hook a Kid on Golf, which is a comprehensive youth golf program designed for recreation agencies or golf courses.

In the Education Division, efforts are made through their respective organizations to train coaches, officials, administrators, and parents. Each is provided with a training session that concludes with signing a code of ethics specific for their particular role as a coach, official, administrator, or parent. The Alliance recognizes the importance of holding each party to the code of ethics and provides guidelines for helping member organizations make individuals accountable for violations. Considering that the NYSCA alone has about 2,500 chapters nationwide, the positive impact of the Alliance is considerable.

A certification in youth sports administration is provided through the Academy for Youth Sports Administrators and is geared specifically for parks and recreation departments. As part of this educational effort didactic and video formats are employed in teaching how to train coaches, officials, and parents with a particular eye on promoting good sportsmanship and creating a supportive atmosphere for the children. The film *Introduction to Youth Sports Administration,* which is a component of this training, is required viewing by all coaches in the El Paso program.

The Parents Association for Youth Sports (PAYS) is a membership organization for parents involved in out-of-school youth sports. The program educates and motivates parents to make their child's sports experience safe and meaningful by encouraging good sportsmanship, positive reinforcement, and keeping youth sports in its proper perspective. During a clinic session parents view a thirty-minute training video, participate in discussion with other parents, and sign the Parents' Code of Ethics pledge. Many leagues require that their parents go through the PAYS training program before their child is allowed to participate in the athletic program.

There are currently about four hundred PAYS chapters nationwide comprised of parks, recreation facilities, or other organizations. Many of these chapters mandate that at least one member of their staff be trained and become a Certified Youth Sports Administrator. The idea is that this person could then train the coaches, officials, and parents.

The experience of the Jupiter-Tequesta Youth League Association in Florida is a testament to the positive impact of the Alliance and in particular the PAYS program. Charged with the responsibility to administer nine different sports programs involving about 6,000 children, Jupiter-Tequesta participated in a pilot project for PAYS. In this league, which includes, among other sports, baseball, basketball, soccer, flag football, wrestling, and softball, there were between ten and fifteen massive fights on the fields among coaches and parents per year prior to PAYS. In the first year of the program the frequency of these disturbingly violent eruptions was reduced to only three relatively minor incidents. Clearly the education, the code of ethics, the accountability, and the disciplinary guidelines for consequences, as well as a general increase in awareness, contributed to this positive trend. Other communities have also reported less and less violence after mandating the PAYS program.

There is a seemingly endless stream of positive efforts being launched by the National Alliance for Youth Sports. It is my hope that you recognize the incredible resource it could be for your efforts to improve your child's sports programs. The last thing I will mention about the

Alliance is the Action Plan it is promoting as a response to the current climate of on-the-field violence:

- An individual must be appointed to act as a supervisor of all youth sports in a community, much the way a school board has a leader.
- Mandate that youth sports administrators who lease park and recreation facilities receive training in all aspects of youth sports management.
- Require volunteer coaches to undergo training in the basics of coaching children to ensure they understand the important role they play in providing a safe and fun experience.
- Require parents to go through a sportsmanship training program so they have a clear outline of their roles and responsibilities, and that proper conduct be defined. Parents sign and agree to abide by a Parents' Code of Ethics.
- Young children should be given the opportunity to develop early motor skills in a structured program before they enter organized sports so they find success, increase self-confidence, and enjoy a lifetime of fitness.

Character Counts and Pursuing Victory With Honor

The Josephson Institute is a nonprofit organization dedicated to improving the ethical quality of society by advocating principled reasoning and ethical decision making. The CHARACTER COUNTS! Coalition is a youth education project of the institute. The purpose of CHARACTER COUNTS! is to fortify the lives of America's youth by teaching them values and modeling ethical behavior. The "Six Pillars of Character" modeled and taught are: trustworthiness, respect, responsibility, fairness, caring, and citizenship. It is recognized by CHARACTER COUNTS! that effective character education requires consistency and repetition "from the family room to the schoolroom to the locker room."

The component of CHARACTER COUNTS! dedicated exclusively for sports is the "Pursuing Victory With Honor" project. Its purpose is to help restore the ennobling tradition of amateur athletic competition with specific programs for players, officials, and coaches. These programs are designed to encourage athletes to exhibit good character on and off the field and to help coaches and other responsible adults to instill and reinforce in young people a commitment to develop and exhibit good sportsmanship.

The "Pursuing Victory With Honor" sportsmanship campaign was kicked off by an impressive conference in May of 1999. At this event were nearly fifty leaders in amateur athletics including Olympic great Dan Gable and John Wooden, the legendary former head basketball coach of UCLA. They spoke in a unified voice for major reforms in the way sports are played, coached, and watched. They generated the Arizona Sports Summit Accord that listed sixteen principles and values to encourage greater emphasis on the ethical and character-building aspects of athletic competition. To date those who have signed on to the accord include a great many state high school interscholastic athletic associations, a number of significant college and university organizations, including the Big Ten and Pacific Ten Conferences, along with a large number of professional organizations, including the U.S. Olympic Committee Coaching Division. It is hoped that principles in the accord will eventually be adopted and practiced widely. The Arizona Sports Summit Accord is in appendix 2.

Like the National Alliance for Youth Sports, CHARACTER COUNTS! reaches quite far in its mission to promote character education. A few of its efforts include:

- In August 2001 CHARACTER COUNTS! hosted the Pursuing Victory With Honor Men's and Boy's Basketball Summit. A number of leaders in amateur basketball came together and emerged with a plan to help transform amateur basketball, from recruiting through tournament refereeing.
- A series of Ethics in Sports Seminars are being conducted around the United States for the purpose of teaching how to build character through coaching, the ethical aspects of sport and sportsmanship, and other professional responsibilities of coaching.
- Beginning in January 2001 the Pursuing Victory With Honor e-mail newsletter began circulation. This semimonthly publication provides a forum for discussion and commentary on issues relevant to ethics in sports. It also includes such interesting ar-

ticles as "Running Up the Score, Running Down the Game," "The True Meaning of Competition," and "Season Ends for Poor Sports."

CHARACTER COUNTS! has a great deal to offer. As with the National Alliance for Youth Sports, it is well worth your time to visit the CHARACTER COUNTS! and Pursuing Victory With Honor Web sites.

Citizenship Through Sports Alliance

The Citizenship Through Sports Alliance (CTSA) was formed out of a collective concern about the decline in sportsmanship, poor ethical conduct in athletics, and a general malaise pervasive in the current sports culture. Given these circumstances, the CTSA seeks to cultivate and nurture a sports culture that values learning respect for self, respect for others, and a respect for sport itself. Citizenship was selected as the medium to accomplish this task because of its far-reaching effect on society. The CTSA's rationale is that because sports in the United States has historically served to bring people together as a community, it can therefore be an effective vehicle for promoting citizenship.

Although it was formally established in 1997 the Citizenship Through Sports Alliance's roots go back to efforts that began in 1988. It is comprised of ten school, college, Olympic, and professional sports organizations that include the NBA, NFL, NCAA, and the USOC. It is the belief of the CTSA that through the collaborative efforts of its member organizations and their athletes, its efforts can have a powerful and transforming impact on our communities. The CTSA's activities are based on six basic principles:

- Promotion of the value of sport
- Promotion of academic and social achievement
- Promotion of the value of diversity
- Promotion of drug-free athletics
- Promotion of ethical conduct
- Promotion of nonviolence

The centerpiece of CTSA efforts is the "It's Up to Us: A Community Organizing Tool Kit," which is in essence a blueprint to help communities teach, learn, and practice good citizenship. This pragmatic "tool kit" provides numerous ideas, activities, and materials that can enable a community to tailor a program to address its particular needs. Among the information provided is a guide to build a community team that includes ways to harness community participation, conduct a needs assessment, and conduct citizen-training seminars. Citizenship activities include those for developing codes of conduct for athletes, parents, and coaches as well as promoting citizenship outside of sports. The CTSA considers giving recognition to those who provide examples of good citizenship an important component in its efforts. Therefore, it suggests that communities offer "The Citizenship Award" to honor outstanding individuals who contribute to the community without fanfare and who do good deeds silently without expectation of reward or honor. It provides a guide for the creation of a citizenship team and criteria for nomination and the selection process. It's Up to Us can be a helpful adjunct to a community's efforts to promote sportsmanship and to increase awareness of the value of personal responsibility and action.

Against the Grain Forum

The Against the Grain Forum is a combined effort of the Mendelson Center for Sport, Character, and Culture at the University of Notre Dame and the Positive Coaching Alliance at Stanford University. The forum is a working group that plans to conduct meetings over the next ten years in an effort to bring together individuals from all aspects of youth sports to formulate ways to enable the culture of youth sports to become more conducive to positive character development. The participants will be a select group of leaders from youth sports, sport psychology, sociology, moral education, media, and the business community.

The specific focus will be on ways to promote character development within sports and its social context. The Against the Grain Forum will serve as a clearinghouse for any information, materials, papers, and books that the participants may wish to distribute. Similar to CHARACTER COUNTS!' Pursuing Victory With Honor summit meetings, the Against the Grain Forum will provide another opportunity for a multidisciplinary gathering for leaders from the world of youth sports to share ideas and issues for the promotion of sound character. The more this topic remains on the national radar screen, the more likely that these noble ideas and efforts will translate with increasing frequency into improvements for all level of sports.

✦ What Makes Sense ✦

If our goal is to make our community a better place by ensuring that the young men who participate in it are grounded individuals with sound character, then it is clear that we can no longer merely stand back and just watch. The forces built into the biology and psychology of our boys really need to be corralled and harnessed. There is ample evidence of what havoc results from boys who lack sound and caring guidance. The need for each of us to take a stand is underscored by the fact that there are more than enough forces in the media and contemporary society that all too easily activate and reinforce the shadows of our boys' personalities.

Fortunately we have the benefit of learning from the fine work accomplished by many of the organizations and concerned individuals cited above. To a person, they will all concede that they do not have all the answers, but see their work to increase sportsmanship and promote character development as part of an ongoing and evolving process. It is very good news that we do not have to reinvent the wheel, but can utilize much of what these programs have already accomplished. Perhaps you will be creative and discover other ways of working toward our common goal of fostering conditions that benefit our boys. I want to encourage you to share what you learn among this growing community of dedicated people, because in a very real sense we are all feeding each other as the revolution in youth and school sports continues.

There is an old saying that advises us to strike while the iron is hot. It is fortuitous that we are living amid a groundswell of public concern about how the behavior of our boys, our boys who are athletes, and some of their parents and coaches has gotten out of hand. The time is right for action on a number of fronts.

Intervening on an Organizational Level

The programs and organizational endeavors described in this chapter provide many of the components that would naturally be included in a comprehensive effort to positively impact on the athletic environment of our boys. We can all benefit in learning from the experience of these worthwhile efforts. I offer the following suggestions when creating and organizing the right program to fit your community, recreational program, or school needs:

- Have a mission statement in place
- Make sure parents, coaches, and players sign an enforceable pledge
- Require parents and coaches to attend sportsmanship training sessions
- Make character education of at least equal value to winning
- Create the expectation that coaching be boy-centered and directed at the whole boy
- Maintain a visible presence in terms of sportsmanship recognition, signage, and sportsmanship and character-building educational materials

Regardless of the setting, it is appropriate to have the organization or school establish a mission statement in terms of its athletics. An example might be to have the sports program be mentally and physically safe, enjoyable, and a character-building opportunity. Once a mission statement is established you can then help shape the organization's actions to be consistent with this mission. If the organization acts in ways counter to the mission, it can then be held to task. In youth sports the mission is necessary in order to establish clear parameters for all concerned. Because many coaches may not necessarily have any further qualifications for being youth sport coordinators than that they are parents, there may be considerable variation in the range of behaviors and attitudes they deem acceptable. Furthermore, enthusiastic parents on the sidelines could also benefit from a clear message as to why we are all involved in this activity. It also sets the stage for increasing cooperation among parents should a league official ever have to respond to their actions.

Although there is a universal need for a mission statement, it is particularly relevant when dealing at the high school, college, and university level for reasons unique to these settings. Sports programs at a number of these institutions tend to be considered somewhat untouchable and privileged. For instance, many big-time colleges are already signatories to agreements that aspire to lofty ideals of sport, but when it comes to their own big-money sports programs, they frequently fail to put them into practice. These are typically large dinosaurlike organizations that have one brain in the head and a smaller one in its tail. They don't necessarily operate in sync. What the community relations department and university office of the president say and what the football coach does in practice may very well be two different things. When a university does have a sportsmanship statement you at least have an established basis for challenging the ways in which the organization steps outside of its own guidelines and goals.

It is also helpful to have a set of clear and reasonable standards as to the kinds of behavior that are expected from coaches, players, and parents. The pledge forms discussed in this chapter and presented in appendix 2 are usable as is or can be modified to fit your organization's particular needs. Furthermore, there must be a mechanism to enforce compliance. If your program and sportsmanship standards have no teeth, then they mean nothing. In the business of creating the best atmosphere for fostering character and integrity in our boys we cannot settle for a nice try. This is where winning is very important.

Continuing with this line of thinking, it seems reasonable to include a sportsmanship training and education program for parents and coaches. One benefit is that these adults might learn how their behavior and attitudes can affect their kids in both negative and positive ways. In coming to understand that what they do matters, coaches and parents might be more mindful of acting according to the guidelines of sportsmanship listed in their pledges. This increase in awareness alone will help to reduce unfortunate incidents on the sidelines and increase the chances for positive experiences for our boys. Experience tells us that as a result of this sort of training there will be less of a need for actual enforcement. However, when a signature on a parent sportsmanship pledge is required along with parental attendance at a SAGE, PAYS, or other sportsmanship education program in order for a child to participate in a chosen sport, teeth are put in a sportsmanship program that might otherwise require only a perfunctory nod. If a parent goes way over the line of reasonable conduct, he or she should not be confronted in the heat of the moment, as that can only serve to inflame the situation. Depending on the circumstance, the officials or league can then afterward make a determination as to a correct course of action, such as no longer permitting a father to attend his son's football games. However, great care must be taken so that the child is not directly or inadvertently penalized for the action of his parent.

A Revolution in Youth and School Sports

All of the above seems to be the bare minimum required for a meaningful sportsmanship and character-building program to actually take flight. These simple efforts can gradually transform the atmosphere of a sports program from the winning-is-everything mentality toward an emphasis on character building. In this spirit I offer an excerpt of an editorial by Rick Burns in reaction to Missouri men's basketball coach Norm Stewart, who had just won his six hundredth game. Stewart was quoted as saying, "The only thing that matters in sport is winning 601." In response Burns wrote:

> As I have moved from NCAA Division III to Division II and to the ambivalent challenge of Division I, I'm gradually feeling the increased pressure to get results. I've found most of my coaching brethren, like tributaries flowing smoothly into the same channel, are buying into the "win at all costs" mentality.
>
> Many need to keep their jobs. Even coaches in "minor/non-revenue/Olympic" sports are being fired for not producing winners. Many of my colleagues look to their seasons with anxiety rather then anticipation. Self-worth and their jobs are tied totally into results. Egos soar or plummet after each win or loss. Winning is euphoria; losing tragedy. The space allotted to other measures of the job (our students' academic success, what kind of human beings we are helping to develop) is shrinking

Rick Burns's statement appeared in the *NCAA News Comment* in June of 1998. At that time he coached women's soccer at Drury College. The comments made by Burns help to underscore what can be a delicate balance between focusing on winning, of which there is nothing inherently wrong, and working to foster character and integrity in our athletes. We can do both. However, because statistically only half of all teams are able to have winning records it would be shortsighted to underdo what is within your ability to accomplish (developing young men with sound character) and overdo what may be beyond your control (having winning or championship seasons).

The time is now to transform athletics into a place where the opportunities to ensure the emotional welfare and character development of our boys are not sacrificed for merely winning. To this end we need to create the conditions that set the tone from the top down and convey the expectation of zero tolerance for abuse by coaches and irresponsibility by players.

Additional support for these efforts can be helpful. Providing literature and signs that will remind all participants of the value of good sportsmanship can help to increase everyone's awareness of its importance. Similarly, issuing a sportsmanship award based exclusively on merit can help to teach an athletic and school community to value more than just winning. In no cases are these efforts cost-prohibitive no matter what the resources are for a community or educational institution.

Including Integrity Sessions

Administrators of recreational leagues, and athletic directors of both high school and college programs need to encourage their coaches to get over their apprehension about recognizing or addressing the psychological aspects that our boys bring into the locker room. The fact is that the psychologies of each of our boys exist, so we might as well actively choose to influence them with the most positive attitudes, beliefs, and behaviors as much as possible. Administrators are vital because they have the ability to impact on so many of our boys through the coaches who are their employees. Therefore they need to convey the importance of character education as part of a coach's job function. Such a progressive administrator should also consider encouraging coaches to implement Integrity Sessions, or a modified form, as standard practice in order to bring the high standards of behavior on and off the field into a concrete and teachable form.

Our boys need action, not lip service. They crave this sort of structure and respond well to it.

Our boys appreciate the fact that what they do and say within the Integrity Sessions really matters. The kind of interaction that occurs in an Integrity Session wherein teammates make commitments and respectfully confront one another has a direct and positive influence on their self-esteem. This helps our boys to feel better about themselves because they are following through and behaving consistently with a set of positive values. Because the emphasis is on building self-esteem based on things that matter, not just for the sake of feeling better, the development of sound character is fostered in our boys. That is reason enough to push our coaches to coach the whole boy in this manner. Integrity Sessions really work. Furthermore, when coupled with sports psychology training, they help individuals to maximize their performance in their sports. Moreover, Integrity Sessions can help lay the actual groundwork to foster character and integrity in our boys. You can probably obtain assistance in setting them up at a reasonable cost by a psychologist who practices in your community. Some may also be in a position to volunteer some of their time.

Big Boys Too

Before we move on it is important to make a statement about college and professional athletics. Because our boys are still growing on their way to manhood through college it is imperative that sportsmanship efforts be much more than lip service. Earlier in *Really Winning* you read how as boys advance in years and in development of their athletic talent they are frequently held to decreasing levels of responsibility for their actions. I hope by now you agree that this practice is absurd. Our high school and college boys need to be held to higher levels of responsibility because they have so much more power to affect their world and the freedom to do so. The same is true for young men who become professional athletes. It is lunacy for owners and coaches not to demand behavior exemplary of men of sound character.

In addition, there is the sense that many Division I money sports and professional teams feel they have the right to be exempt from displaying sportsmanship and producing young men with sound character. Sure, the colleges and professional teams "support" sportsmanship efforts with money and endorsements, but to quote George Bush senior from his debates with Jimmy Carter a few years back, "Where's the beef?" We need to demand that the actions of these high-profile athletes and their programs match their words. We need to let the university board of trustees, the professional owners, and the television networks and their advertisers know that the overemphasis on winning the gold (and anything less is losing), and the in-your-face, taunting, and otherwise undignified behavior is simply not acceptable. When enough individuals vote with their dollars, and follow it up with a letter informing the interested parties, these changes will occur.

The Choice

It is not so important what you choose as a course of action for your child, sport, community, or school, just as long as you make a choice to take action. Of course what you seek to accomplish needs to be grounded in the reality of what you face. If your community youth, school, or college sports programs are in the Dark Ages when it comes to promoting character and sportsmanship, then you must be realistic in your efforts to make a change. A reasonable timetable for the gradual introduction of various sportsmanship programming, tailored to your community, will ensure that you and your colleagues will not become too discouraged and burned out. If that were to happen, it would surely be a worst-case scenario, as it could lead to losing heart and giving up on what is a most necessary cause. If sportsmanship and character building have not been on people's minds, then you must put it on the agenda at every opportunity and wherever a positive influence may impact our boys. Among the potential targets are the township recreation committee, community youth sport associations, board of education, parent-teacher association, city council, as well as the college and university board of trustees. If the organizational structures for sportsmanship are already in place in your youth sports, high school or college sports program, but exist in name only, find a way to become a part of the activation process. We want to make sure you and those who come after you keep a steady eye on the target of bringing fun back to youth sports and school sports and of utilizing the opportunity that sports provides to foster character and integrity in our boys.

Life, however, is not so simple as to permit us to introduce such sweeping changes in one fell swoop. Circumstances vary, but the one thing that is constant in terms of implementing change is working to influence the attitudes and beliefs that people hold. Our efforts to promote character education and to integrate the expectation that our boys, along with their coaches and their parents, behave with integrity and good sportsmanship will succeed if we are persistent in knocking on all these doors with a consistent message: this is what we expect, anything less does not measure up, so let's do the right thing and make some changes. With consistency and perseverance even the most entrenched ways of doing things and the kind of thinking that perpetuates this behavior can be transformed. Because our efforts are grounded in sound values and common sense it is all the more reason that we will succeed.

Let's Go for the Win: Your Presence Matters

In order for us to be successful in our efforts to create the conditions that foster the development of character and integrity in our boys, it ultimately comes down to standing up as an individual and taking action. Some may coach a team, become a league official, become a team parent, join a sportsmanship committee, or write a letter. Taking action in this way is consistent with the Citizenship Through Sports Alliance's emphasize on using citizenship as a medium through which to promote character. Participating as a responsible member of the community in the specific way that is right for you is what is required to bring about change. You cannot leave it for the next guy to do because it won't get done. The reason it won't get done, as the old saying goes, is that *unless* you are part of the solution, you *are* part of the problem.

Becoming involved with your son's sports programs or even being the chairman of the community sportsmanship committee will not add up to a hill of beans unless you put this learning into action in your relationship with your own child. You need to be a good teacher and a good role model, but you also need to be involved in creating the kind of personal relationship that will foster sound character in him.

If you are involved with our boys as a parent or as a coach, you must remember that they need you to be present with them as a person. You need to talk with and listen to them with respect, just as you need to convey a clear expectation as to the kind of behavior you want from them. All of what you now know about the psychology of boys needs to be brought into your interactions with them. You must also be approachable and this can be done while being friendly but also firm. In addition, you must be a person of your word. This requires you to follow through with whatever it is you said you would do, whether it's bringing oranges to the next soccer game, enforcing a team violation by benching a player who missed his study sessions, or agreeing to help your son build a model airplane. When your actions reflect your values as a man of sound character, you become the best of all teachers. Our boys will remember far more from the things you do than the words you say. When you model the right way to be you make it easier for them to comply with the demands you impose upon them to behave with a sense of integrity. If you model being a man of sound character when working with older boys, you will make their transition to using Integrity Sessions with serious intent a much easier and more natural process. However, it must be noted that we need not take any heroic actions. Sometimes being present means merely showing up, but not in body only. If your son is playing a sport, he needs you to be there and needs you to want to be there. So don't just try to be there; *be there*. This is part of what choosing to lend ourselves to our boys means.

When we remember to act like a person with character and integrity we not only gain the satisfaction of being the best person we can be, but we do our boys the favor of showing them the way to manhood. Boys will be boys and we need to let them have fun while playing within bounds. They are looking for us to help them do so. Our boys will benefit the more we follow through. And then we will all be really winning.

Appendix 1

Bibliographical

and Internet References

Listed below are a number of books that I believe you will find particularly helpful in understanding our boys. They have been cross-referenced among several specific areas of interest. They will be followed by a listing of Internet references relevant to the issue of character development and sportsmanship.

Bibliographical References

BOYS: PSYCHOLOGICAL, SOCIAL, AND PHYSIOLOGICAL DEVELOPMENT

Elium, D., and Elium, J. 1994. *Raising a Son: Parents and the Making of a Healthy Man*. Berkeley: Celestial Arts.

Erikson, E. 1963. *Childhood and Society*. New York: Norton.

———. 1968. *Identity: Youth and Crisis*. New York: Norton.

———. 1980. *Identity and the Life Cycle*. New York: Norton.

Golding, W. 1954. *Lord of the Flies*. New York: A Perigee Book.

Gurian, M., and Henley, P. 2001. *Boys and Girls Learn Differently: A Guide for Teachers and Parents*. San Francisco: Jossey-Bass.

Gurian, M. 1998. *A Fine Young Man: What Parents, Mentors, and Educators Can Do to Shape Adolescent Boys into Exceptional Men*. New York: Tarcher/Putnam.

———. 1996. *The Wonder of Boys: What Parents, Mentors, and Educators Can Do to Shape Boys into Exceptional Men*. New York: Tarcher/Putnam.

Keen, S. 1991. *Fire in the Belly: On Being a Man*. New York: Bantam Books.

Kindlon, D., and Thompson, M. 1999. *Raising Cain: Protecting the Emotional Life of Boys*. New York: Ballantine Books.

Kivel, P. 1999. *Boys Will Be Men: Raising Our Sons for Courage, Caring and Community*. Gabriola Island, B.C., Canada: New Society Publishers.

Miller, A. 1983. *For Your Own Good: Hidden Cruelty in Child-Rearing and the Roots of Violence*. New York: Farrar, Straus and Giroux.

Mones, P. 1991. *When a Child Kills*. New York: Simon & Schuster.

Moore, R., and Gillette, D. 1991. *King, Warrior, Magician, Lover: Rediscovering the Archetypes of the Mature Masculine*. San Francisco: Harper Collins.

Newberger, E. H. 1999. *The Men They Will Become: The Nature and Nurture of Male Character*. Cambridge, Massachusetts: Perseus Books.

Pollack, W. 1998. *Real Boys: Rescuing Our Sons from the Myths of Boyhood*. New York: Owl Books.

Trachtenberg, P. 1998. *The Casanova Complex: Compulsive Lovers and Their Women*. New York: Poseidon Press.

Yeoman, A., and Woodman, M. 1998. *Now or Neverland: Peter Pan and the Myth of Eternal Youth*. Toronto: Inner City Books.

CHARACTER EDUCATION AND ETHICS

Armstrong, L., and Jenkins, S. 2000. *It's Not About the Bike: My Journey Back to Life*. New York: Penguin Putnam, Inc.

Bradley, B. 1998. *Values of the Game*. New York: Broadway Books.

Gough, R. W. 1997. *Character Is Destiny: The Value of Personal Ethics in Everyday Life*. Roseville, California: Prima Publishing.

Gough, R. W. 1997. *Character Is Everything: Promoting Ethical Excellence in Sports*. New York: Harcourt Brace College Publishers.

Guroian, V. 1998. *Tending the Heart of Virtue: How Classic Stories Awaken a Child's Moral Imagination*. New York: Oxford University Press.

LaFontaine, P., Valutis, E., Griffin, C., and Weisman, L. 2001. *Companions in Courage: Triumphant Tales of Heroic Athletes*. New York: Warner Books.

Miller, A. 1983. *For Your Own Good: Hidden Cruelty in Child-Rearing and the Roots of Violence*. New York: Farrar, Straus and Giroux.

Mones, P. 1991. *When a Child Kills*. New York: Simon & Schuster.

Newberger, E. H. 1999. *The Men They Will Become: The Nature and Nurture of Male Character*. Cambridge, Massachusetts: Perseus Books.

Plato. 1994. *Republic*. (Robin Waterfield, trans.) Oxford: Oxford University Press. (Original work published c. 370 B.C.).

Ralbovsky, M. 1974. *Lords of the Locker Room: The American Way of Coaching and Its Effect on Youth*. New York: Peter H. Wyden Publisher.

GIRLS: THINGS WORTH KNOWING

Bassoff, E. 1998. *Cherishing Our Daughters: How Parents Can Raise Girls to Become Strong and Loving Women*. New York: Dutton.

Gurian, M. 2002. *The Wonder of Girls: Understanding the Hidden Nature of Our Daughters*. New York: Pocket Books.

Gurian, M., and Henley, P. 2001. *Boys and Girls Learn Differently: A Guide for Teachers and Parents*. San Francisco: Jossey-Bass.

Silby, C., and Smith, S. 2000. *Games Girls Play: Understanding and Guiding Young Female Athletes*. New York: St. Martin's Press.

Simmons, R. 2002. *Odd Girl Out: The Hidden Culture of Aggression in Girls*. New York: Harcourt Brace.

HUMAN DEVELOPMENT

Bly, R. 1988. *A Little Book on the Human Shadow*. San Francisco: HarperSanFrancisco.

Bugental, J.F.T. 1965. *The Search for Authenticity*. New York: Holt, Rinehart and Winston.

Campbell, J. 1949. *The Hero with a Thousand Faces*. Princeton: Princeton University Press.

Erikson, E. 1963. *Childhood and Society*. New York: Norton.

———. 1968. *Identity: Youth and Crisis*. New York: Norton.

———. 1980. *Identity and the Life Cycle*. New York: Norton.

Golding, W. 1954. *Lord of the Flies*. New York: Perigee Book.

Gurian, M., and Henley, P. 2001. *Boys and Girls Learn Differently: A Guide for Teachers and Parents*. San Francisco: Jossey-Bass.

Jung, C. G., ed. 1964. *Man and His Symbols*. Garden City: Doubleday.

Smith, C. D. 1990. *Jung's Quest for Wholeness: A Religious and Historical Perspective*. Albany: State University of New York Press.

Yeoman, A. 1998. *Now or Neverland: Peter Pan and the Myth of Eternal Youth.* Toronto: Inner City Books.

OPTIMAL PERFORMANCE PSYCHOLOGY

Benson, H., and Klipper, M. Z. 2000. *The Relaxation Response: 2000 update edition.* New York: WholeCare.

Blanchard, K., Carlos, J. P., and Randolph, A. 1999. *The 3 Keys to Empowerment: Release the Power Within People for Astonishing Results.* San Francisco: Berrett-Koehler.

Cameron, J. 1992. *The Artist's Way: A Spiritual Path to Higher Creativity.* New York: Tarcher/Perigee.

Csikszentmihalyi, M. 1990. *Flow: The Psychology of Optimal Experience.* New York: Harper Perennial.

Goldratt, E. M. 1992. *The Goal: A Process of Ongoing Improvement.* Great Barrington, Massachusetts: The North River Press.

Kalupahana, D. J. 1987. *The Principles of Buddhist Psychology.* Albany: State University of New York Press.

Hendricks, G., and Wills, R. 1975. *The Centering Book.* Englewood Cliffs: Prentice-Hall.

Houston, J. 1982. *The Possible Human: A Course in Enhancing Your Physical, Mental, and Creative Abilities.* Los Angeles: J. P. Tarcher, Inc.

Lynch, J., and Huang, C. A. 1998. *Working Out, Working Within.* New York: Tarcher/Putnam.

Murphy, S. 1997. *The Achievement Zone: An Eight Step Guide to Peak Performance in All Areas of Life.* New York: Berkley.

Parcells, B., and Coplon, J. 1995. *Finding a Way to Win: The Principles of Leadership, Teamwork, and Motivation.* New York: Doubleday.

SPORTS IN GENERAL

Armstrong, L., and Jenkins, S. 2000. *It's Not About the Bike: My Journey Back to Life.* New York: Penguin Putnam, Inc.

Benedict, J. R. 1998. *Athletes and Acquaintance Rape.* Thousand Oaks: Sage Publications.

Bradley, B. 1998. *Values of the Game.* New York: Broadway Books.

Engh, F. (1999). *Why Johnny Hates Sports: Why Organized Youth Sports Are Failing Our Children and What We Can Do About It.* New York: Avery Publishing Group.

Feinstein, J. 2000. *The Last Amateurs: Playing for Glory and Honor in Division I College Basketball.* New York: Little, Brown and Company.

Gough, R. W. 1997. *Character Is Everything: Promoting Ethical Excellence in Sports.* New York: Harcourt Brace College Publishers.

LaFontaine, P., Valutis, E., Griffin, C., and Weisman, L. 2001. *Companions in Courage: Triumphant Tales of Heroic Athletes.* New York: Warner Books.

Parcells, B., and Coplon, J. 1995. *Finding a Way to Win: The Principles of Leadership, Teamwork, and Motivation.* New York: Doubleday.

Ralbovsky, M. 1974. *Lords of the Locker Room: The American Way of Coaching and Its Effect on Youth.* New York: Peter H. Wyden Publisher.

Shulman, J. L., and Bowen, W. G. 2001. *The Game of Life: College Sports and Educational Values.* Princeton: Princeton University Press.

Wooden, J. R., and Jamison, S. 1997. *Wooden.* New York: McGraw Hill.

SPORTS PSYCHOLOGY

Campbell, J. 1949. *The Hero with a Thousand Faces.* Princeton: Princeton University Press.

Engh, F. 1999. *Why Johnny Hates Sports: Why Organized Youth Sports Are Failing Our Children and What We Can Do About It.* New York: Avery Publishing Group.

Epstein, M. 1995. *Thoughts Without a Thinker: Psychotherapy from a Buddhist Perspective.* New York: Basic Books.

Hogg, J. M. 1997. *Mental Skills for Young Athletes: A Mental Skills Workbook for Athletes 12 Years and Under.* Edmonton: Sport Excel Publishing Inc.

Jensen, P. 1994. *The Inside Edge: High Performance Through Mental Fitness.* Toronto: Macmillan Canada.

Lynch, J., and Huang, C. A. 1998. *Working Out, Working Within.* New York: Tarcher/Putnam.

Murphy, S. 1997. *The Achievement Zone: An Eight Step Guide to Peak Performance in All Areas of Life.* New York: Berkley.

Parcells, B., and Coplon, J. 1995. *Finding a Way to Win: The Principles of Leadership, Teamwork, and Motivation.* New York: Doubleday.

Ravizza, K., and Hanson, T. 1995. *Heads-Up Baseball: Playing the Game One Pitch at a Time.* Indianapolis: Masters Press.

Rotella, B., and Cullen, B. 1997. *The Golf of Your Dreams.* New York: Simon & Schuster.

Silby, C., and Smith, S. 2000. *Games Girls Play: Understanding and Guiding Young Female Athletes.* New York: St. Martin's Press.

Singer, R. N., Murphey, M., and Tennant, L. K., eds. 1993. *Handbook of Research on Sport Psychology*. New York: Macmillan.

Suinn, R. M. 1986. *Seven Steps to Peak Performance: The Mental Training Manual for Athletes*. Toronto: Hans Huber Publications.

Weinberg, R. S., and Gould, D. 1999. *Foundations of Sport and Exercise Psychology*. 2nd edition. Champaign, Illinois: Human Kinetics.

Internet References

Athletes for a Better World
www.AforBw.org

Center for Sports Parenting
www.sportsparenting.org

Character Counts
Josephson Institute of Ethics
www.charactercounts.org

Citizenship Through Sports
  Alliance
www.sportsmanship.org

El Paso Parks and Recreation
  Sports Department
powellpj@ci.el-paso.tx.us

The Institute for the Study of
  Youth Sports
Michigan State University
www.ythsprts@pilot.msu.edu

Dr. Jim Mastrich
www.drjimmastrich.com

Mendelson Center for Sport,
  Character, and Culture
University of Notre Dame
www.nd.edu/~cscc/index.html

Michigan High School Athletic
  Association
www.mhsaa.com

Mid New Jersey Youth Soccer
  Association
www.mnjysa.org

MomsTeam.Com
www.MomsTeam.com

The National Alliance for Youth
  Sports
www.nays.org

Positive Coaching Alliance
Stanford University
www.positivecoach.org

Sports P.L.U.S.—Positive
  Learning Using Sports
www.sportsplus.org

Men Mentoring Men
www.menmentoringmen.org

Appendix 2

Relevant Documents

What follows is a list of documents relevant to various aspects of sports psychology and the promotion of character, integrity, and sportsmanship:

The Mental Preparation Checklist
Integrity Sessions for Athletes: Goals and Ground Rules
Physical and Mental Standards: Football Wide Receivers
ISYS Bill of Rights for Young Athletes
SAGE The Mission
SAGE Coach Sportsmanship Pledge
SAGE Player Sportsmanship Pledge
SAGE Parent Sportsmanship Pledge
NAYS Pre-season Parents' Checklist
NAYS/PAYS Parents' Code of Ethics
CHARACTER COUNTS! Arizona Sports Summit Accord

The Mental Preparation Checklist

1. *Create a mental strategy and execute it.*
   Develop and carry out your mental strategy.
   Do *not* focus on results.
   Do focus on your strategy.
   Focus only on what you can, not what you can't, control.

2. *Use imagery and mental rehearsals.*
   See yourself mentally as performing perfectly and being in the right frame
   of mind.
   Do consistent run-throughs in your mind's eye.

3. *Set daily goals.*
   Identify clear daily goals as you move toward the event.

4. *Target your optimal level of arousal, nutritional and fitness training.*
   Get to know in advance what your appropriate level of arousal is on a
   scale from 1 to 10.
   Get to know your own level of nutritional and fitness training needs.
   Practice getting to these states on a daily basis.
   Use relaxation techniques, tapes, and imagery to learn to achieve the op-
   timal level of arousal.

5. *Use self-talk and personal affirmations.*
   Repeat positive, affirmative statements about the way you wish to per-
   form.
   Use short specific phrases for maximum impact.

6. *Practice quality; quality practice.*
   Perfect mental practice moves us toward increased performance.
   Do the right thing in your head first. Be as precise as possible.

7. *Develop and follow a pre-event ritual.*
   Create your own way of self-organizing before a big event.
   Develop and follow your own pre-event ritual.

8. *Run simulations.*
   Do complete run-throughs, preferably in the environment where the event
   will take place or in a similar environment.
   Imagine yourself there.

9. *Make mental preparation part of your overall preparation.*
   As an individual or with a team, incorporate proper mental preparation
   into your rehearsal schedule.

Source: *The Inside Edge* by Peter Jensen

Integrity Sessions for Athletes:
Goals and Ground Rules

in•teg•ri•ty

1: an unimpaired condition: SOUNDNESS
2: firm adherence to a code of esp. moral or artistic values: INCORRUPT-
   IBILITY
3: the quality or state of being complete or undivided: COMPLETENESS
   syn see HONESTY.

©1989 Merriam-Webster, Inc.

GOALS

THE PURPOSE OF THE INTEGRITY SESSIONS IS:

TO PROMOTE THE FULFILLMENT OF OUR POTENTIAL AS
QUALITY INDIVIDUALS AND SOUND ATHLETES;
   AND TO HELP EACH MEMBER OF THIS UNIT ACHIEVE AND
MAINTAIN AN INCORRUPTIBLE STANDARD OF PHYSICAL AND
MENTAL CONDITIONING THAT THEY BRING TO EVERY PRAC-
TICE AND EVERY GAME;
   AND THAT WE EACH PROMOTE THIS BY DEMANDING THE
BEST FROM OURSELVES AND EACH OTHER ON AND OFF THE
FIELD. IN THIS WAY WE BECOME A MORE COMPLETE AND UN-
DIVIDED UNIT.

GROUND RULES

1. *Self-disclosure:* You are asked to be open about yourself. This means that
you are to talk about yourself in such a way as to get the real you (rather than
a facade) across to your teammates. What you say about yourself should
constitute a kind of invitation to your teammates to involve themselves with
you.
   Let the concept of being present guide you. Being present means listening

to your gut; if it is stirring, it's telling you to speak up. Being present means making a public commitment about your weekly practice goals, following through, and owning up to areas of deficiency. Being present means you owe it to your teammates, especially in Integrity Sessions, to tell them about yourself and to tell them what you feel and think about them and their approach to practice, the game, as well as to life off the field. When you speak, try to be concrete and specific. For instance, when speaking about yourself, say "I." Do not use the general "you" when you are talking about your feelings, thoughts, or actions.

2. *Listening:* It is amazing to discover how poorly we listen to others. We ask you to examine your ability to listen to others. Listening involves tuning in to persons rather than just ideas. Listening is picking up *all* the cues that others emit, both verbal and nonverbal. Facial expressions, gestures, a shrug of the shoulders, bodily positions—all of these are sources of communication. Often, too, we communicate by the way we say things. You are also asked to become sensitive to these additional messages sent to and from you. You are asked to respect your teammates' comments about you. If they are conveyed with an "I" statement, then you needn't feel defensive; everyone has a right to their own thoughts, perceptions, and feelings. Furthermore, this feedback is a valuable source of information for you to use in improving yourself.

3. *Support:* It is difficult for people to "put themselves on the line," that is, to approach each practice and every game with an unrelenting eye toward quality, as well as in Integrity Sessions to engage with teammates in meaningful self-disclosure and to express feelings and thoughts responsibly. We need to support these courageous acts of our teammates.

You and your teammates need each other's support in order to make a sincere attempt to fulfill the contract to approach practice and game situations with integrity. When someone "invites you in" by being open about themselves, or their perceptions of you, you may find it difficult to respond. Perhaps your best response is to admit that you are uncomfortable, that you are at a loss for a response, or that you have not followed through, but will recommit to do so. This can be supportive in itself, because it is honest. Ultimately, because we are a unit, we owe it to each other to lend support to each other. We need to give support in the form of acknowledgment for what the other has achieved, as well as encouragement and confrontation if the other has not, in your estimation, lived up to making a complete and honest effort.

4. *Confronting others:* Sometimes you will find it impossible to agree with what another person is saying or doing. If this is true, tell them so as honestly as you can, and tell them why. This is a confrontation. Confrontation is, basically, an invitation to another to examine or reflect upon personal behavior in the context of the team. The *way* you confront someone is very important. The cardinal rule is that you confront another because of a concern for that person and the team, and out of a desire to involve and reveal yourself with that person. When we confront our teammates we are inviting them to expect the same level of accountability from us.

5. *Responding to confrontation:* If confrontation is responsible, that is, if it really is an invitation to self-examination, then obviously the best response is self-examination. However, when we are confronted, even by someone who is concerned and wants to become involved with us, our instinctive response is often twofold: to defend ourselves and to attack the confronter. Therefore, we must try to listen to what the one confronting us is saying and not just to the feelings that are being evoked within us. If what is being said comes from a sincere desire to become involved with you, and if the confrontation is in the best interests of the team, then it is to your advantage to listen, to examine yourself, and to respond responsibly to the confronter. This is difficult, but frequently rewarding. Just as rising water raises all boats equally, when our standards as a unit rise, the integrity of each, as individuals, also rises and this will be reflected on the field and in all areas of our lives.

Physical and Mental Standards
(Football Wide Receivers)

INTEGRITY IN PRACTICE
WHAT YOU BRING TO PRACTICE,
YOU'LL BRING TO THE GAME.

Physical Standards

- Dress fully before you leave the locker room.
- Dress only in team issue, as one unit, with one goal: a united and stronger team.
- Dress quickly and get out on the field.
- All run once you hit the practice field.
- No running out of bounds if in pads.
- Go after every ball (don't dive in practice if on turf).
- Compliment and affirm your teammates for their efforts and achievements.

Mental Standards

- Choose to want to be on the practice field.
- Understand that giving in to resistance to practice with integrity is to surrender to the coward inside.
- Accept/surrender to coaching and understand your defensiveness as fear based.
- Choose to ask self, coach, and teammates how you can be a better player.
- Choose to help teammates to learn to be better players.
- Choose to be unselfish.
- Choose to be proactive in taking responsibility for yourself.
- Do not accept negativity from a teammate, and confront him on it.

INTEGRITY IN A GAME SITUATION

Physical Standards

- Dress fully before you leave the locker room.
- Dress only in team issue, as one unit, with one goal: a united and stronger team.
- The Style of Play of Excellence challenges us: to lift each other up after every play *figuratively* by affirming and complimenting your teammates and fostering a positive attitude and to lift each other up after every play *literally* by going to the ball carrier and pulling him up, even if on the other side of the field.
- No running out of bounds if in pads.
- Go after every ball in all situations with no exceptions.

Mental Standards

- The Style of Play of Excellence is about regularly calling on all the 5 Skills of Mental Fitness, especially maintaining a positive mental attitude, and reframing all crises and challenges as opportunities to grow and excel.
- The Style of Play of Excellence allows us to feed off the energy we each generate.
- Recognize that every moment, every event, and every play is an opportunity to excel.

INTEGRITY OFF THE FIELD

Physical Standards

- Approach academics with the same focus and purpose as in preparing for a game.
- Engage in relations with women with respect for them, for yourself as an honest man, and with the knowledge that you are a reflection of this team. Remember that one who has real power knows he does not have to exploit it.
- If you observe teammates placing themselves in positions that may compromise their integrity, know that you owe it to them to help them by calling them on their actions.
- Demand a high standard in how you take care of yourself, including your approach to nutrition, sleep, who you affiliate with, and any possible dealings with drugs and alcohol.

Mental Standards

- To approach all aspects of your life (athletic, academic, interpersonal, and intrapersonal) with high standards. Don't settle for less than excellence from yourself in all areas. When we strive to achieve our best, we become better.
- Don't deny your fears, instead face your fears with the integrity of a warrior, don't hide from them. Be open to learning what your fears have to teach you. Meet them head-on and don't be afraid to ask for help, support, and guidance so that you can complete your mission.

© 1998 Dr. Jim Mastrich, Sports Psychologist

ISYS Bill of Rights for Young Athletes

The Bill of Rights for Young Athletes was developed in the 1980s by Dr. Vern Seefeldt, professor emeritus at the Institute for the Study of Youth Sports, and by Dr. Rainier Martens in response to growing concerns regarding the abuse of young athletes. This bill has been used by a number of national organizations as guidelines for coaches and parents.

1. Right to participate in sports.

2. Right to participate at a level commensurate with each child's maturity and ability.

3. Right to have qualified adult leadership.

4. Right to play as a child and not as an adult.

5. Right of children to share in the leadership and decision-making of their sport.

6. Right to participate in safe and healthy environments.

7. Right to proper preparation for participation in sports.

8. Right to an equal opportunity to strive for success.

9. Right to be treated with dignity.

10. Right to have fun in sports.

Reprinted from *Guidelines for Children's Sports* (1979) with permission from the National Association for Sport and Physical Education (NASPE), Reston, Virginia.

SAGE Sportsmanship Program
The Mission

To remind us that the game is for the kids, that respect for others is a lesson we can help teach, and that setting a good example is more important than winning.

The SAGE program in brief:

1. Parents and players sign separate Sportsmanship Pledge forms spelling out appropriate conduct and the reasons why good sportsmanship is so important.

2. Preseason mandatory coach-ref meetings are used in part to reinforce SAGE.

3. Mandatory preseason parents' meetings away from the fields are held to explain how we can increase the fun and learning process for the kids.

4. Clubs oversee the selection of two parent representatives for each team (team SAGE representatives) who become visual reminders of the program at matches. They attend a special seminar on sportsmanship and then are given colorful SAGE T-shirts.

The team SAGE reps are NOT ENFORCERS of the SAGE program. There should be no confrontations. If a few people are loud and negative, that's NOT the time to talk to them about sportsmanship. The team SAGE reps are visual, not oral reminders.

Increasing awareness of the program due to all the visual reminders should help all coaches, players, referees, and parents. We should all think more about the goals of fun and respect for everyone, along with helping kids feel good about themselves. Other goals include improving skills, encouraging players to try their best to help the team do as well as it can, and also helping them learn to interact with others in a team situation.

Any parent, coach, player, or ref can spread the word informally about examples of good or bad sportsmanship. Clubs should let the league know about examples of good sportsmanship, even if they seem insignificant. Clubs take whatever action on poor sportsmanship they believe necessary. This action might include a conversation with those involved, suggesting or mandating that they attend a sportsmanship seminar, or the last thing any of us wants, suspension from attending matches.

5. Brochures with reminders about the dos and don'ts of good sportsmanship are distributed periodically to spectators at matches. In addition, signs, buttons, decals, and bumper stickers are used as reminders at the fields and elsewhere. We encourage spectators to wear the buttons when at the fields.

6. Just before matches begin, brief meetings led by club or league officials are held at the fields with spectators to review appropriate behavior. Brief meetings with others involved at the games may also be added.

SAGE Coach Sportsmanship Pledge

Please read and sign this pledge form indicating your support for making this a positive experience for everyone.

1. Keep in mind that the main reason kids play is to have fun and we have an obligation to keep it fun.

2. We can only expect them to try their best.

3. Find reasons to praise each player often to help them feel good about themselves. If they learn new skills and show good sportsmanship, even if they're not great players, they should be complimented to help their confi-

dence, which can improve their play. They should keep in mind that it is okay to not be one of the best players. Everyone is not great at everything.

4. Let them know your club and league's policy on playing time. We might need a reminder that if they don't play much, they won't gain the extra confidence which helps them improve.

5. Some of us, sometimes, get angry and critical when our players make mistakes. We should be calm and offer suggestions in a friendly tone of voice. Too much criticism can reduce their enthusiasm. That criticism can even cause excellent players to sometimes lose some of their interest in trying to improve.

Our natural competitive spirit, frustrations we feel from other parts of our lives, and our normal desire for glory can occasionally make us loud and negative with the kids when they don't fulfill our expectations. Once in a while our expectations may be unrealistic.

6. To reduce our frustration as coaches and the players' as well, try asking the players for volunteers to repeat in their own words what we just tried to teach. Sometimes we think we're explaining it clearly but they're not getting it.

7. While we want our team to try hard to be successful, studies consistently show that winning is not as important to the players as having fun. If we help the players understand that winning is just one of the goals, they can have a positive experience even when they're not winning.

8. If we win most of our games consistently, we are not playing tough enough competition and so our kids cannot improve as much as they would. That's because having to play as hard as they can against good competition is a great way to raise their intensity and skills, and that carries over to future games.

9. Learning to accept losing is an important lesson in life that we, along with parents and others, can help teach. We don't succeed at everything. We just try harder next time. Losing can help prepare us for the setbacks that happen in other parts of our lives.

10. We should not criticize referees. They deserve respect whether or not they are outstanding at what they do. Sometimes they make mistakes, as we all do. We sometimes think they made a mistake when they didn't. They don't change their calls. But many referees do quit because of the abuse they take from coaches, parents, and players. Yet we wonder why there is a shortage of referees.

11. We should not worry about whether others view us as great teachers of the game or less than great. We are giving our time and doing our best. If we are making it a positive, fun experience for the kids by teaching without anger, we are fulfilling our mission.

Signed

_____

S. A. G. E.: Set A Good Example

Mid-New Jersey Youth Soccer Association

SAGE Player Sportsmanship Pledge

1. Remember that we play the game mostly because it is fun. My opponents play for fun as well.

2. We should always try to help our team be successful, but it is okay to lose. The fun we have during the game is far more important than the score at the end. Also, losing teaches many valuable lessons just as winning does. We are sometimes not successful in other parts of our lives and losing in sports helps prepare us to accept that and we should just come back with enthusiasm the next time.

3. If we win almost all our games, it can mean that we are not playing good enough competition. Our intensity and skills improve most and carry over to future games when we play against good teams.

4. It is okay not to be a great player. Always try your best. That is all that can be expected.

5. Don't sound angry or frustrated when giving advice to teammates. They will consider suggestions more seriously if we use a pleasant tone of voice. It helps to speak in a friendly way. Also show respect to opponents, coaches, and spectators.

6. Help a teammate calm down if they are too angry so that they remain in the game and continue to have fun.

7. When another player says something inappropriate or is too rough, most of the time a confrontation can be avoided. If you respond when it is not necessary, it doesn't mean you're cool or tough. Lowering oneself to the irresponsible player's level risks hurting the team by your possibly facing ejection from the match or being removed by the coach.

8. Recognize that referees try to do the best job they can, just as you are. They make mistakes just as you do. Do not criticize their decisions. It is not surprising that many referees quit because of the abuse they take and yet we wonder why there are not enough referees. Show the same respect to them that you want for yourself.

9. By joining the team, make a commitment to attend practice and games and display good sportsmanship. One cannot expect as much playing time without meeting those commitments.

10. I can help my family by reminding them not to argue with referees or coaches and to show respect and good sportsmanship at all times.

Signed,

_____

(date) _____

S.A.G.E.: Set A Good Example

Mid-New Jersey Youth Soccer Association

SAGE Parent Sportsmanship Pledge

We respectfully ask you as a condition of your child's participation in the program, to please read and sign the following Parent Sportsmanship Pledge:

(signed) _____

(date) _____

Parents or Guardians: (signed)_____

(date)_____

1. It is often difficult for parents to see their children in situations where they are being evaluated, especially at a very young age. But if we spend our time worrying too much about how they're doing, we are missing what should be a wonderful experience for us as well as them.

If they're not great players, we will love them anyway for who they are. Find reasons to praise them for their accomplishments on the field, big or small, and know that they will be great at other things.

2. The game is for the kids. We shouldn't let our natural competitive spirit and normal desire for glory turn into angry yelling at the kids when they don't fulfill our expectations. Sometimes our expectations may be unrealistic. If they're having fun as well as gaining confidence by learning skills, and being coached by a person who is teaching and mentoring without anger, that should satisfy us.

3. Winning is only one of many goals. Fewer than half the teams competing win their games on any given day (counting ties) and as studies have consistently indicated, children play mainly for the fun of it. Kids almost unanimously rate the fun they have during the match much higher than the score at that single moment when the game is over.

4. We must also remember that it is okay to lose because life is not just about winning. We suffer setbacks at times. Learning to accept defeat gracefully and come back enthusiastically next time is an important lesson to teach. As long as children try their best, they are winners on another level even when they lose the game.

5. Coaches and referees deserve respect. They make mistakes as we all do, but whether they're great at what they're doing or not, we have a responsibility to set a good example to help teach respect to our children. Yelling criticism at referees, coaches, or players is inappropriate and that behavior must be subject to penalties from the club, including the last thing the club wants to consider: possible suspension from attending matches. Children often reveal that they are embarrassed when their parents shout out criticism.

Referees do not change their calls but many do decide to quit because of the abuse they take from parents, coaches, and players. Yet we wonder why we don't have enough referees.

Coaches are giving of their time and effort, and if they are making it a positive, fun experience, we should respect them for that.

6. Some of us are more emotional, which is good in some ways. Some of us are calmer, which also is good in some ways. When we are emotional—

perhaps sometimes because of frustrations in other parts of our lives—it is harder to keep ourselves under control. It can become a problem in this setting when we yell at the kids. When they think we're angry, it can make them nervous and lower their self-esteem. As a result, they may not perform as well as they can. Sometimes we don't even realize how angry we sound because, for one thing, our children don't always talk about their feelings. They may tell someone else.

7. When someone makes unsportsmanlike comments to other spectators, children, coaches, or referees, it is often best to ignore them unless they're good friends. In general, when someone is excited and negative, that is not the time to talk about sportsmanship. We should avoid confrontations at all costs.

8. Even if our child has outstanding ability, we shouldn't look too far into the future. We need to be realistic about the question of whether they will get a lot of playing time in high school or college. And considering the rapidly increasing number of good players coming out of high school, we need to be aware there are relatively few college soccer scholarships, and competition for spots on the roster will be intense.

9. Know the level of commitment expected and the policy on playing time. If you have any questions, it is often best to ask the coach during a quieter moment, not at a game.

10. If we keep the game in the proper perspective, we can realize that children usually have FUN as long as we support their effort. Putting them under pressure by being overly critical is not a good idea. If they become anxious about their performance, they may be hesitant to try new skills, they may not reach their potential, and their interest in the game may decline.

11. The experience of watching children play youth sports is over all too soon. Why not relax and have fun simply knowing that the kids are having fun and we're having a good time together?

NAYS Pre-season Parents Checklist

PRESENTED BY THE NATIONAL ALLIANCE
FOR YOUTH SPORTS
10 THINGS EVERY PARENT SHOULD ASK
THEIR CHILD'S COACH

Parents, it's that time of year again. As summer arrives you know what that means—cookouts, mosquitoes, sunburns—and an endless string of youth baseball and softball games and practices. Millions of children nationwide will once again descend on local fields to participate in Little League programs. There will be colorful uniforms, post-game ice creams and—sadly—plenty of unhappy children, too.

More than 70 percent of children quit sports because of unpleasant experiences in which the coach—despite the best intentions—is often guilty of causing emotional or physical harm. The National Alliance for Youth Sports, America's leading advocate for positive and safe sports for children, offers 10 questions parents should ask coaches before signing their child up to help ensure they have a fun and rewarding experience.

1. How important is winning to you? There's no denying that winning is important, that everyone likes to win and that we should all strive to win. But when winning emerges as the only goal, and it overshadows the essence of doing your best, exhibiting good sportsmanship and playing within the rules, that's when the seeds of trouble have been planted. A win-at-all-cost coach can ruin a child's season and create havoc with an entire program.

2. What's your main focus going to be? If the word fun doesn't pop up immediately, look out—this is a clear sign that serious problems loom.

3. Have you been certified? A parent would never enroll their child in a school with untrained teachers. So why is it any different when it comes to enrolling children in sports programs with untrained coaches, where the consequences can be equally severe. Simply put, a first-year volunteer with no coaching experience who has been certified is more likely to be a positive influence on the children than someone who has coached for several years but who doesn't understand the dos and don'ts of working with children.

4. Will all the children get to play different positions? Coaches are often guilty of stereotyping kids without even realizing it. An overweight child is often thought of as a catcher while the team's best player automatically winds up at shortstop or on the pitching mound. To fully experience the sport children need the opportunity to play a variety of positions. Forcing them

into one position at an early age infringes on their growth, cuts down on their learning and oftentimes spoils their entire experience.

5. Will there be equal playing time for everyone? The dreaded bench is pretty uncomfortable—especially to a child's psyche. If a youngster is stuck on the bench they're not going to be learning or having any fun. Studies show that children overwhelmingly would rather play for a losing team than sit on the bench for a winning team.

6. Are you familiar with all the safety rules and equipment? Injuries are as much a part of sports as grass stains and they are going to happen. But by using all of the available safety equipment, and teaching only proper sports techniques, the number of injuries—and their severity—can be greatly reduced.

7. Is my child going to be properly supervised at all times? Don't treat the coach as if he or she is a baby-sitting service. Too often parents view practices as an opportunity to run a few errands, but it's not fair to expect the coach to monitor 15 or 20 6-year-olds. Find out if the coach would like some help. It's a good idea for all the parents to take turns helping out at practice. It'll also be an eye-opening experience on what it's like to coach children.

8. Will there be a preseason parents meeting? It's critical that coaches and parents are on the same page before the season begins. At this meeting coaches can explain their philosophy, get to know the parents and address any questions or concerns. Open communication from the beginning eases parental fears and paves the way for a fun and enjoyable season.

9. What are you going to teach my child? There's more to youth baseball and softball than simply learning batting stances, sliding fundamentals and fielding techniques. Many youngsters automatically put their coaches on a pedestal. So, it's important that coaches take advantage of the opportunity and put it to good use by talking about good sportsmanship, the dangers of alcohol and tobacco, fair play, ethics, the importance of doing well in school, as well as a number of other areas.

10. Remember, the volunteer coach of your child's team is sacrificing his time and energy to coach. It's an enormous responsibility and if parents can alleviate some of the workload—arranging carpools, setting up post-game treats, assisting with team fund-raisers—the chances for a smooth-running season for everyone involved are greatly enhanced.

NAYS/PAYS Parents' Code of Ethics

PARENTS ASSOCIATION FOR YOUTH SPORTS
NATIONAL ALLIANCE FOR YOUTH SPORTS

I hereby pledge to provide positive support, care, and encouragement for my child participating in youth sports by following this Parents' Code of Ethics:

I will encourage good sportsmanship by demonstrating positive support for all players, coaches, and officials at every game, practice, or other youth sports event.

I will place the emotional and physical well-being of my child ahead of my personal desire to win.

I will insist that my child play in a safe and healthy environment.

I will require that my child's coach be trained in the responsibilities of being a youth sports coach and that the coach upholds the Coaches' Code of Ethics.

I will support coaches and officials working with my child, in order to encourage a positive and enjoyable experience for all.

I will demand a sports environment for my child that is free from drugs, tobacco, and alcohol and will refrain from their use at all youth sports events.

I will remember that the game is for youth—not adults.

I will do my very best to make youth sports fun for my child.

I will ask my child to treat other players, coaches, fans and officials with respect regardless of race, sex, creed or ability.

I will help my child enjoy the youth sports experience by doing whatever I can, such as being a respectful fan, assisting with coaching, or providing transportation.

I will read the National Standards for Youth Sports and do what I can to help all youth sports organizations implement and enforce them.

Pursuing Victory With Honor:
The Arizona Sports Summit Accord

On May 25, 1999, nearly 50 influential leaders in sports issued the Arizona Sports Summit Accord to encourage greater emphasis on the ethical and character-building aspects of athletic competition. It is hoped that the framework of principles and values set forth will be adopted and practiced widely. The Accord is the result of a summit conference convened May 12–14, 1999, in Scottsdale, Arizona. The summit—"Pursuing Victory With Honor"—was sponsored by the Josephson Institute of Ethics, the CHARACTER COUNTS! Coalition, and the United States Olympic Committee, Coaching Division.

PREAMBLE

At its best, athletic competition can hold intrinsic value for our society. It is a symbol of a great ideal: pursuing victory with honor.

The love of sports is deeply embedded in our national consciousness. The values of millions of participants and spectators are directly and dramatically influenced by the values conveyed by organized sports. Thus, sports are a major social force that shapes the quality and character of the American culture.

In the belief that the impact of sports can and should enhance the character and uplift the ethics of the nation, we seek to establish a framework of principles and a common language of values that can be adopted and practiced widely.

IT IS THEREFORE AGREED:

1. The essential elements of character-building and ethics in sports are embodied in the concept of sportsmanship and six core principles: trustworthiness, respect, responsibility, fairness, caring, and good citizenship. The highest potential of sports is achieved when competition reflects these "six pillars of character."

2. It is the duty of sports leadership—including coaches, athletic administrators, program directors and game officials—to promote sportsmanship and foster good character by teaching, enforcing, advocating and modeling these ethical principles.

3. To promote sportsmanship and foster the development of good character, sports programs must be conducted in a manner that enhances the

mental, social and moral development of athletes and teaches them positive life skills that will help them become personally successful and socially responsible.

4. Participation in athletic programs is a privilege, not a right. To earn that privilege, athletes must conduct themselves, on and off the field, as positive role models who exemplify good character.

5. Sports programs should establish standards for participation by adopting codes of conduct for coaches, athletes, parents, spectators and other groups that impact the quality of athletic programs.

6. All sports participants must consistently demonstrate and demand scrupulous integrity and observe and enforce the spirit as well as the letter of the rules.

7. The importance of character, ethics and sportsmanship should be emphasized in all communications relating to the recruitment of athletes, including promotional and descriptive materials.

8. In recruiting, educational institutions must specifically determine that the athlete is seriously committed to getting an education and has or will develop the academic skills and character to succeed.

9. The highest administrative officer of organizations that offer sports programs must maintain ultimate responsibility for the quality and integrity of those programs. Such officers must assure that education and character development responsibilities are not compromised to achieve sports performance goals and that the academic, emotional, physical and moral well-being of athletes is always placed above desires and pressures to win.

10. The faculties of educational institutions must be directly involved in and committed to the academic success of student-athletes and the character-building goals of the institution.

11. Everyone involved in athletic competition has a duty to treat the traditions of the sport and other participants with respect. Coaches have a special responsibility to model respectful behavior and the duty to demand that their athletes refrain from disrespectful conduct including verbal abuse of opponents and officials, profane or belligerent trash-talking, taunting and unseemly celebrations.

12. The leadership of sports programs at all levels must ensure that coaches, whether paid or voluntary, are competent to coach. Minimal competence may be attained by training or experience. It includes basic knowledge of: 1)

the character-building aspects of sports, including techniques and methods of teaching and reinforcing the core values comprising sportsmanship and good character; 2) first-aid principles and the physical capacities and limitations of the age group coached; and 3) coaching principles and the rules and strategies of the sport.

13. Because of the powerful potential of sports as a vehicle for positive personal growth, a broad spectrum of sports experiences should be made available to all of our diverse communities.

14. To safeguard the health of athletes and the integrity of the sport, athletic programs must discourage the use of alcohol and tobacco and demand compliance with all laws and regulations, including those relating to gambling and the use of drugs.

15. Though economic relationships between sports programs and corporate entities are often mutually beneficial, institutions and organizations that offer athletic programs must safeguard the integrity of their programs. Commercial relationships should be continually monitored to ensure against inappropriate exploitation of the organization's name or reputation and undue interference or influence of commercial interests. In addition, sports programs must be prudent, avoiding undue financial dependency on particular companies or sponsors.

16. The profession of coaching is a profession of teaching. In addition to teaching the mental and physical dimensions of their sport, coaches, through words and example, must also strive to build the character of their athletes by teaching them to be trustworthy, respectful, responsible, fair, caring and good citizens.

Index